Class, Codes and Control

Primary Socialization, Language and Education
Edited by Basil Bernstein
University of London Institute of Education
Sociological Research Unit

A catalogue of other series of Social Science books published by
Routledge & Kegan Paul will be found at the end of this volume.

Class, Codes and Control

Volume 3
Towards a Theory of Educational Transmissions

Basil Bernstein

Professor in the Sociology of Education
Head of the Sociological Research Unit
University of London Institute of Education

Revised edition

ROUTLEDGE & KEGAN PAUL

London, Henley and Boston

First published in 1975
by Routledge & Kegan Paul Ltd
39 Store Street,
London WC1E 7DD,
Broadway House,
Newtown Road,
Henley-on-Thames,
Oxon RG9 1EN and
9 Park Street,
Boston, Mass. 02108, USA
Set in Times New Roman
Second edition 1977
Printed in Great Britain by
Redwood Burn Ltd
Trowbridge and Esher

ISBN 0 7100 8666 0

Contents

Acknowledgments

The publishers and Professor Bernstein would like to thank the following for permission to reprint material in this volume:

New Society for 'Open schools—open society?', originally published in *New Society*.

The Open University for 'The sociology of education' from *Eighteen Plus—the Final Selection*, 1972, and 'Sources of consensus and disaffection in education' from *Perspectives on the Curriculum*, 1972.

The Royal Society for 'Ritual in education', *Phil. Trans*. B, 1966, 251 (772), p. 429.

Collier-Macmillan for 'On the classification and framing of educational knowledge', in *Knowledge and Control*, ed. M. F. D. Young, 1971.
OECD (CERI) for 'Class and pedagogies: visible and invisible', Paris, 1973.

Introduction to second edition

In the Introduction to the original edition (p.28) are the following sentences: 'I am also fully aware that the thesis is limited in focus and depth. For example, the relationships between codes, ideologies and economic structures is hardly worked out.' I would not claim that this has been fulfilled in the revised edition, but I hope a step in this direction has been taken. The paper 'Class and pedagogies: visible and invisible' has been considerably extended to include a more rigorous definition of the distinguishing features of the two pedagogical forms. The section on the class assumptions of invisible pedagogies has been elaborated and is now, I hope, more rigorous and detailed. There is an attempt to develop a classification of agents of symbolic control in terms of their function. A new chapter has been added ('Aspects of the relations between education and production') where the concepts classification and framing have been applied to education and production and their interrelationships. The analysis presupposes the previous two chapters and focuses upon the relative autonomy of, and dependence of, education on the mode of production with special reference to that fraction of the middle class who function in the agencies of cultural reproduction (particularly education) rather than in production. The contradictions which are created by different structural relationships between education and production are made explicit. In a note to this paper, some derivations are applied to the socio-linguistic code thesis.

It has been pointed out that class plays a crucial role in the analysis, yet no formal definition is given. The definition underlying the general discussion is: class relations constitute inequalities in the distribution of power between social groups, which are realized in the creation, organization, distribution, legitimation and reproduction of material and symbolic values arising out of the social division of labour.

Introduction

In a way, the series of papers in this volume follow an approach similar to the papers in Volume 1. Each one develops from the last, and there is, I hope, an evolution of the concepts. Whereas the sociolinguistic thesis represented an attempt to clarify the basic concept of 'code', the papers here represent a search for the basic concepts themselves. In the sociolinguistic thesis, I started with the crucial concepts; in the papers on transmission, I had to find them. From another point of view, the sociolinguistic thesis focuses upon the reproduction of class relationships as these shape the structure of communication, and its social basis in the family, whereas these essays represent an attempt to sketch the effect of class relationships upon the institutionalizing of elaborated codes in the school. Much of the criticism of the sociolinguistic thesis fails to take into account the essays in this book. Yet it is the case that the series started *at the same time* as the major SRU research, in 1964. Whereas the sociolinguistic thesis played little or no part in any of my formal teaching at the Institute of Education, the papers in this volume were all given as lectures to students reading for the sociology of education papers in the then Academic Diploma in Education. I am clearly very grateful to the Diploma students who were at the Institute between 1963 and 1970, for their criticism was not only academic, but informed by the everyday practice of teaching, often under impossible conditions. I owe much to these students.

I wanted to set the analysis of the school against a broader canvas of changes in forms of social control. Yet I did not want to lose sight in the analysis of the grim consequences of class relationships. There are two strands in the paper—one explicit and the other

1

implicit—power and control, but it is only towards the last papers that I felt I had begun to find concepts which would permit their inter-penetration. More of this later. In a way, I did not think that it was too difficult to understand how it was, at the surface level, that the structure and inter-actions within the school distributed success and failure so unevenly and so painfully. I was, however, dissatisfied with the application of sociology to the analysis of the school, and with the research. I am well aware of the importance of, and need for, descriptive research which maps the vicissitudes of a problem, yet one wants to grasp somehow the underlying principles of the map itself. However, I have always found it difficult to move towards a more general macro-analysis until I had some grip upon the local relationships at the micro-aspect. The journey here was almost identical with that of the sociolinguistic thesis, which remained a micro-analysis for many years, with only hints as to its macro-institutional features. The papers follow a similar style and it is only towards the end that the analysis opens up. The analyses of the early chapters are indeed no more than sketches which take as their concern changes in the form of social control. The school is abstracted from its wider constraints rather like a figure relieved of its ground. I do not know why this happens, it certainly is not because I am unaware of the wider context, as students know. I think it is possibly because I am sensitive to inter-actions and once these are part of my experience, I can begin to intuit what I take to be the structural principles which they embody. But it takes a long time, at least for me, to condense experience into a concept, and even longer to extract from the concept what one has not in the first place directly experienced. Yet as we are all part of society, that experience is in us. When a set of concepts do not work, it is as if one's own sense of the social is obscured. When they do, then one's own biography is continuous with the formulation. Concepts, I believe, for some, look outwards and inwards. Their generality finds its springs in the analysis of inner space. I am sure this is not the case for all; or perhaps for some, the relationship between the conceptual world and the inner world is more attenuated and so less transparent. The relationships between concepts and the conceptualizer are not only the product of the intellectual market place, nor a *simple* reflection of the ideological ambience although clearly neither of these two forces can *ever* be discounted. It is sometimes as if the condition for re-arranging is the re-arrangement of parts of oneself, yet the re-arrangements of parts of oneself can only be done when the concepts have been formed. Outside and inside are linked by a tense dialectic. When this tension slackens, one is doing no more than performing arabesques around the past or, and perhaps most painful of all, the transformation is complete, because the concepts themselves, and the intellectual tradition of which they are necessarily a part, have created a language too limited for any further inner exploration. The initial condensing has itself become a principle of denial. Terms like implicit/explicit, intimacy/distance, visible/invisible, positional/personal (which never are simply dichotomies, but are *dialectically* related) may no longer intensify inner contradictions. Perhaps it may be useful to trace the origins and vicissitudes of the underlying structure of analysis which I hope is the organic basis of this volume. The difficulty is that such an approach may appear pretentious, for I am acutely conscious of how slight are the early pieces in the book.

The first paper, 'Sources of consensus and disaffection in education', had its origins in a number of different sources. At the time, in the early 1960s, we were beginning to get a picture of how the stratification features within schools affected the careers of pupils. The shift away from the studies of the family to the characteristics of schools had begun. At the same time, sociologists of education were beginning to apply organizational theory to schools. Attention was also focusing upon pupils' informal relationships with various peer groups. I felt, then as now, that it was important to keep together in one analysis the inter-actions between the family and the school, and to show the variations in this relationship, both within and between social classes. I wanted to indicate the variety of pupil responses to the roles the school created and to show how variations in the role of pupil had consequences for the type of involvement in the family. At the same time, I was not very hopeful of the possibilities of applying organizational theory to schools, and I wanted to develop a different approach which placed at the centre of the analysis the principles of transmission and their embodiment in structures of social relationships. I aimed at a form of analysis which could be applied to families, pupils and teachers and to their inter-action. I distinguished that *structure* of social relationships which controlled curriculum, pedagogy and evaluation from that structure of social relationships which controlled the transmission of the moral order. Instrumental and expressive did not refer to roles (as in Parson's analysis of family relationships), but to structural relationships of control. I took Merton's means-ends schema outlined in his essay 'Continuities in the study of suicide', and derived from it a typology of involvements in the role of pupil which were themselves markedly influenced by Goffman. Douglas Young had previously applied the role involvements of embracement, attachment and estrangement to work roles. There was no analysis of the specific contents of the two orders instrumental and expressive, but it was clear to me that as their forms changed, so would the contents. This paper has a functionalist ring about it, and the general form of the analysis is somewhat mechanical, but I would still argue that the analysis would raise necessarily questions of conflict rather than questions of equilibrium. Looking back, one can see the problems of a means-ends distinction and the problems of what constituted the basic unit of analysis; a pupil within a given curriculum, if so, which, etc. . . ? However, the paper set me thinking of different forms of integration and changes in the forms of such integration, and so directed me again to the *Division of Labour in Society*, which was also one of the major starting points of the code thesis. Then, as now, I am not very concerned about flaws in the analysis, or ambiguity in the structure of the concepts. So long as the analysis keeps moving, I believe that I can clear up some of the conceptual mess. In fact, of course, one rarely can do this without research. Conceptual elegance is attractive, but only when it has the living quality which comes from empirical exploration.

The second paper, 'Ritual in education', was written for a Conference on Ritual convened by Julian Huxley. Lionel Elvin, the then Director of the Institute of Education, and Richard Peters encouraged me to prepare a paper for the conference. It had to be written rather quickly. This paper, although, perhaps, of little consequence in itself as a piece of analysis, looking back now, was critical to what followed. I wonder what would have happened if Lionel Elvin had not asked me to write on this subject. I certainly had no ideas about the question of ritual, but I did see a connection between forms of ritual and a restricted code, between forms of ritual and positional and personal forms of social control. I had of course read Waller's incredible book *The Sociology of Teaching*. At the back of my mind, possibly stemming from the first paper, were the different principles of control created by stratified as against differentiated structures, and the notion of one imbedded in the other. I was also playing with the idea that bureaucracy could take different forms. Somewhere round the corner was also the issue of what happened when the *basis* of the expressive order changed, but not the instrumental. What happened to Catholic schools, for example, after Vatican II? Two years later Mary Douglas and myself offered a research proposal to the SSRC to study changes in the moral orderings of schools. It was in fact turned down. I regard the Ritual paper as setting out conceptually what became almost an obsession: to try to understand the origins and consequences of different modalities of control. It was the sharp focusing upon principles of control which was probably responsible for the abstracted analyses of schools.

It might be worth spelling out in some detail the distinctions made in the Ritual paper, for they re-appear, albeit transformed, in the later papers. The expressive order outlined in the first paper is analysed in some detail. Two forms of transmission are delineated, which correspond to the family types positional and personal. These arise out of two different concepts of the pupil: one where he/she is regarded as possessing fixed attributes, the other where the pupil is regarded as possessing variable attributes which undergo development according to the milieu. Positional transmission is sharply bounded, with well-marked consensual and differentiating rituals, and is relative to person-focused transmission (therapeutic), a very much condensed communication, where the basic messages of power are elements of an explicit social structure. The curriculum for the able pupils is bureaucratized and is realized as sets of routines. The differentiated structure is viewed as a means of social control for the less able. As structures change from stratified to differentiated, so does the emphasis shift from the significance of adult-imposed rituals to pupil-generated rituals, from rituals celebrating dominance to rituals celebrating participation. Thus, according to the paper, a shift from stratified to differentiated changes the power relationships of pupils and the peer group becomes an important source of identity, relation and order. It follows that the contents of learning are increasingly drawn from the contents of the peer group, but these become elements of the instrumental order for the purpose of social control. I considered at the time that the shift from stratified to differentiated was connected with changes in the division of labour. This was too glib a conclusion. It has been said of late that the sociology of education of the early sixties did not consider the problematics of education, but took these 'for granted'. I do not think that this applies to this paper. Indeed, slight as the paper is, it was one of the first in England to draw attention to changes in the bases of social order in schools and opened up a range of questions somewhat before large secondary schools exhibited weak stratification features.

It was the Ritual paper which brought me into contact with Professor Mary Douglas, who was attending the Huxley meeting. She came up to me after the paper, delivered the following and disappeared: 'It's the Convent of the Sacred Heart all over again! See you in September.' It was then late June. What could one do, except read her work. I was well-equipped when we met in September. I valued enormously the friendship which developed, for the sociolinguistic thesis and study of the school had left me somewhat isolated. Up to a point, such a relation can be productive, but it can also lead to institutional paranoia. Despite the different focus of our research, we drew on a common tradition which I found confirmed the direction I was taking. It was a great relief to talk to somebody without having to protect the vulnerability which was the delicate centre of one's activity. I understood the categories Professor Douglas was using, and the work they were doing, although I sometimes got lost amongst the pygmies and the many societies in the anthropologist's Aladdin's cave. Over the years we drew upon each other's work whilst retaining our individual focus and growth. I used the concepts of purity and mixing of categories as a starting point for the analysis of educational knowledge in the paper 'Open schools—open society?'.

I feel, again, that these remarks are so pompous when one considers the brevity and slightness of that paper. But I am now looking back and its significance as a local analysis is not the point at all, it was what it opened up, a direction that could be taken, future contours which at that time were only dimly grasped. Professor Douglas was at work on the first edition of *Natural Symbols*, and we discussed endlessly her basic dimensions of group and grid. I felt that although those were very powerful dimensions, they did not contain the power components of the analysis I was working towards, neither were they capable of introducing the dynamics I required in my own research. The concepts of classification and frame arose out of this dialogue, and I believe re-acted upon Professor Douglas's formulations.

Professor Douglas even now says, to my chagrin, that she does not understand 'framing'. It is very rare to have an intellectual dialogue which is not at some point transformed into symbolic cannibalism; my formulation can eat up yours.

The 'Open schools—open society?' paper was in one sense a polemic against the application of organizational analysis to the school. It was, of course, never seen in this way. It attempted to integrate structural and inter-actional features of transmission and to point towards both power and control components. It made explicit how much I owed to Durkheim's *Division of Labour in Society*. It dissolved the distinction between instrumental and expressive orders, and freed me from the dichotomy. Of perhaps supreme importance, as I have written elsewhere ('A brief account of the theory of codes'), it forged explicitly the connection between the sociolinguistic thesis and the work on the structure of the transmission of educational knowledge; for at *one* level the concepts of mechanical and organic solidarity underlay both. It also showed, though this was not made explicit, that there was in principle a variety of ways by which elaborated codes could be institutionalized in education. It brought very clearly to me that behind the early papers on the school was a developing analysis of the social assumptions of elaborated codes. Although I made it evident at the beginning of the paper, indeed in the first paragraph, that I was discussing what existed at the level of educational ideology, rather than what existed at the level of day-by-day practice of schools, the paper was taken in some quarters as a description of the facts! I did find it useful to extract the bones of the paper and present in diagrammatic form the oppositions between 'open' and 'closed', instrumental and expressive orders. The idea here was to produce a scale of degrees of openness and closure which one might take to schools. One could examine the concomitant changes in the expressive order with different degrees of change in the instrumental order, and of course vice versa, with respect to different sections of the schools population. Again, I would insist that this quadrant, like many others in the paper, is not simply a matter of dichotomizing, but that the positions are those of conflict. I have appended this diagram to the first paper in this volume.

I have included in this collection the first draft of what became the Classification and framing paper. One year separated the first draft from the final version. Again, the process was to simplify the structure of the previous paper. This was done by taking as the key relationships, curriculum, pedagogy and evaluation, and through the concepts of open and closed, distinguishing two different transmission structures, collection and integrated. The basic ideas were scattered in embryonic form in earlier papers. They crystallized in the Curriculum paper, and the power relationships were brought firmly into the analysis. It is again true that in this sketch there was little connection with any institutional or ideological features outside of the school, but as I have written earlier, I seem unable to widen the analysis until I get a grip upon the specifics of transmission in local agencies. I feel that if I get the concepts right for this analysis, they will serve as unit concepts for the next level of the analysis, but if they are not sufficiently fundamental, they cannot function as unit concepts and therefore no more general analysis is possible. At the back of my mind was the need to develop a pair of concepts (because I do not believe it can be done with one) which operate analytically at different logical levels and which could hold together (it is somewhat ridiculous, but one has to add here not in a functionalist way), structural and inter-actional levels in such a way that change could be initiated at either level. That is a pair of concepts which would allow for responsiveness to and change in structure, but which would also indicate that there was at any one time a limit to negotiation. It was important that such concepts could be applied to a range of transmission agencies (minimally to the family and to education), for only if this was possible could one analyse the inter-relations and, even more important, could one show at a more general level of analysis sources of change of transmission agencies themselves. The concepts should also illuminate the social basis of communication if they are to have any significance for the shaping of mental structures.

In the process of expanding the Curriculum paper, I tried to develop concepts which would fulfil the above specifications. The relative strengths of classifications and frames determined for me the regulative principle of the transmission at a most general level. The concepts could be used at the level of classroom encounter, at the level of codes, and as a means of broadly characterizing transmission in different societies. The relationships between inside the school and outside could also be included in the same analysis.

We have found that it is possible to transform positional and personal family types into the language of classification and frames, and certain sociolinguistic texts can also be described in the same language.

It is the case that, because the concepts are defined without reference to content, the analysis has limitations. Yet they do create the possibility of sensitive analysis. For example, where the frame is strong on the pacing of knowledge (the rate of expected learning), then time is scarce. This has two implications. The student learns that only certain kinds of questions can be put at any one time, and the teacher learns to provide a certain kind of answer. Thus as frame strength over pacing changes, so does answering and questioning behaviour. Second, strong frames are more likely to produce a reproduction of previous knowledge on the part of the student than to encourage the student to go beyond what has been. Thus, on the whole, where the classification and framing is relatively strong the time-dimension of the pedagogy is that of the past. On the other hand, where the classification, and in particular the framing, is relatively weak, then the time-dimension of the pedagogy is likely to shift towards the present. With such a coding of educational knowledge, one would expect that the transmission would be more oral, and the learning a co-operative rather than a privatized activity. Where the classification and frames were relatively strong, one would expect that if a pupil presented some work to the teacher which the teacher thought was unexpectedly good, he/she might say, 'That's a very good piece of work. Did you do it by yourself?' Whereas if the classification, and especially the framing, was relatively weak in the same situation, the teacher might say, 'That was really exciting. Did you do it by yourself?' If the pupil said that he did, the teacher might then add, 'You might have got even more out of it if you had talked it over with some of the group.' Many of the derivations are not given in the paper. I tried also to raise questions about changes in the modality of social control with changes in the coding of educational knowledge. For in this area there is a lot of romanticism, and so the paper goes on to attempt an analysis of forms of implicit control which in turn becomes the major theme of the paper which follows.

Chapter 5 has been reprinted from *Class, Codes and Control* volume 1 in order that the reader can see its antecedents and later development. The basic structure of the paper is built upon two ideal typical social structures which are necessarily in conflict with each other. Indeed, the second is an attempt to change the first. The first social structure is predicated upon the rule 'Things must be kept apart'. Now the stronger this rule, the stronger the classification and framing which controls its transmission. Thus the control will be hierarchical and the criteria explicit and highly specific. Pollution is likely to occur wherever there is an attempt to reduce the apartness of things. For the apartness of things is the major means whereby repetition takes place. Although the criteria are explicit and highly specific, socialization into the apartness of things renders the latter taken-for-granted events or practices, and therefore they are less likely to be experienced as problematic. The strong Cs and Fs which control the transmission place the emphasis upon the past, and therefore they do not encourage a seeking for a different order of things. This rule tends to create strong social types, with explicit distancing techniques. There are strong constraints upon making public subjective experience.

The second social structure is predicated upon the rule 'Things must be put together', which is the inverse of the first rule and therefore is necessarily in conflict with it. How much so depends upon how much is to be put together. This social structure is a potential change matrix; it is not a *terminal* state. It can also be, and is more likely to be, an interrupter rather than a change matrix (see chapter 6). Here, control is less obviously hierarchical, indeed control may appear to inhere in a person, rather than in a formal position. The criteria transmitted which refer to members of this social structure, *not* to individuals outside of it, are likely to be very general and *apparently* less specific and consensual. Control is implicit and transmitted through weak classification and weak framing, although the framing and classification between inside and outside the social structure will be extremely strong. Thus this social structure encourages relationships, be they internal to the person or external, to be made public and the foci of inquiry. This leads to the possibility of continuous surveillance; in which case there is no privacy. The time-dimension of the transmission will be the present tense. Members of the group will experience effervescence and spontaneity of behaviour. However, deviancy is likely to be much more visible, for it is difficult for an individual to distance himself. Strong, well-marked social types are less likely to be produced, for here selves are inextricably inter-related. The socialization will be deeply penetrating. The fundamental principle of order will rest upon an explicit *ideology* which directs the putting together of things.

I realize that the above models of conflicting social structures, predicated upon antithetical rules employing different forms of socialization seem far removed from the substantive and even analytic content of the paper, (chapter 5), yet they served for me a number of purposes. I could disconnect the class analysis from the analysis of forms of social control. Yet, at the same time, certain elements in the models could be used for substantive analysis. From another point of view, variations in the strength of boundaries are only the surface realizations of continuities and discontinuities which are generated by underlying rules. It is a matter of considerable sociological and sociolinguistic interest how it is that certain rules generate distinctive texts. It then becomes important to understand the different forms of socialization into distinctive underlying rules. For these underlying rules are not learned as a consequence of any one practice, but they are somehow inferred by the socialized from a range of social relations. In this sense, the socialized is always active in his own socialization. He both acquires the ground rule *and* he responds to it; I think that these underlying rules give rise to coding procedures. The process of cultural reproduction is accomplished by the controls on the selection and institutionalizing of these underlying rules, which create ways of experiencing, of interpreting and telling about the world. I believe that the structure of socialization is not a set of roles, but classification and framing relationships. It is these, I think, that shape the mental structures, by establishing coding procedures which are predicated upon distinctive rules. These rules are acquired in the process of exploring the classification and framing relationships. However, and it is a big however, behind any given classification and framing, are the power relationships and the fundamental principles of social control. *Thus from this point of view, power and control are made substantive in the classification and framing which then generate distinctive forms of social relationships and thus communication, and through the latter initially, but not necessarily finally, shape mental structures.* Power maintains the classification (that is the *insulations*, the *boundaries* between things, be they relationships internal to the individual, or external). Power, however, may be realized through frames of different strengths. Framing regulates inter-action and it is *always present*, even though the socialized and socializer may consider they are eliciting from each other a process of endless negotiation, of spontaneity, of unique authorship. In other words, frame strength regulates the modality of the socialization. We can therefore have a situation where the power relationships remain unchanged, but they are realized through a change in frame strength.

This brings me to a fundamental limitation of the Classification and framing paper. It is not possible with the analysis as it stands in that paper to deal with the specific contents of a strong classification and framing form of socialization, which means that one cannot analyse its ideological basis. Indeed, in the paper the ideological basis of educational knowledge codes with varieties of strong classification and frames of different strengths is *assumed*. In other words, I started the paper knowing, or at least thinking I knew, about the ideological basis of collection codes. The ideological basis was therefore *implicit*, but not explicit in the argument. For this reason, the purely *structural* concepts of classification and frame could do so much work. Integrated codes were analysed in relation to collection codes and were seen from two points of view; first, as technological devices to cope with problems of social control, or changing concepts of skill or the fragmentation of knowledge at the higher levels; second, as potential change matrices to bring about a change in the distribution of power and principles of social control. Thus, groups with radically different ideologies might find themselves supporting integrated codes. I might add here that the only place I have ever seen institutionalized integrated codes as a change matrix is the new university in Denmark, Roskilde, and I was pleasantly surprised to learn that the paper was considered by those responsible in the design of the university.

I realize that I have now discussed this paper at some length, but it is to give some idea of its significance for me. It should not be taken as an indication of its objective significance. I felt I had transcended the early formulations of imperative, positional and personal modalities of control (1962) which were both too descriptive and too narrow in their focus. They also collapsed into one concept, structural and inter-actional components. They could not serve as unit concepts for a logically higher level of analysis. Within the sociolinguistic thesis, their value was confined to the analysis of only one context, i.e. the regulative context. They were incapable of dealing with the realizations of both object and person relationships. It seems to take so long before one's intuition really does useful conceptual work. What is it that is mediating or usually blocking that relationship? One knows when concepts have gone dead on one for they become clichés. Perhaps there is at their basis a metaphor which is felt rather than known, a condensation of experience which one is not altogether happy to make explicit and so one settles for an imprecise formulation which can so easily become a trap. We cannot reflect the world, how it is, and any sociology which attempts this, which attempts to understand the practices whereby individuals construct order by disconnecting these practices from the structural relationships of which they are the outcome, is inevitably a sociology without history; either of members or of the sociologist. It is therefore a sociology without conflict. In the same way I am not sure that we need special procedures like 'bracketing' to make the word strange or problematic. Methodological devices, or moral imperatives as to how we are to approach what we address, may enable us intellectually to place our own motivation beyond suspicion and those of others not, yet they are not in themselves the source of the sociological imagination. This rests in the end on our sense of the social in us, filtered through, because of our training, the *dialectic* of the sociological tradition which continuously reflects back to us, albeit in a cracked mirror, the possibilities of man. To be aware of the various forms constraint can take is not to diminish the possibility of man, is not to see man as passive, is not to underwrite the stability of power relationships, it is to raise to our consciousness its own shaping; that is to experience the sociological paradox, which is the crucible in which the imagination is forged.

The final paper in the series, 'Class and pedagogies: visible and and invisible', took its origins from a footnote in the previous paper 'Variations in the development of class structures affect the classification and framing of educational knowledge'. I also wanted to attempt to sketch the structural origins of educational transmissions regulated by weak classifications and weak frames. At the same time, at a more *general* level, I wanted to keep going the exploration of implicit forms of control which I believed were at the bottom of so-called spontaneous behaviour. In the previous paper, collection and integrated codes were kept apart and it was argued that, at least at the secondary level, weak forms of integration would be available to the 'less able', usually working-class pupils, whereas the 'able' would experience collection codes as they progressed through their educational career. In other words, *symbolic property* is generated by *strong* not weak classification. I was also somewhat apprehensive that the argument could be used to justify *existing* weak classification and weak framing procedures for working-class children in infant/primary schools. Finally, I was beginning to think of sliding together the two models outlined previously so that one could be imbedded in the other. This clearly would lead to a modification of the two original types. This was tantamount to the belief that behind weak classification is strong classification, *but* that under particular conditions their relationships could be creative; a kind of continuous reaching beyond existing boundaries. I am beginning to see here one of the problems these papers represent, it is as if two rather different kinds of analysis are always going on which are not kept apart; general problems of control and analyses of *class related* modalities of control.

The paper was triggered off by Henri Nathan (OECD:CERI), who was the author of an exciting programme concerned to focus various disciplines on what he called the Learning Sciences. He invited me to submit a paper to a seminar concerned with theoretical aspects of the process of scholarization. However, it did not stop there. Henri Nathan continuously bombarded me with questions I could not answer. All the questions centred round the artefacts of learning. He had already written a paper entitled 'Stable rules', which showed amongst other things the inability of learning theories to contribute to our understanding of what schooling was about. At the time, I held a temporary position at the École Pratique des Hautes Études, attached to the Centre de Sociologie Européenne, directed by Pierre Bourdieu. I have a boundless respect and admiration for the work of Bourdieu and of his colleagues who work with him at the Centre. Within a decade, this group has produced probably the most important single body of work in the area of the sociology of education and culture. It is a great misfortune that only a very tiny part of this corpus of work is available in translation. This is also a personal statement, for I am unable to read French. Despite this inability, I was surprised to find during my stay in Paris, and my subsequent return the following year, an immediate intellectual rapport. I am sorry that the reason for this rapport was because Bourdieu and his colleagues read and speak English. They therefore understood the problem which I was trying to tackle, whilst I could only intuit theirs. Yet I found no difficulty in sensing quickly the broad outline of their approach and in recognizing the work of their fundamental concepts. Bourdicu, of course, draws upon a more varied intellectual tradition than my own, and he is concerned with the principles of social and cultural repro- duction, and the conditions and contexts which act selectively upon the form it takes. His work encompasses both theoretical and empirical studies of the structure of reproduction, and the position and functions of its specialized agencies and personnel. Although Durkheim is not as central to Bourdieu's thesis as he is perhaps to mine, it was this shared element which provided the relationship. In discussion with the group at the Centre, it became clear that our work was complementary. Whereas they were concerned with the *structure* of reproduction and its *various* realizations, I was essen- tially concerned with the *process* of transmission. This may be a necessary condition for an intellectual meeting, but in itself it is not sufficient. There has to be a common discourse in which both problems are set. This was evidenced in a startling fashion. Cham- boredon, a member of the Centre, had just completed an important paper entitled 'L'école maternelle'.[1] He gave it to me to read during my first week at the École, and I was too embarrassed at my lack of French to admit to him that I was unable to read it. I did however scan it, in the hope of an occasional clue which would save my face. There were not too many. When we discussed the paper we found that the points I was trying to make were entirely complementary to the paper. Whereas I was focusing upon the process, Chamboredon was explicating the structure. I think these two papers represent for me the importance of a common dis- course, generating a common problematic, yet differing in terms of foci.

I am certain this is the crucial productive basis for comparative research and co-operation. So much comparative research, and, indeed, co-operation in research activity, proceeds on the basis of a low-level specification of a problem rather than a problematic. This is then followed by low level 'hypotheses' which carry no logical necessity because they are not derived from higher order, more general propositions. International meetings are called to create common 'instruments', procedures of standardization, and to 'iron out' the 'bugs' arising out of the translation of the instrument into twenty-five languages. Over the next three years there is a series of meetings to 'monitor' the research; finally the 'data' is discharged from each local computer and enters the Consolidated International Correlational Matrix. Volumes are published, the first of which contains a chapter on the difficulties of comparative research. Unfortunately, the above is not a parody, much comparative research in education is based upon this method. The 'instrument' destroys any possibility of understanding the form the problematic takes in different societies; indeed it ensures that the question is never the object of study. What I believe is required for basic comparative research is that the various groups adopt their own perspective on the *problematic* and within each perspective each group has the responsibility of creating procedures which can be made public and so subject to criticism. We might then have an understanding of how variations between societies shape the realization of the problematic. Of course, this does not rule out the common collection of gross data about the attributes and position of social groups; although even this apparently simple task has many difficulties.

Central to the argument presented in the Class and pedagogies paper is the notion that educational transmissions embody class ideologies which are crucial to the cultural reproduction of class relations. However, this process of reproduction is not a simple one and it can take various forms. In this paper I tried to make explicit what was implicit in the previous one; that is, I tried to integrate both the form and the content of the transmission. Originally (1962) I had distinguished between two contradictory forms of socialization within middle-class families, positional and personal. I rejected out of hand the distinction between authoritarian and democratic because the latter concepts are too crude. I suggested that these family types arose out of the shift of emphasis in the division of labour from the production of goods to the production of services in societies where there was a diverse range of legitimizing beliefs; that is, where value consensus was low. Goldthorpe and Lockwood in their important paper 'Affluence and the class structure' showed theoretically the movement within the middle class from radical individualism to instrumental collectivism. Miller and Swanson in their book *The Changing American Family* distinguished between entrepreneurial and bureaucratic families and they attempted to show empirically differences in the forms of socialization. Melvin Kohn, working more descriptively, also attempted to plot empirically the relationships between occupational roles and family socialization into values. Parsons, in an early essay which was a critique of Reisman's thesis, also tried from his perspective to examine changes in the cultural shaping and function of agencies of transmission.

The most wide-ranging and systematic work is being carried out by Bourdieu and his group, who have been investigating the shaping of the intellectual field by different fractions of the middle class. Their most recent empirical work, for example, is a study of the social composition of students attending the Grandes Écoles, and their different cultural perspectives.

There is, of course, an extensive literature on ideological variation within the middle class and its relation to variations in the structural position of the members, but rarely have these interrelationships been systematically linked to conflicting forms of socialization. Clearly, a major defect of the Class and pedagogies paper is the very imprecise specification of what is called the new middle class. This group has had a long historical evolution, but I was more concerned with developments over the past fifty years and in particular since 1945. The basic fractions of the middle class which interested me were that fraction which reproduced itself through ownership or control of capital in various forms and that fraction which controlled not capital but dominant and dominating forms of communication. The latter group's power lies in its control over the the transmission of critical symbolic systems: essentially through control over *various* forms of public education and through control over what Bourdieu calls the symbolic markets. I am clearly aware of the need for a precise structural location of this fraction of the middle class. I think that the theoretical and empirical work of Bourdieu and his colleagues would provide the structural principles of such an analysis.

There is a more serious difficulty in this paper which arises out of the attempt to distinguish two forms of organic solidarity within the middle class. One can of course ask why try to do this in the first place? Why use this Durkheimian perspective? It is because I have yet to find *any* social theorist whose ideas are such a source (at least to me) of understanding of what the term *social* entails. One day American and some British sociologists of education will learn what is there to be learned in Durkheim rather than to be used for sterile posturing.

It is clear that in advanced industrial societies, especially in the West, there has been a considerable increase in the division of labour of social control based upon specialized modes of communication (symbolic control). This has created a vast range of occupations dedicated to the symbolic shaping and re-shaping of the population. With this increase in the division of labour of symbolic control, I suggest there has also developed a change in emphasis in the *form* of socialization; from the creation of strongly bounded but specialized *individuals* to more weakly bounded but specialized *persons*, Durkheim foresaw this as a development of organic solidarity, and he was concerned with its consequences for inner discipline. I do not think that he quite saw that this development carried its own *structure* of integration, nor did he see its social function: to shift the relationships between visible and invisible forms of control. None of this is of course new.

From another point of view, I was very impressed with the spectrum of British public schools, which over the last hundred years has created a range of social types out of the beatings of Harrow and the subtle spontaneity of Summerhill. The British middle class can not only ensure its privileged position in education, but through the public school system it can select which social type. In a way, the British public school system is a system for generating not a finite range of sentences, but *social types*. I know of no other middle class which has the possibility of such a differentiated form of socialization. The effect of this on the internal structure and culture of this class is something worthy of prolonged study. The distinction between individualized and personalized forms of organic solidarity, in part, but only in part, arose out of this consideration. One can place those forms of organic solidarity in the context of class and in the context of opportunity for social mobility arising out of increases in the division of labour of social control.

In essence individualized organic solidarity rests upon ownership/ control over specialized physical resources, although it would include entrepreneurial professional occupations such as lawyers, medical consultants, solicitors, accountants. Personalized organic solidarity rests upon ownership/control over dominant and specialized forms of communication. According to the argument, two conflicting forms of transmission of reproduction of class are created by these modalities. That fraction of the middle class which has gained access to the area of symbolic control (specialized and dominant forms of communication) selects from prevailing forms of the socialization of the young those forms which encourage children to display their diversity and to learn the subtleties and strategies of inter- and intra-personal control. Such forms of socialization are legitimized by a group of theories thought to be progressive within the spectrum of the social sciences. From one point of view this is the origin of the 'spontaneous' child apparently putting it together in his own way. From another point of view, such a form of initial socialization enables parents to screen the child's possibilities so that they, and the child later, can take advantage of the diversification of the occupational structure of symbolic control. The paper hints that there are many consequences of the cultural output of personalized organic solidarity.

There is an important economic integration between the *out-put* of these two forms of solidarity. This integration may be seen if we consider changes in the control over workers through the application of the social sciences to business management studies and to the training of personnel officers and if we consider changes in the control over consumption through the intensive and wide-ranging activities of agencies of mass persuasion. Burns and Stalker, many years ago, in their book *The Management of Innovation* suggested that the type of product and its market situation influenced what here would be called the classification and framing of the work task and the nature of its administration. Burns and Stalker distinguished between firms in terms of their modes of solidarity: mechanical and organic. In the economic sphere, the basic relationships have remained unchanged, but there has been a change in the modality of control. In a way, the economic sphere represents from this point of view an imbedded control. When the crunch comes, it is still unemployment.

The major argument of the paper, then, is that conflicting pedagogies have their origins within the fractions of the middle class and so an unreflecting institutionalizing of *either* pedagogy will not be to the advantage of the lower working class.

However, behind these substantive issues is a concern to try to understand the relationships between modes of social integration and symbolic structures through the study of the process of their reproduction and change. This concern, which focuses upon transmission, raises a number of problems. It seems to me that one requires three levels of analysis and concepts which allow the transformation of one level into another. I do not find the customary distinction between macro and micro (two levels) or between sociology, social psychology, psychology (three disciplines), helpful; indeed these distinctions, and more often cleavages, work against any solution. This is not the place to develop the argument at any length, perhaps I can briefly outline what I mean. The first level of such an analysis would consist of an analysis of the distinctive features of the macro-institutional relationships and the distinctive features of dominant and dominating cultural codes. The second level would consist of the analysis of the distinctive features of the transmitting agencies and their inter-relations. Here one is analysing the *matrix of transmission,* and the nature of the relationships between transmission matrices, e.g. family, work, education, leisure (see chapter 6). The third level would consist of an analysis of the distinctive features of the interpretative principles, the codes and codings through which the mental structure reveals itself.

I should emphasize that because words like structure, codes, principles, are used, this is not to suggest a mechanical or simple process of transmission and reproduction. On the contrary, we should ask how it is that only at particular times is the relation between transmission and reproduction simple and complete. The distribution of power and the principles of social control *create structural relations* but these relationships contain contradictions, ambiguities, cleavages and dilemmas which inhere in the symbolic realizations of structural relations and in this way enter into mental processes to become · the seeds of change. Further, because one distinguishes three levels in this formal way, it certainly does not follow that if this were to be institutionalized as an approach, it would necessarily create anything except an approach; and we already have enough approaches. I am rather suggesting that any theory, or rather attempt at theorizing, must be capable of producing concepts which hold together *and* facilitate the transformation of one level into another.

I am not happy with the terms given to distinguish the two modes of organic solidarity within the middle class, but in terms of the particular problematic, there must be some characterization of the structure of social relationships which elicits the codes and codings of the mental processes. I have used Durkheim because I believe he gives the clue to this problem. In terms of the problem in the Class and pedagogies paper, the method if presented diagrammatically would look roughly like Figure I.1.

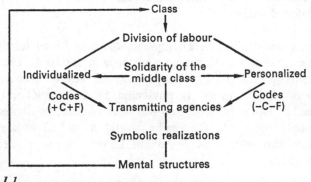

Figure 1.1

Finally the question arises as to whether there is an inconsistency between the Classification and framing paper and the Class and pedagogies paper. In the former, both collection and integrated codes are subject to a sociological analysis. The argument suggests that in *principle* there are advantages to a transmission regulated by a weak classification and weak framing to both staff and pupil, but that there are also questions of social control, including of course the strategies of spurious casualness. I distinguished between the theory of integrated codes and its likely practice *and* the constraints upon the institutionalization of such codes. I also distinguished between the different motives of the supporters of integrated codes. However, for the reasons given earlier, there is no analysis of *one* ideological basis of weak classification and framing, nor is there a concept of imbedded pedagogy.

In many ways I find the Class and pedagogies essay strange. It lacks the rather tight conceptual basis of other essays in this or the first volume. There are a number of ideas which are not properly developed and they spill over into a series of notes at the end of the paper. The paper shows very clearly the difficulty I have in separating very general questions of control from specific class-related forms. I am well aware that the analysis is not under control; there are too many things going on. What is required now is extensive research on a broad front. Pre-school education is about to be started; there is some diversification at the secondary level. Is it to be 'plus ça change, plus c'est la même chose'?

The relationship between sociolinguistic and educational codes

Finally, I would like to draw together the major inter-relationships between the essays in Volume 1 and those in this book. The outline of the linkage was given in a paper entitled 'A brief account of the theory of codes', which is published in the second edition of Volume 1. However, that account was necessarily limited, as I could not expect that the reader would have had access to the essays in this volume. The general thesis consists of two inter-related strands:

(1) How class regulates the structure of communication within the family and so the initial sociolinguistic coding orientation of the children.

(2) How class regulates the institutionalizing of elaborated codes in education, the forms of their transmission and therefore the forms of their realization.

Now (2) is often ignored by those who evaluate the research, yet this volume shows that there has been a series of papers which, since 1964, have attempted an analysis of education as an agency of social control. Clearly there are crucial *inter-actions* between (1) and (2). The realizations of elaborated codes transmitted by the family are *themselves* regulated by the form of their transmission in the school. The class assumptions of elaborated codes are to be found in the classification and framing of educational knowledge, and in the ideology which they express.

It may be helpful to distinguish analytically the three levels of the general thesis. I have set these out diagrammatically. Level I refers to the *macro-institutional* level. Level II refers to the *transmission* level. It refers to any one transmitting agency, e.g. the family, pre-school group, secondary school. Level III refers to the *textual* level. It refers to the forms of *specific* social relationships in Level II and focuses sharply on the selection of meanings which activate linguistic coding. At this level, we are asking what ground rule lies behind the production of the text. At Level II the major unit is a specific *agency*, at Level III the major unit is a specific text. Thus, in principle, we should be able to move from the distinguishing features of a specific text (Level III) to the distinguishing features of the agency (Level II) to the distinguishing macro-institutional features (Level I). I say 'in principle' because I know of no theory which enables us to make this progression other than in extraordinarily gross terms: even at one point of time. One of the difficulties is that theories which are relatively strong at the macro-institutional level are very weak for the analysis of the *process* of transmission. Whereas theories which are relatively strong for the analysis of the latter are very weak for the analysis of the former. The theory in those volumes focuses upon the *principles* underlying the process of interiorization and exteriorization, yet the focus must be such that the social relationships which this process rests upon are not abstracted from the wider institutional and cultural situation. This problem is often conceptualized as the problem of the relationships between macro and micro sociology (no sociologist would call the latter social psychology). However, this kind of distinction is itself a product of strong classification and strong framing within the division of labour of sociological knowledge. Such strong insulation makes it extraordinarily difficult to grasp how contradictions, cleavages, ambiguities and dilemmas are constituted in the individual. It is almost as if there is a self-defeating principle at the centre of sociological activity, which finds its expression in terms of distinctions like macro and micro and substantively in terms of the polemics both within and between these two levels.

I will try briefly to set out the three inter-related aspects of the thesis (see Figure I.2).

Level I—Macro-institutional

Class acts fundamentally on the division of labour by structuring its moral basis; that is, by creating the underlying relationships of production, distribution and consumption. Class relationships regulate the transmission, participation in and the possibility of changing the dominant cultural categories. The thesis focuses upon the consequences of the above for only *two preparing agencies*, the family and the school. It examines more specifically the acquisition of coding principles in the family and the school which are thought

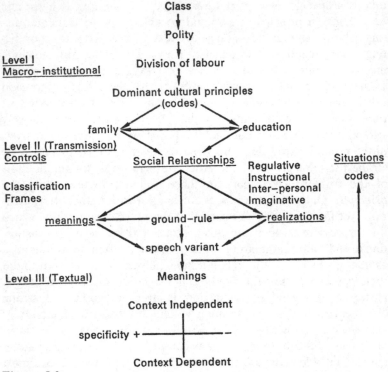

Figure 1.2

to shape consciousness. Such shaping, however, contains the cleavages, which inhere in the specific features of class relations. Thus Level I is concerned with the *origins* and *distribution* of *dominant principles of interpretation (codes)* as these are initiated and maintained by the family and education. I should say immediately that this is a programme rather than what so far exists.

Level II—Transmission

This aspect refers to the *substantive* analysis of the structure of *agencies* of transmissions of which the family and education are crucial. The basic proposition here is that the structure of social relationships determines the principles of communication and so the shaping of forms of consciousness. It follows that changing the structure of social relationships can change the principles of communication and so change forms of consciousness. In more specific terms, the form of the social relationship transforms the potential semantic into a specific semantic which activates the form of its realization *and* the conditions for the realizing of one pattern rather than another. The concepts used for the analysis of transmitting agencies are those of classification and framing. The argument here is that as the classification and framing within *and* between agencies change, so does the social basis of communication and its realization. It is important to add here that we would be vitally concerned with not only the relationships between the family and education, but also work and leisure. In order to operationalize the thesis at the transmission level, I have distinguished analytically four situations crucial to its exploration, regulative, instructional, imaginative and inter-personal (see Volume 1, chapter 9). Thus, if one were studying the family empirically, one would examine, *at least*, the classification and framing of these four situations, and the speech variants they produced. As classification is defined in terms of the *strength of insulations* it necessarily points towards hierarchy and to the latter's symbolic realization. It is the major concept at this level, because the concept translates power into the symbolic structure. From this point of view, where there is a strong insulation between social groups in the acquisition of elaborated codes, this is a critical realization of strong classification. Framing, on the other hand, regulates the *modality* of the socialization *into* the classification *and* to the response to it. There can be discontinuity or continuity in the strengths of classification and framing at different periods of time both within and between different socializing contexts. It is also important to bear in mind that the strengths of classification and frames can vary independently of each other so that one could in principle have an agency regulated by weak classification but *strong* framing. Such a form of transmission, if it successfully reproduced itself, would ensure that only one structure of *inter-relation* was permitted. At a higher level of abstraction we would have here the paradox of weak classification generating strong classification. In more substantive terms, such a transmission (weak classification), according to the theory, should rest upon a single explicit ideology (which would reduce insulations and establish inter-relations) but the strength of the *framing* would constrain the options available to *both* the socializer and the socialized.

At the transmission level, these concepts would be used for the analysis not only of preparing agencies (family, school) and repairing agencies (prisons, hospitals, etc.) but all agencies regulating the transmission of symbolic systems crucial to cultural reproduction. However, in these two volumes, the analysis is limited to the family and education. Thus one of the forms of the reproduction of class relationships is through strong classification of elaborated codes produced through class acting upon *both* the family and the school. It is important to add yet again that class does not simply regulate the distribution of elaborated codes, but it also regulates their *realizations*.

Level III—Textual

This aspect refers to the production of specific *texts* in the above four situations. It states in the most *primitive* way the criteria for distinguishing at the semantic level whether the text is realized through an elaborated or a restricted variant. In order to move to the concept of code, at the empirical level, it is necessary to examine the type of variant in the four situations. This is not the place to discuss the specifics of the sociolinguistic analysis which may be derived from this primitive formulation. I can only refer the reader to essays in Volume 2 and in particular to the forthcoming SRU monograph edited by Diana Adlam, *Codes in Context*, to be published by Routledge & Kegan Paul, and the final SRU monograph, *Familial Transmission and Socialization*.

I must emphasize that the distinction between levels is analytic. Clearly, according to the thesis, aspects (1) and (2) are invisibly present in Level III. It must also be emphasized that changing elements of a situation can change its semantic and so linguistic realization. This follows from the thesis *but* the production of an elaborated variant does not in *itself* indicate that a *code* has been changed. Any more than exposure to a *local* and limited weak C/F pedagogical relation in a school is an indication that the basic collection code has *not* been acquired. If the super-ordinate code is elaborated, then the variant stands in relation to the code as a figure to its ground. In this sense an elaborated variant in a restricted code is different from such a variant in an elaborated code. In the same way the realizations of restricted variants vary according to the super-ordinate code. There is a dialectical relationship between the coding of intimacy and the coding of distance; between local subjectivities and the making objective of their grounds and conditions. This is equivalent to saying that class regulates the distribution and realizations of elaborated codes but *only* the realizations of restricted codes. In other words, *all* individuals possess a restricted code, but the significance of its realizations vary according to whether it is the major code.

Deficit

From the point of view of the *general* thesis, I would like to examine yet again some aspects of the deficit debate. I take deficit 'theory' to be a set of propositions which attempt to account for educational failure by locating its origins solely in surface features of the child's family and local community. The unit of such theory is a child and the distinguishing features are indices of a pathology. The only historical aspects of such theories tend to be developmental aspects of the child. Perhaps one can call such theories abstracted geneticist. The changes which flow from such theories are usually limited to changes either *within* the family or *within* the local teacher-taught relationships. Their assumptions make it difficult to raise a general problematic about the fundamental structure and changes in the structure of the reproduction of forms of consciousness. In other words, deficit theory fails to examine how the distribution of power and the principles of social control regulate the distribution of, the reception to, participation in, and change of dominant cultural categories. *I would argue that whether a theory is deficit or otherwise cannot be reliably inferred from low-level diagnostic statements, but only from an examination of its fundamental problematic.*

My view is very clear. Class acts crucially on all agencies of cultural reproduction and therefore on *both* the family and the school. I know of no class society which *deliberately* and *rationally* attempts to ensure that all social groups can participate equally in the creation, production and distribution of what are considered as value, goods and services. From this point of view, it must necessarily follow that lower working-class children are today crucially disadvantaged. But this is not to say that the children, families and communities must be viewed as so many pathological deficit systems; that their forms of consciousness are pathological or at best irrelevant. Class is a fundamental category of exclusion and this is reproduced in various ways in schools, through the social context and forms of transmission of education. Thus, I find myself in the position of stating that working-class children, especially lower working-class children relative to middle-class children, are crucially disadvantaged, given the way class relationships affect both the family and the school, but that their forms of consciousness, their way of being in the world, must be active in the school, for without such expression there can be little change in the children or in the society. The steps required to validate this inclusion will also, in the end, involve a restructuring of education itself. Yet it is also the case, according to the thesis, that the code which facilitates the *systematic* examination of, and change in, the boundaries of experience is not initially made available to the children as an *essential* part of their socialization within the family. *The contradiction is that where such a code plays an essential role in family socialization, its realizations are shaped by the ideology of class.* My intellectual position is not comfortable; neither is the reality.

I see my research as different from American sociolinguistics, because I have come to this field from a different intellectual tradition. The debate the research has triggered off in the USA has been, on the whole, conducted at a fairly trivial level, because it has not been placed in the wider problematic of cultural reproduction and change. I would agree that my own research style has not always helped to clarify the terms of the debate, but I would submit that it has persistently pointed to the crucial problematic. I am also fully aware that the thesis is limited in focus and depth. For example, the relationship between codes, ideologies and economic structures is hardly worked out.

It is about time we put the 'deficit' debate into some kind of historical perspective, or continue it in order to see the dialectics of the intellectual field in Western societies. The people working in the deficit field were psychologists; themselves an outcome of the prevailing socialization into their discipline. They were working in a field of relatively low status within the various branches of psychology; and this acted selectively on those who entered it. Many of them were drawn from the applied (but not theoretical) areas of developmental, educational and clinical psychology. It is a matter of interest that the high status linguists, sociologists and anthropologists were not to be seen in this area until at least the mid-1960s. Where were they in the mid-1950s, when this field originally became a funding area? Why wasn't education a major area of theoretical concern to them? What made them wake up? One has to see the USA developments in terms of the structural relationships which determined who did what, how they did it, and when. Only if we take a historical perspective to the application of social science can we begin to understand the application of social science to the current problem; and, initially, we are all part of this history. It is not enough to see deficit 'theorists' as defenders of American or British liberalism. We have to account for who they were and what they did. *And this holds for those who reacted against this work* and the *form* of the reaction.

In order to understand this, we have to know about the hierarchical structuring of research problems, about the divorce of theory from practice, the nature of theory and the form of socialization into the various disciplines of social science. Those sociolinguists who reacted against the early work fought the deficit people by showing that Blacks clearly possessed sociolinguistic competencies, but their analyses rarely used concepts higher than 'context', 'speech community', 'interpretative rules', 'language variety'.

The major import of this research was to shift the problem to the school, but if the deficit people ignored the socio-ideological context of both the home and the school, American sociolinguists of the mid-1960s have produced no *systematic* analysis of the transmission of educational knowledge. The strong insulations between foci of theory and practice can only be transcended by social theory which can explain the present fragmentation, for the present fragmentation only leads to *internal*, rather minor, confrontations and heresy-spotting, which obscures the critical problem.

The thesis presented in Volumes 1 and 3 is so constructed that it brings explicitly into the foreground fundamental questions of the *nature and process of social control*. It is unsentimental about social control and it refuses to stop short of analyses of progressive or radical modalities of socialization. Its concern is to remind us continually to seek out the sources of repression, the boundaries, be they visible or invisible, which reduce the power of the dialectic between the past, present and future, *whatever* the social arrangement. It offers *one* interpretation of how the category class is constituted in our consciousness and inasmuch as it is successful in its endeavour, we can see a little how things can be different, and also our relationships to things. I am also aware that I have rarely made this explicit in the papers, but this has been because my central concern has been to drive the conceptual elements towards greater explicitness and operational precision. It may be that success here has also been limited. The thesis is optimistic (despite indications of the stability of power relationships) in that it asserts categorically (and it always has done this) that there is a causal relationship between the structure of social relationships and the structure of communication. However, it does not deny, and it would be foolish to so deny, the pervasiveness of the stability of power relationships and the many forms of their transformation.

The approach does provide some strategies of change of educational institutions—change in alignment of groups, interests and power as the classification and framing change their values. It also indicates what are likely to be new forms of social control and the new attributes of the person which may become candidates for labels. It attempts to reveal the ideological basis of forms of socialization within the family and the ideological basis of apparently 'progressive' pedagogies in the school. To my mind, it raises the basic issue that we can change the *social* means of the reproduction of class relationships, but not necessarily change the cultural means of such reproduction. It points to the question that although family and school are not themselves major levers of radical change— those lie in economic and political structures—family and education shape mental structures and so forms of feeling and thinking which may militate for or against changes in cultural reproduction. It therefore raises as a major problematic the relationships between social and cultural reproduction.

The most economic formulation of the argument developed in this volume would be as follows. Any *formal* educational experience entails *de-contextualizing* and *re-contextualizing*. In ways we do not properly understand, informal everyday experience, everyday communication within the family and peer group, creates procedures and performances fundamental to formal education. However, formal education selects, re-focuses and abstracts from such experience and in so doing de-contextualizes. But the social principles (codes) which regulate the form re-contextualizing takes, also determine the process of the de-contextualizing. Indeed, this process may be such that it prevents effective re-contextualizing. When one talks of context independent relationships (elaborated codes) it is always with the knowledge that such relationships have been mediated through the social principles controlling the re-contextualizing process. We can formalize this description as shown in Figure I.3.

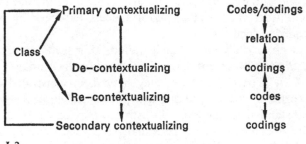

Figure I.3

Primary contextualizing occurs in the family and peer group of the child/pupil. This process *regulates* the acquisition of procedures and performances by means of which the child is able to offer and receive appropriate communication. (I have deliberately avoided the term competency because such a term involves complex often intractable issues). Inspective of the origins of procedures, the performances they create at the *level* of primary contextualizing are *context dependent*. Such performances are imbedded in, take their significance and specific meaning from local contexts. Further these performances have an underlying *structure* even though from the point of view of the child each may be initially experienced as a specialized activity. The child's performances within his peer group form a structure of activities which are often very different from the structure of his activities with adults. The skills the child acquires cannot be abstracted from the social basis of their inter-related contexts which elicit and shape their usages. The social basis may differently orientate children towards context independent meanings.

Formal education acts selectively, abstracts from, and re-focuses procedures and performances acquired through the process of primary contextualizing. This process of selection, abstraction and re-focusing leads to *re-contextualizing*. At this level, the activities, meanings and social relationships, their inter-relationships, their sequencing, their evaluation and above all their relation to the procedures and performances acquired through primary contextualizing are a function of the *code* underlying the process of re-contextualizing. However, such a code regulates the form and range of the process of *de-contextualizing*. Analytically it is not possible to distinguish between de- and re-contextualizing; empirically the *form* de-contextualizing takes may make very different demands on different groups of children, which affects the extent to which children acquire the performances required by the re-contextualizing code.

Once such a code has been acquired, this leads to *secondary contextualizing*. Meanings have been put together and of course separated in a particular way, they have been generated by distinctive forms of social relationships; power and control have been made substantive in the symbolic structure released by the code regulating re-contextualizing. Eventually secondary contextualizing, that is the *codings* of the educational code informs adult transmissions at the level of primary contextualizing *(and, of course, much else)* and so the child's experience of the de-contextualizing process. The thesis is one attempt to understand how class acts differentially upon the process of primary contextualizing *and* re-contextualizing so as to reproduce itself.

From another point of view, I have tried to develop a way of thinking which integrates structural and interactional categories so that a theory of transmission might be possible.

Acknowledgments

To research students, especially to those who see tutorials as a skiing slope towards a precipice; to members of staff of the Department of the Sociology of Education and particularly to Wally Brandis of the Sociological Research Unit and to Pat Dyehouse of the Department of the Sociology of Education.

I am indebted to the following for making the research possible: DSIR, the then Ministry of Education, the Nuffield Foundation, the Ford Foundation, the Grant Foundation and the SSRC.

Note

1 Published as 'Le Métier d'enfant', in *Revue Français de Sociologie*, *XIV*, pp. 295–335, 1973.

References

BERNSTEIN, B. (1962), see chapter 8 in *Class, Codes and Control* vol. I.

BERNSTEIN, B. (1973), 'A brief account of the theory of codes' in *Social Relationships and Language*, Open University: Educational Studies: Language and Learning Block 3; also in *Class, Codes and Control* vol. I, Routledge & Kegan Paul, revised edition 1974.

BOURDIEU, P. (1972), *Current Research* (of the Centre for European Sociology, École Pratique des Hautes Études), Maison des Sciences de l'Homme, 54 Boulevard Raspail, Paris VI.

BURNS, J. and STALKER, G. M. (1961), *The Management of Innovation*, Tavistock Press.

DOUGLAS, M. (1966), *Purity and Danger*, Routledge & Kegan Paul.

DOUGLAS, M. (1970), *Natural Symbols: Explorations in Cosmology*, Barrie & Rockliff, The Cresset Press.

GOLDTHORPE, J. and LOCKWOOD, D. (1963), 'Affluence and the class structure', *Sociological Review*, vol. XI, pp. 133–63.

KOHN, M. (1959), 'Social class and parental values', *AJS*, vol. 64, pp. 337–51.

MILLER, D. and SWANSON, G. E. (1958), *The Changing American Parent*, New York, John Wiley.

NATHAN, H. (1974), *Stable Rules: Science and Social Transmission*, Studies in the Learning Sciences, Centre for Educational Research and Innovation, OECD.

PARSONS, T. (1964), 'The Link between Character and Society' (with W. White) in *Social Structure and Personality*, The Free Press, Collier Macmillan Ltd.

WALLER, W. (1965), *The Sociology of Teaching*, Science Editions, John Wiley.

Part I Changes in the moral basis of schools

Chapter 1 Sources of consensus and disaffection in education[1]

I want to talk about some of the consequences of education where the school acts as a major source of social, occupational and cultural change. It is well known that the school transforms the identities of many of the children: transforms the nature of their allegiances to their family and community, and gives them access to other styles of life and modes of social relationships. I am going to present an analysis of being a pupil as this role is formed and transformed by the school. The child's response to the school is likely to transform the way in which he thinks and feels about his friends, his community, and society as a whole.

I shall first examine the culture of the school, particularly of the *secondary* school, and I shall try to establish what this school culture is transmitting to the pupils. Second, I will classify different kinds of family settings in terms of a family's perception of the school culture; how they regard it, see it and understand it. Third, I shall consider various ways in which a pupil may be involved in the school and I shall try to indicate how the culture of the school and the form of its transmission may shape the child's involvement in his role as pupil. Finally, I shall consider some consequences both for the child and for society of these various involvements in the role of pupil. The major factors affecting the behaviour of pupils in school are four: the family setting and social origins of the child, the age group or friendship patterns of the child, the school itself, and the pupil's perception of his occupational fate. Any analysis of the pupil's involvement in his role must take into account these four factors—family, age group, school and work—and show the relationships between them. The analysis should hold irrespective of the type of secondary school—grammar, secondary modern or comprehensive—and, in principle, should be capable of extension to other countries; in fact wherever a school is an agent of cultural change.

First, I shall consider the culture of the school and the kind of behaviour the school transmits to the pupil. What are the procedures, practices and judgments that the school expects the pupil to master? There are two distinct, but in practice inter-related, complexes of behaviour which the school is transmitting to the pupil: that part concerned with character training and that part which is concerned with more formal learning. On the one hand, the school is attempting to transmit to the pupil images of conduct, character and manner; it does this by means of certain practices and activities, certain procedures and judgments. On the other hand, the school is transmitting to the pupil facts, procedures, practices and judgments necessary for the acquisition of specific skills: these may be skills involved in the humanities or sciences. These specific skills are often examinable and measurable by relatively objective means. The image of conduct, character and manner is not measurable in the same way. Among the staff there may be a fair degree of agreement about the learning,[2] but there is more room for doubt and uncertainty about the image of conduct, character and manner which the school is trying to transmit.

I propose to call that complex of behaviour and activities in the school which is to do with conduct, character and manner the *expressive order* of the school, and that complex of behaviour, and the activities which generate it, which is to do with the acquisition of specific skills the *instrumental order*.

The relations between these two orders are often a source of strain within the school. The instrumental order may be transmitted in such a way that it distinguishes sharply between groups of pupils. Children may often be streamed off from each other in terms of their ability, in order to assist the development of specific skills in some. Thus the instrumental order of the school is potentially and often actually, divisive in function. It is a source of cleavage not only between pupils, but also between staff (depending upon the subject taught, the age, sex, social class and stream of the pupils).

The expressive order attempts to transmit an image of conduct, character and manner, a moral order which is held equally before each pupil and teacher.[3] It tends to bind the whole school together as a distinct moral collectivity. The more the instrumental order dominates schools in England, the more examination-minded they become and the more divisive becomes their social organization. The greater the emphasis on this type of instrumental order, the more difficult it is for the expressive order to bind and link all the pupils in a cohesive way. It is quite likely that some pupils who are only weakly involved in the instrumental order will be less receptive to the moral order transmitted through the expressive order. In this situation, the children may turn to an expressive order which is pupil-based, and anti-school. It is also likely that a strong involvement in the instrumental order may lead, under certain conditions, to a weakening of the pupil's involvement in the expressive order and the values it transmits.

There are a number of influences which affect the form and the content of the instrumental order (see Appendix A). Major influences are, of course, the economy and the class structure. However, it is likely that any change in the school leaving age or any change in the length of the *average* educational life will have major implications for both the form and contents of the instrumental order.[4] This is too large an issue to be discussed in this paper.

The instrumental order itself may be unstable when society is undergoing rapid technological change. Different subjects may be introduced into the curriculum and some may lose their status. There may also be a change in the means through which the instrumental order is transmitted, in the teaching methods, and this may lead to instabilities within the school.

The expressive order of the school is legitimized by notions of acceptable behaviour held outside the school, but these notions of acceptable behaviour may not be equally held by *all* groups within a society. This may be complicated by the fact that in a fluid, changing society, the very image of conduct, character and manner, the moral order itself, may be unclear and ambiguous. There are at least two sorts of strain in a school's expressive order; first, the moral order may not be acceptable to certain groups within the school, and, second, despite the clarity of the image within the school, the image outside the school may be ambiguous. The weakening of the school's expressive order is likely to weaken the school's attempt to transmit behaviours working for cohesion between staff, between pupils, and between pupils and staff.

So much for a very brief discussion about these twin aspects of the school. (A more extensive account will be found in Bernstein *et al.*, 'Ritual in education', 1966). We shall now present a framework for analysing the pupil's initial involvement in the school. We shall do this by means of a classification of families. We shall classify families according to their understanding of the *means* whereby the expressive and instrumental orders are transmitted and their acceptance of their ends (i.e. their goals). (See Figure 1.1.)

In Figure 1.1 there is a thick black line, at one end of which there is a negative sign and at the other end of which there is a plus sign. This represents the involvement of the pupil as this is initially affected by the family. The child at position 1 is highly involved in the school, and in both orders. If he is initially at position 4, then the situation is more difficult both for the child and for the school. If a family *understands* the means whereby the instrumental order is transmitted (the day-by-day procedures involved in the acquisition of specific skills) then the parents can help to support the child at the level of *means. This does not mean that the family accepts the goals of the instrumental order.* Similarly, a family may understand the *means* whereby the expressive order is transmitted (the day-by-day procedures whereby the moral order of the school becomes available to the child) but this does *not* mean that the family accepts the goals or *ends* of the expressive order. If a family accepts and understands the *means* and the *ends* of both of these orders, then the child would be at position 1. Other things being equal, a child from such a family starts off initially highly involved as a pupil. This is quite likely, but not necessarily, to be a middle-class family.

Let us take position 2. This refers to the family which understands the *means* whereby these two orders are transmitted, but it does not accept the ends. It does not accept, for example, the examination structure, or the necessity of the linkage between education and occupation, or the image of conduct, character and manner. It may hold a different concept of learning, and it may not accept, say, the grammar school concept of appropriate conduct. We can expect here a clash between home and school at the level of ends, which may also lead to a clash at the level of means. A child from such a family would, compared to position 1, have a reduced involvement and so we have placed him at position 2.

Position 3 is a very important one. This is a family which accepts the ends of the instrumental order, but has little understanding of

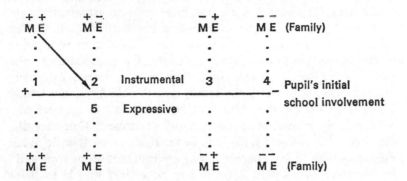

Legend

Instrumental: Facts, procedures, practices and judgments which lead to the acquisition of skills and sensitivities.

Expressive: Image/images of conduct, character and manner *and* their evoking activities.

M = means: *Understanding* by the family of *means* used by the school to transmit the instrumental and expressive orders.

E = ends: Acceptance by the family of ends or goals of the expressive and instrumental orders, i.e. *acceptance of the school's moral order* and *occupational placement through examinations* or equivalent forms of assessment.

1 — M E: Understanding of means, acceptance of ends.

2 — M E: Understanding of means, non-acceptance or rejection of ends.

3 — M E: No or little understanding of means, but acceptance of ends.

4 — M E: No or little understanding of means *and* non-acceptance or rejection of ends.

5 — M E (instrumental)
    M E (expressive)   Understanding of means, of both orders, acceptance of ends of instrumental order *but* rejection of ends of expressive order.

It should be realized that pluses and minuses really are scales. It is, of course, possible to complicate the diagram. We could distinguish further between families who understand the means by which the two orders are transmitted but who do not *accept* them. For example, parents could understand the new mathematics, but not agree with this particular approach. On the whole, in terms of the diagram, if there is a disagreement at the level of means, there is likely to be a disagreement at the level of ends.

Figure 1.1 The family's effect on the pupil's involvement in school

the means used to transmit it. Similarly, it accepts the ends of the expressive order, but has no idea how, in fact, this order is transmitted. The family wants the child to pass examinations, to get a good job, and also to conform to a standard of conduct often different from the one the family possesses. This is often an aspiring working-class family. For such a family, the procedures of the school are often a closed book. This makes for an extremely difficult position for both the family and the child, for the family is likely to deliver the child to school and fail to support him appropriately in matters of learning and adjustment. Consequently, the child's involvement is likely to be relatively more difficult. What must it be like to be a parent if you are insulated from your child in this way? What must it be like to be a child unable to share his school experience with his family? This is extremely painful for the parents, and for the child. Here the school is driving a wedge between the role of the child in his family and his school role. I am not suggesting this goes on in all schools; I am saying it is a possibility in this situation of position 3.

Position 4 is where the family is very negative and uninvolved in both the means and the ends of the two orders of the school. These are families in England found more often in what Newsom calls 'the slum and problem areas'. The child's initial involvement in the school from this point of view is likely to be very weak.

There is a further position of interest. This is the case of a family which understands the means by which the instrumental order is transmitted, and accepts the ends—occupational placement of the child—but it is negative towards the expressive order because it feels that the school's image of conduct, character and manner may carry the child away from the family and the local community. This family would like the child to get on, but is uneasy of the social consequences. This family is ambivalent and the child is likely to have mixed feelings, so his initial position is likely to be position 5 .

Earlier we said that the classification could be complicated if we considered situations where a family understood the means of transmission of instrumental and expressive orders, but rejected them. Perhaps we should give an illustration of this type of family. Imagine a family where the parents held a different concept of education and its function in society. It is likely that a child in this family would find himself in a situation where the school represented one way of life and his family another. Such a conflict would critically affect his response to the school and therefore the nature of his involvement. If position 4 represents a working-class family in a relation of alienation to the society, then the family we have just described may represent a middle-class family in a relation of alienation to the society.

We have now set out a classification of families in terms of their relationship to the school's instrumental and expressive orders at the levels of means and ends. We have discussed six possible relationships, but it is quite clear that the classification could yield a very great number of possible relationships. The weaker the insulation between social groups in society, the more likely we shall need to take advantage of the classification's potential delicacy. The advantage of the classification scheme is that it does not start with the social class position of the family, but with the culture of the school. As a result, we could use the classification scheme in any society. After we have applied it we are likely to find an association between social class and the family's relation to the school. We should also be able to distinguish families, according to their relationship to the school, *within* each social class. Another advantage of this scheme, is that it directs our attention to the school itself; for we cannot proceed empirically unless we know from the *beginning* the culture of the school.

The task of the school is to get all the pupils towards position 1, despite the varying attitudes of the families and the initial role involvements these create in the pupils. This makes of crucial importance the procedures used to transmit these two orders, because they can affect the children's involvement in the school quite dramatically.

Now we will turn away from the family and its initial affect on pupil involvement, and turn to how the pupil comes to define his own role. We can understand a little about how a pupil defines his own role by seeing how he relates to these two orders: the instrumental and the expressive. These different ways of relating to these two orders are not necessarily a function of a pupil's specific psychology, or of his family setting, but they are often shaped by the school. This means that what goes on in a school, its procedures, can influence the pupil's role and also affect his view of society.

We shall now set out five types of pupil role involvements. It is important to realize that there is no necessary progression from one role to another. A pupil can, early in his career, form one role which he maintains for the whole career. He can also shift across roles. (See Figure 1.2.)

As with the diagram illustrating family settings (Figure 1.1), Figure 1.2 can also be further complicated. For example, we could have a situation where a pupil *understands* the means whereby the instrumental and expressive orders are transmitted, but does not accept them. This would give us two types of alienation. One where there was no understanding of the means and no involvement in the ends (position 5), and a type where there would be understanding, but *rejection* of the means whereby the two orders were trans-

		Instrumental means	ends	Expressive means	ends
1	Commitment	+	+	+	+
2	Detachment	+	+	+	−
3	Deferment	....			
4	Estrangement	−	+	+	+
5	Alienation	−	−	−	−

Legend

means: <u>understands</u> the means (+ −: YES NO)

ends: <u>accepts</u> the ends (+ −: high/low involvement)

Figure 1.2 Types of involvement in the role of pupil[5]

mitted. This would represent the alienation of those who the school considered were able children. In the same way, we might need to distinguish two types of detachment. Given the contemporary situation, our schools probably contain alienated middle-class and alienated working-class pupils *and* detached middle-class and detached working-class pupils. *We must bear in mind the class origins of these two different forms of alienation and detachment.*

'Commitment' refers to a role where the pupil is strongly involved in both orders. He is, clearly, not a saint, but his behaviour is appropriate and committed. He is a loyal member of the school, and works well. It is important to point out that a pupil in this situation of what I call 'commitment' conducts his behaviour in an unself-conscious manner and spontaneously produces the behaviour accepted by the school in both its expressive and instrumental orders.

'Detachment' is a more interesting situation. It refers to a role where the pupil is involved in the instrumental order, but he is cool or negative towards the expressive order. He might even go through the motions, or verge towards rejection. This may well be the bright working-class pupil who realizes that if he accepts the expressive order of the school, the image of conduct, character and manner, this may make his relations with his family and community and friends, difficult or strained. On the other hand, he wants to do well; he is eager to learn and pass examinations. This may lead to a cool, apparently uninvolved, attitude to social relations and values. The staff may find it difficult to get through to a pupil involved in this role. In general he is likely to come from a home where the expressive order is not in step with that of the school, or he may belong to an anti-school peer group.

We would add here that a school with a weak expressive order and a dominant and highly divisive instrumental order is likely to move a number of pupils to a role involvement of 'detachment'. This is the kind of pupil who can self-consciously manipulate his role. He is the kind of pupil or person who could, where necessary, turn on the proper relations, the appropriate behaviour. This pupil is able to distance himself from his role.

Position 3 is 'Deferment'. This is a situation where the pupil is, so to speak, deferring his commitments to or involvement in both orders; he is watching the state of play. This is a form of role involvement which is not unusual in the early stages of a pupil's career in a new or different school. It is also a role where there is a discrepancy in outlook between the home and the school; it may apply to working-class children who find themselves at a grammar school, almost as a bonus. These children, I suggest, will be watching the state of play, not quite clear, a bit perplexed or bewildered, not coming down one way or the other. The important factor here is the length of time they maintain this role. This will depend upon the school's inducting procedures. An increasing dependency on an anti-school peer group may well occur in the case of a pupil who maintains this role for any length of time. If the culture of the family and school are very different, then the pupil's peer group is likely to be antagonistic towards the school and this may cause the pupil to move towards alienation.

There is a further type of role involvement: estrangement. Here the pupil is involved in the instrumental order at the level of ends, but he cannot manage its demands; he cannot manage the learning, he does not understand the *means*. It is all a bit too difficult for him. He is, however, highly involved in the expressive order and joins willingly in school activities. He takes up a position of responsibility within the school, plays his part in sports and after-school activities, and behaves well in class. His behaviour is consonant with the image of conduct, character and manner, and he displays his acceptance of the moral order of the school. But his failure in the instrumental order at the level of means may be particularly wounding. He may be placed in a lower stream and among pupils who are only weakly involved, or who might even reject the expressive order to which this pupil is committed and by which he lives. It is likely that this pupil's family and school are in step. However, the pupil's blighted aspirations, combined with a low stream, coupled with his loyalty to the school, may make his school experience particularly painful and damaging. The problem for this pupil in a situation of estrangement is that his relationship to the school entirely depends upon his relation to the expressive order. If that relation weakens, he may well shift and move down towards alienation. It would be interesting to know whether children in role involvements of estrangement develop some form of personality disturbance.

The last role is alienation. This is where the pupil does not understand, and rejects both the instrumental and expressive orders of the school. He is positively in opposition. In the case of detachment and estrangement there is a shadow across one aspect of the role, but in the case of alienation the pupil is related to the school only in terms of conflict or sullen acceptance. The family of such a pupil is likely but not necessarily, to be out of step with the school. The pupil in a role involvement of alienation is likely to forge strong relations with an anti-school peer group and this will serve to set up a vicious circle holding him to his alienated role.

We can use this framework to examine the inter-relationships between the home and the school. Let us imagine that a pupil is in a role involvement of commitment in his family; that is, he unself-consciously and spontaneously accepts the instrumental and expressive orders realized in his family. In terms of our definitions he has internalized the aspirations of the family as these refer to educational success and as these refer to standards of conduct, character and manner. For the sake of argument, let us assume he is a middle-class child. If this child moves to a pupil role involvement of estrangement in the school, we might expect a shift in his role involvement in his family to estrangement, as a result of his failure to achieve family expectations as these apply to educational success. Such a shift in his role involvement in his family may in turn affect many other areas of his life. In the same way, if we take a working-class child who is in a role involvement of commitment in his family and who finds himself in a role involvement of commitment at school, is this likely to lead to a shift in his family role involvement of commitment to one of detachment, or even alienation? We could, in principle, consider a number of other shifts in the school role involvements and seek out their possible consequences for the role involvement in the family. This analysis points to the importance of examining the effect of role shifts in the school upon the home.

The same framework might be used in order to examine the peer group or friendship patterns of the pupils. Is it likely that pupil role involvements structure friendship patterns? In other words, do pupils in role involvements of commitment, detachment, deferment, estrangement, alienation, select their friends in similar role involvements? If this were to be the case, then a change in pupil role involvement would lead to a change in the friendship group and this, of course, would set up a number of other changes.

Finally, we might apply the same framework to the staff of the school: the teachers. Teachers who accepted the instrumental and expressive orders of the school could be said to be in a role involvement of commitment. Teachers who accepted the instrumental order of the school, but not its expressive order, could be said to be in a role involvement of detachment. These might be, for example, some of the science teachers and craft teachers. New teachers in the school could be said to be in a position of deferment. Teachers for whom there were no *promotion* prospects, but who accepted the school's expressive and instrumental orders, might be said to be in a position of estrangement. Finally, teachers who were hostile to the school's instrumental and expressive orders could be said to be in a position of alienation. Is it likely that teachers in similar role positions would form friendship groups, and perhaps form pressure groups, of various types?

We might also consider the relationships between teachers in one role position teaching pupils in another. Simply for purposes of illustration, we could consider the following:

Teacher's Role	*Pupil's Role*
Commitment	Alienation
Estrangement	Detachment
Alienation	Commitment
Deferment	Deferment
Detachment	Estrangement

Clearly, a large number of permutations are possible, and there is no space in this short paper to discuss the outcomes of discrepancies between teacher's and pupil's roles, and discrepancies between pupil's roles and their family roles.

I have tried to use the same conceptual framework for families, pupils and teachers and to show the dynamics of their inter-relationships. Perhaps one important consequence of this analysis is that we can see that there is a range of possible role positions; many analyses simply divide children into the academic and non-academic, or the delinquent and the achieving. This analysis also points to the critical importance of both the organizational structure and the knowledge structure of the school *and* the principles of transmission. In other words *how* the expressive order is transmitted, *how* the instrumental order is transmitted, *what* is transmitted by both, what the official and unofficial goals are, of both orders, will structure the role positions of teachers and pupils, affect the nature of teacher and pupil relationships and their respective friendship and pressure groups and affect the pupil's relationship to his family and community.

Commitment, detachment, deferment, estrangement and aliena-tion—these role involvements are sociological in the sense that the forces shaping them may well be independent of the specific psychological attributes of the pupils. They represent possible ways pupils and teachers will relate to the school. Two sets of forces shape the pupil's role; the first depends upon the family's relation to the expressive and instrumental orders of the school, the second upon the procedures the school uses to involve the pupil in both of its orders. Here we can begin to see the area of autonomy of the school. Irrespective of the family, the school is an independent force in the pupil's definition of his role. What the school does, its rituals, its ceremonies, its authority relations, its stratification, its procedures for learning, its incentives, rewards and punishments, its very image of conduct, character and manner, can modify or change the pupil's role as this has been initially shaped by the family. *Thus the number of pupils initially involved in a particular role can be modified or changed by the school itself.*

I would like finally to look at the significance of these types of role involvements from a different perspective. A school is a microcosm of society. Socialization into the school and the type of socialization affects socialization into the society as a whole. In society, groups are differently ranked in terms of prestige, and this prestige is usually ranked according to economic function, type of work. Here we have a divisive principle of social organization. In a school with a dominant instrumental order, the divisive element is also strong, and pupils may be ranked invidiously in terms of their position, in that order. In this way, pupils come to know, to accept, reject or come to terms with, the class system before they are formally part of it.

The expressive order of the school is often a formalization, crystallization, even idealization, of an image of conduct, character and manner reflected by some, but not all, groups in the wider society. The expressive order of the school has some relation, but not a direct one, to what sociologists call the style of life. The nature of the pupil's involvement in the expressive order of the school and the particular *form* of the school's expressive order affects his perception and behaviour when he leaves.

My point is simple. The more important a school is in re-ordering an individual's place within society, the more can the type of involvement in the role of pupil have critical consequences for society. In pluralistic societies like ours, where there are many and conflicting images of conduct, character and manner, and where technological change is rapid, the school system is subject to many pressures. These pressures are translated to the pupil in terms of the character of his role involvement. The external pressures of the society as a whole are crystallized out and felt and experienced by the child in terms of each of these five roles he moves towards. The school system need not necessarily be a passive mediator or, at worst, an amplifier for these general social pressures.

Notes

1 A shortened version of this paper appeared in the *Journal of the Association of Assistant Mistresses*, 17, pp. 4–11, 1966.
2 This is no longer true today. See chapter 5.

3 In fact, it is likely that where the instrumental order involves strong cleavage between pupils, *different* standards may be expected of different groups of pupils.
4 This relation of the instrumental order to work is much more complex than has been indicated. The linkage between the two is often through the licences to practice (examinations) in different parts of the system, issued by schools, universities etc., rather than through specific contents (subjects).
5 This classification focuses upon types of consensus and disaffection. We may need to extend the classification to include a pupil's relation to the school of *indifference*.

References

BERNSTEIN, B. (1967), 'Open schools, open society?' *New Society*, 14 September. Reprinted as Chapter 3 in this volume.

BERNSTEIN, B., ELVIN, H. L. and PETERS, R. S. (1966), 'Ritual in education', *Philosophical Transactions of the Royal Society of London*, Series B, 251, No. 772.

FORD, J. (1969), *Social Class and the Comprehensive School*, Routledge & Kegan Paul.

GOFFMAN, E. (1961), *Encounters*, Bobbs Merrill.

HARGREAVES, D. (1968), *Social Relationships in a Secondary School*, Routledge & Kegan Paul.

KING, R. (1969), *Values and Involvements in a Grammar School*, Routledge & Kegan Paul.

LAMBERT, R., BULLOCK, R. and MILLHAM, S. (1970), *A Manual to the Sociology of the School*, Weidenfeld & Nicolson.

YOUNG, M. (ed.) (1971), *Knowledge and Control*, Collier-Macmillan.

Appendix A: Additional notes

Note 1

We can summarize the typology of pupils' roles as in Figure 1.3 :

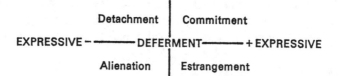

Figure 1.3

I am grateful to Dr R. King for the above form of presentation.

Note 2

The reader will have noted that the distinction between means and ends is used for the allocation of families and pupils to different positions in the classification schemes, but that only *ends* are used for the allocation of pupils to roles within their family. This has been done to reduce the complexity of the analysis. Further, when we considered the involvement of the teacher at the level of *means* in his teaching role, we indicated that this was in terms of his acceptance or rejection of the *means* used to transmit the instrumental and expressive orders. It does not make sense to talk about the teacher's understanding of the means. Presumably he is paid because he does understand the means.

Note 3

In this analysis we have imposed a goal upon the instrumental order, i.e., examination success, which may not be the official goal of the school. This immediately raises a number of questions. How do we distinguish formal or official goals or ends from the informal and unofficial goals which guide actual practice? Further, we need to take into account whether a school offers a common curriculum for all of its pupils or whether curricula are carefully graded according to various sub-groups of pupils. It is likely that in stratified societies we shall find a range of curricula in a secondary school which form a hierarchy of relative prestige. For the purpose of this analysis, we should take as the ends or goals of the instrumental order the ends or goals of that curriculum which enjoys the highest prestige. We are likely to find that such a curriculum is a critical stepping stone to high ranking positions in the society. (See Bernstein *et al.*, 1966, 1967, 1971; Young, 1971).

Note 4

It might be considered that the means-ends schema used in the paper *assumes* agreement about ends and therefore implies a consensual model. However, it does not seem to me unwarranted to assume that one of the major goals or ends of the instrumental order is to provide access to the acquisition of valued skills relevant to valued occupational positions. Indeed the secondary school system is subject to the controls of the economy and the entry qualifications of higher educational establishments. This is not to say that this must necessarily be the case, or that there is general agreement that it ought to be the case. I indicate in the paper that the goals or ends of the school's expressive order may well be problematic. Indeed, much of staff-student-pupil protest is a response to the moral socialization of the school and its implicit and explicit conceptions of appropriate conduct. The argument may also appear to understate the power of individuals to change the terms of their encounters. On the other hand it is quite clear that the analysis points to the possible patterns of conflicting interests which schools may create, but it leaves open the form of their resolution. The form of their resolution depends ultimately upon the weakening of the controls of the economy and higher education upon the organizational and knowledge properties of the school.

Appendix B: Instrumental and expressive orders

Instrumental and expressive orders refer to the *social structures* which control the transmission of skills and morals. Instrumental and expressive orders may each be distinguished in terms of the strength of the boundaries they create. We may then scale these orders on a dimension of open and closed. Where these orders are closed, definitions of roles, groups, subject boundaries and sequence, relationships with the outside, are explicit and strong; where these orders are open, definitions of roles, groups, subject boundaries and sequence, relationships with the outside, are implicit and blurred. It may well be the case that within *one* school the instrumental order for one group of pupils (e.g. the élite) may be closed and for another group of pupils (e.g. the less able) it may be open. Thus the *social composition* of the groups of pupils and teachers who share the similar role involvements *and* the numbers in any given role involvement may be a function of the degree and *scale* of openness of the instrumental and expressive orders of the school.

Figure 1.4 on page 53 shows in ideal typical form differences in the social structures of open and closed instrumental and expressive orders.

Figure 1.4

Formal Controls
ORDERS: INSTRUMENTAL

Mixing of Categories	Purity of Categories
Teaching groups: Heterogeneous—size and composition varied	Teaching groups: Homogeneous—size and composition fixed.
Pedagogy: Problem setting or creating. Emphasizes *ways of knowing*	Pedagogy: Solution giving. Emphasizes *contents* or states of *knowledge*
Teachers: Teaching roles co-operative/inter-dependent. Duties *achieved*. Fluid points of reference and relation. Subject boundaries blurred (inter-related)	Teachers: Teaching roles insulated from each other. Duties *assigned*. Fixed points of reference and relation. Subject boundaries sharp (less inter-relation or integration)
Curriculum: Progression: deep to surface structure of knowledge. Common curriculum	Curriculum: Progression: surface to deep structure of knowledge. Curriculum graded for different ability groups
Pupils: Varied social groups reducing *group* similarity and difference—increased area of choice. Aspirations of the *many* raised. Fluid points of reference and relation	Pupils: Fixed and stable social groups emphasizing *group* similarity and difference—reduced area of choice. Aspirations of the *few* developed. Fixed points of reference and relation

TYPE—OPEN

(1) Ritual order celebrates participation/co-operation
(2) Boundary relationships with outside blurred
(3) Internal organization: wide range of integrative sub-groups with active membership and success roles across ability ranges. If prefect system—wide area of independence from staff, but limited exercise of power. Range of opportunities for pupils to influence staff decisions, e.g. opportunities for self-government
(4) Teacher-pupil authority relationships: Reward and punishment less public and ritualized. Teacher-pupil relationships of control—inter-personal

ORDERS: EXPRESSIVE

Mixing of Categories

TYPE—CLOSED

(1) Ritual order celebrates hierarchy/dominance
(2) Boundary relationships with outside sharply drawn
(3) Internal organization: narrower range of integrative sub-groups with active membership and success roles confined to high ability range. If prefect system—under staff control and influence, but extensive exercise of power. Limited opportunities for pupils to influence staff decisions, e.g. limited opportunities for self-government.
(4) Teacher-pupil authority relationships: Reward and punishment public and ritualized. Teacher-pupil relationships of control—positional

Purity of Categories

Chapter 2   Ritual in education

Introduction

Ritual in animals generally refers to a rigid pattern of motor acts which function as signals controlling behaviour between animals in specific situations. Ritual in humans generally refers to a relatively rigid pattern of acts, specific to a situation, which construct a framework of meaning over and beyond the specific situational meanings. Here, the symbolic function of ritual is to relate the individual through ritualistic acts to a social order, to heighten respect for that order, to revivify that order within the individual and, in particular, to deepen acceptance of the procedures which are used to maintain continuity, order and boundary and which control ambivalence towards the social order.

Ritual will be considered as an expression in action as distinct from thought of man's active attitudes towards these non-empirical aspects of their reality, which are expressive of ultimate values.

First, we shall examine these notions as they relate to a school as a social form and, second, we shall examine the effect of changes in the function of the school on ritualizing processes.

The school as a social form

Although there is clearly only one order within a school, it is useful to distinguish two different orders of relation which control both its transmission and the response to the transmission: an instrumental order which controls the transmission of facts, procedures and judgments involved in the acquisition of specific skills, and an expressive order which controls the transmission of the beliefs and moral system. Both of these orders can be distinguished in terms of the forms of social relation which control the transmissions. The forms of social relation of the instrumental order are bureaucratic,[1] whilst the forms of social relation of the expressive order are non-bureaucratic. Differences in the patterns of social relations of these two orders will become clear during the ensuing discussion. The expressive order can be considered as a source of the school's shared values and is therefore potentially cohesive in function, whilst the instrumental order, on the other hand, is potentially divisive. It is the expressive order which is the major mechanism of social consensus and thus under certain conditions is prone to extensive ritualization. The rituals of the expressive order may be divided into two main groups: consensual and differentiating.

(a) Consensual rituals

These are the rituals which function so as to bind together all members of the school, staff and pupils as a moral community, as a distinct collectivity. These consensual rituals give the school continuity in time and place. They recreate the past in the present and project it into the future. These rituals also relate the school's values and norms to those held by, or alleged to be held by, certain dominant groups in the non-school society. The consensual rituals give the school its specific identity as a distinct and separate institution. They facilitate appropriate sentiments towards the dominant value system of the wider society. They assist in the integration of the various goals of the school within a coherent set of shared values, so that the values of the school can become internalized and experienced as a unity. In general the consensual rituals consist of assemblies and ceremonies of various kinds together with the consensual lineaments of dress, the imagery of signs, totems, scrolls and plaques for the revivifying of special historical contexts and other symbolic features. An important component of the consensual rituals is the ritual of punishment and reward.

(b) Differentiating rituals

These are concerned to mark off groups within the school from each other, usually in terms of age, sex, age relation or social function. The differentiating rituals deepen local attachment behaviour to, and detachment behaviour from, specific groups; they also deepen respect behaviour to those in various positions of authority, and create order in time.

These two main types of rituals are major mechanisms for the internalizing and revivifying of social order. They function to maintain continuity, order, boundary and the control of dual loyalties and ambivalence. The rituals control questioning of the basis of the expressive culture and so are conditions for its effective transmission and reception. They buttress the formal authority relations and evoke respect through the ritualization of difference and similarity of function; they create continuity in individual and social time and relate the value system and its derived norms to an approved external order.

To give an illustration: the school is a community related to, but different from, kin and local community. It is a stage in the emancipation of the pupil towards his acceptance of a wider referent group. Problems of divided allegiance and relation on the part of pupil, kin and school are partly solved by ritualizing, so sharpening the boundaries between the different groups. The consensual rituals and their inductive subsets facilitate detachment behaviour from family and local community and attachment behaviour to the school. For parents these rituals transform the child into pupil. The consensual rituals of the school orient the pupil to special classes of behaviour and give him a specific consciousness of age, sex, school and kinship status. The separation of statuses—for example, in possessing a distinct school and family status—increases the degree of control the school can exert on both the pupil and the kin.

Within the school the problem of ordering, integrating and controlling the heterogeneous population is assisted by the differentiating rituals and their initiating or inducting subsets. There are at least four types of such differentiating rituals.

(1) AGE DIFFERENTIATING RITUALS

These help to differentiate groups in time by marking out age status as of special significance. The age rituals often function as *rites de passage*. They may become sources of conflict where such *rites de passage* have been weakened in the non-school society.

The age rituals often reinforce the class as the basic unit of social organization and in this way serve to regulate local attachment behaviour to persons, territory and property. They also serve to impersonalize the relations between different age groups, controlling and focusing clashes or crushes.

(2) AGE RELATION RITUALS

These are essentially concerned with authority relations. Often the age groups are marked off from each other in terms of different approach behaviour to those in formal authority. A cluster of rituals normally group round the prefect system, marking it off as a separate system of social control. These rituals serve to increase distance and thus boundary between unequals. They strengthen commitment to basic values and control feelings of ambivalency and dual allegiance.

(3) SEX RITUALS

These are consensual in single sex schools but differentiating as far as the non-school society is concerned. Conceptions of the masculine are celebrated by such rituals. They cohere round sporting activities[2] but may appear as approach behaviour to female members of staff or to visitors. In dual sex schools they become differentiating rituals reinforcing sex typing. In boys' schools and particularly in girls' schools, these rituals may also control sexual display behaviour. However, it is as well to remember that the black stockings of the 1930s have become signs of sexual display in the 1960s.

(4) HOUSE RITUALS

These are the rituals which delineate fictional communities within the school, and each community has its own set of consensual and differentiating rituals, together with their inductive subsets. The whole is supported by the lineaments of dress, the imagery of signs, totems, the associations and sentiments invoked by scrolls, plaques, chants, etc.

One further point should perhaps be made. Cognitive difference between boys, as this finds expression in ability, is often transformed into a component of consensual ritual if it is related to the school, or into a component of the differentiating ritual if it is related to a particular class. Sporting prowess is similarly transformed. The consensual and differentiating rituals then function to assist in the creation of a unique identity for the school, in defining and regulating boundary behaviour, continuity, and order, and in controlling ambivalence and dual allegiances. These rituals both facilitate the transmission, reception and internalization of the values of the expressive order and relate these usually to an approved value system outside of the school. The rituals also serve to prevent questioning of the values and of the social order which transmits them.

So far, then, we have been considering not what necessarily exists, for schools vary in the degree to which the expressive order is ritualized, but the critical points of ritualization. The more a school resembles a total institution (that is where the life of the pupil is almost wholly spent in the school, as in a boarding school) the greater the ritualizing of its expressive order. It is also likely that day schools in countries with a single, explicit political or religious ideology are likely to display extensive ritualization, especially schools in those countries which are currently undergoing, or have recently undergone, rapid technological change. In this case ritualization within the school is a major means through which such single ideologies are transmitted and social cohesion maintained under conditions of rapid social change. The school itself symbolizes and celebrates the social order to come.

Industrialization and responsiveness to ritual in schools

In advanced industrialized societies the social purpose of the school becomes one of educating for diversity in social and economic function. In this situation it is worthwhile examining the forces which may have critical consequences for the pupil's responsiveness to consensual and differentiating rituals. We are thinking here particularly of the situation in Britain.

Differentiating rituals

In the school these rituals tend to mark out specific groups in terms of age, sex, age relations, and house. The latter may perhaps be regarded as the school equivalent of community. The process of industrialization reduces the significance of the family as a determiner of occupational status. It affects age relations (authority relations) by dissolving customary boundaries, mutual spheres of freedom and control, and renders more implicit and informal the transfer of adult responsibilities to the young, so that effective regulation of the young becomes problematic. Moreover, family rituals, which mark out as of special social significance changes in age status, weaken. In fact, age as a social status comes to have an important achieved element. Early adolescents, by various accessories (cosmetics and dress) present themselves as middle adolescents in order to achieve youth group identity, whilst fifty-year-olds attempt to present themselves as members of a younger age group. Thus there is a compression in that part of the age span which is socially significant. At the same time sex typing of the young is reduced and sex status is less significant as a restriction on occupational function. The net effect of changes in the significance of age, sex, age relation, and family status for the ordering of social relations is to increase the possibility of innovation within a society and to widen the area of individual choice. At the same time this creates problems of assuring cultural continuity for those transmitting the society's culture, and creates problems of boundary, order ambivalence and thus of identity in the young.

Further, age and sex tend to become less relevant as general social categories for distinguishing and separating groups within the school. This can be seen in the development of vertical integration in the primary school, where children between the ages of five to seven years are placed together to form one educational group. At the secondary level, on the other hand, and especially in comprehensive schools, children are placed in sets according to the single criterion of the ability they display in each subject. In this way the social unit for school organization becomes both less homogeneous in terms of age and sex and more differentiated. In addition, the changes in age relations (authority relations) are likely to make the authority of the teacher in expressive spheres conditional rather than automatic.

Thus, differentiating rituals in the school in terms of age, sex, age relation and house membership are not matched by adult-regulated differentiating rituals in similar areas in the family setting or community; the organizational procedures of the school make its social unit often less homogeneous and the units themselves more differentiated; the authority of the teacher in expressive spheres becomes conditional.

Consensual rituals

These are the rituals which, it was said, function so as to bind together all members of the school, staff and pupils as a moral community. They assist in the integration of the various goals of the school, within a coherent set of shared values, so that the values of the school can become internalized and experienced as a unity. In pluralistic, industrialized societies, there is often considerable ambiguity in their central value systems. This can lead to a sharp discrepancy between the clarity of the value system of the school and the ambiguity in the value system of the society. This tends to weaken responsiveness to the school's expressive order, and thus also to its ritualization. The need to exploit intellectual ability leads to overt and covert selection procedures in order to increase the proportion of children who pass examinations. This often leads to a sense of failure, and sometimes alienation, in the children who are less able. This situation is further complicated by the task the school has (especially the grammar school) of assimilating the children of parents who do not share, or who often do not understand, the expressive order of the school. Here, the acceptance of the school's expressive order may also require a reorientation of the normal procedures a pupil uses to relate in his family setting and local community.

Thus the response to the consensual rituals is likely to be weakened because of ambiguity in the society's central value systems, the divisive consequences of covert and overt selection procedures and the increase in the social heterogeneity of pupils at selective secondary schools.

It is likely that the social basis for the ritualization of the expressive order of the school will be considerably weakened and the rituals may come to have the character of social routines. We might also expect a switch from the dominance of adult-imposed and regulated rituals to the dominance of rituals generated and regulated by youth. It would seem, then, for the reasons given, that there is likely to be a marked change in the pupil's responsiveness to consensual and differentiating rituals whilst organizational changes in the schools may not facilitate their development.

Ritual and changes in school structure

We have been considering how the expressive order of the school is transmitted and we have suggested that a major means of its transmission is through its ritualization. We have indicated that the pupil's responsiveness to ritualization of the school's expressive order is likely to be weakened in state schools in our contemporary, pluralistic society. We now want to consider changes in the structure of the school as a social form and the consequences for changes in the *means* through which the expressive order is transmitted. Ritualization is likely to be highly developed in schools where pupils are ordered and grouped on the basis of a fixed attribute or an attribute which is thought to be fixed. This fixed attribute can be sex, age or IQ. If IQ is considered as a fixed attribute, then this acts to produce divisions within an age/sex group. Thus if a fixed attribute is taken as a basis for ordering relationships within a school, then a fairly explicit vertical and horizontal form of social organization develops. We shall call such a structure a stratified one. This structure facilitates ritualization of the expressive order, and especially so if the school is insulated from or can insulate itself from the community of which it is a part. This can often be facilitated through the ritualization of relationships at its boundaries. However, if the basis for ordering relationships among the pupils is not a fixed attribute, then the school structure ceases to be stratified and becomes differentiated. This is the case where cognitive ability is seen as a process rather than a substance. A process which does not develop in a uniform way in all pupils, nor in a uniform way in all subjects, but a process which can be shaped and modified by the social context. If cognitive ability is perceived in this way, then a school will not develop explicit vertical and horizontal organizing procedures. Ideally, pupils will achieve different positions in a range of groups or sets, membership in which is less likely to be related to age or sex but more likely to be related to special proficiency in a particular subject. The notion of education for diversity receives institutional embodiment in the differentiated school. The shift from stratified to differentiated schools may not always involve a change in the content of the expressive order but it does involve a change in the *means* by which it is transmitted. As vertical and horizontal organizing procedures become less relevant, the structural basis for consensual and differentiating rituals becomes much weaker. The values of the expressive order in stratified schools are translated through ritual into elements of its social structure, whereas in differentiated schools the values tend to be psychologized and issue in the form of inter-personal relations. This changes also the basis of social control.

Ritual involves a highly redundant form of communication in the sense that, given the social context, the messages are highly predictable. The messages themselves contain meanings which are highly condensed. Thus the major meanings in ritual are extra-verbal or indirect; for they are not made verbally explicit. Ritual is a form of restricted code. The expressive order, then, in a stratified school is transmitted through a communication system which is verbally both highly condensed and highly redundant. The expressive order of a differentiated school is likely to be transmitted, not through ritual and its restricted code, but through a communication system where the meanings are verbally elaborated, less predictable and therefore more individualized. If the basis for social control through ritual is extra-verbal or indirect, impersonal and non-rational, then the basis for social control where ritual is weakened is likely to be personal, verbally explicit and rational. A major source of control in stratified schools is the internalizing of the social structure and the arousal and organization of sentiments evoked through ritual, signs, lineaments, heraldic imagery and totems. In differentiated schools there is likely to be a weakening of ritual and its supporting insignia. The social structure is then unlikely to be experienced as a unity, and social control will come to rest upon inter-personal means. It will tend to become psychologized and to work through the verbal manipulation of motives and dispositions in an inter-personal context. We shall call this form of social control, this form of transmission of the expressive order, *therapeutic*. In the differentiated school both teacher and taught are exposed and vulnerable in a way very different from their relationships in a stratified school. One might wonder whether the stratified, ritualized school does not evoke *shame* as a major controlling sentiment in the pupils, whereas the differentiated, personalized school might evoke *guilt* as the controlling sentiment. The stratified school is, perhaps, also more likely to communalize failure, whereas the differentiated school is more likely to individualize failure. Thus changes in school structure and in the means used to transmit the expressive order may have important socializing consequences.[3]

This shift in school structure from stratified to differentiated can be understood as a shift from a social order resting upon *domination* to one resting upon *co-operation*. This shift itself is probably related to a similar shift in the character of work relations in an advanced industrialized society.[4] However, this shift in school structure entails not only problems of order, boundary, continuity and ambivalence for pupils but also a shift in consensus, within the school, from that based upon shared ends or values to that based upon shared means or skills. This possibility must finally be considered.

The instrumental order of the school and the basis of social consensus

The more the social purpose of education is to educate for diversity in economic and social function, the more likely it is that the school will shift from a stratified to a differentiated form. We have argued that the response to the expressive order is likely to be weakened, and social control to be based upon therapeutic rather than ritual procedures. Inasmuch as the school is a major instrument of the division of labour through its control over the occupational fate of its pupils, it has taken on a pronounced bureaucratic function. Here it subordinates pupils' needs to the requirements of the division of labour through the examination system. The teacher-pupil relation, where the pupils are selected as potential examinees, often becomes almost one of contract with limited commitment on each side. Knowledge is rationally organized by the teacher and transmitted in terms of its examination efficiency. Control over such pupils stems from control over their occupational or higher educational fate. Such control is bureaucratic. The instrumental order of the school is likely to be transmitted through bureaucratic procedures which affect curriculum, the transmission of knowledge and the quality of the pupil-teacher relation.

For the non-examination children the school functions not so much as a delicate instrument of the division of labour but much more as an instrument of social control regulating the behaviour of such pupils, their emotional sensitivities, their modes of social relation to what is considered acceptable to a section of the society to which they often feel they do not really belong. The school is regulating style of life. The teacher here can be likened to a social worker concerned with the transmission of social skills. Indeed this conception of the role of teacher is explicitly recognized. The control over such pupils is not so much bureaucratic as it is therapeutic, resting upon personal, verbal, rational, techniques. Conformity within the school is obtained through the transmission of occupational and social skills. Social order within the school comes to rest upon shared techniques or skills rather than upon shared values. Here we have a dominant instrumental culture transmitted either through bureaucratic or therapeutic procedures.

Educating for diversity of economic and social function in pluralistic societies often involves a strengthening of the instrumental and a weakening of the expressive order of schools within the state system. Problems of continuity, order, boundary and ambivalence become socially active as the school moves to a differentiated form, or as stratified schools become de-ritualized. Pupils are then likely to generate their own consensual and differentiating rituals in order to assist in the development of a transitional identity. What is novel is that the organizational setting of the school, its focus upon attributes of selected pupils, its emphasis upon skills, the bureaucratization of learning, the individualizing of failure, is facilitating the dominance of the informal, autonomous youth group as the major source of shared values and sentiments. This shift from adult-imposed to the dominance of pupil-generated and regulated rituals is likely to weaken still further the transmission of the school's expressive order.

Inasmuch as the school is more and more closely linked to the demands of the occupational system the more probable it is that the tendencies discussed will be strengthened. Indeed the viability of the differentiated school may be lost so that it becomes simply a disguised form of the stratified type. In fact it may be that the only means available to weaken the dominance of the instrumental order is to challenge the élitist assumptions and functions of the contemporary British university system. It is the small percentage of the age group in Britain at present attending higher education which is responsible for overt and covert selection procedures, the bureaucratization of knowledge, the divisive nature of the instrumental order in all schools—stratified or so-called differentiated—and the shift of educational resources and rewards towards the élite pupils and away from the less successful. If the number of places at the higher levels of education were greater than the number of students available to fill them (which would make selection procedures less relevant), then the schools would at least possess a degree of autonomy over their procedures, curriculum and organization. Educating for diversity under contemporary social conditions inevitably reduces the possibilities of social consensus at the level of ends within the school. It may be that, in a period of heightened social change, continuity in the transmission of culture can only be obtained at the cost of a false yesterday or a mythical tomorrow.

Conclusion

We have attempted to analyse the role of consensual and differentiating rituals in British state schools, with some reference to problems of continuity order, boundary and ambivalence. We have suggested that these rituals facilitate the transmission and internalization of the expressive order of the school, create consensus, revivify the social order within the individual, deepen respect for and impersonalize authority relations. They also serve to prevent questioning of the values the expressive order transmits. We have argued that the social basis for the transmission and response to ritual has been weakened within the school as a result of changes in age, sex, age relation and family status in the society and through changes in school organization and social composition. We have also suggested that educating for diversity in economic and social function under contemporary social conditions increases the dominance of the school's instrumental order, which may switch the focus of ritual from the celebration of ends to that of means. We have argued that bureaucratic and therapeutic forms of social control may develop, and that this probably will facilitate youth-generated and regulated rituals which will tend to replace adult-imposed and regulated rituals as the source of shared values and sentiments. Finally, we have suggested that if the school is to be more than a passive mediator of, or at worse, an amplifier for, general social pressures, a way must be found for attenuating the relationship between the educational and the occupational system.

Notes

1 The expressions of knowledge may be ritualized, e.g. the rituals of assessment.
2 Sport is also a medium for celebrating the subordination of conflict/competition to rules. Such celebration becomes a part of consensual rituals.
3 It should be possible to distinguish *within* forms of stratified or differentiated schools in terms of the degree and kind of stratification or differentiation. Some stratified schools may well display differentiating features and differentiated schools may well have sections which are stratified.
4 The shift from stratified to differentiated is not necessarily related to changes in the character of the occupational order. The American high school started as a differentiated form with a relatively weak instrumental order and a strong expressive one. The function of the latter was that of integrating the large immigrant population into the American society. Further, one would not expect, for example, Soviet schools to display marked differentiating features, as such features would weaken the transmission and reception of the political ideology transmitted through the school's expressive order.

References

DOUGLAS, M. (1966), *Purity and Danger*, Routledge & Kegan Paul.
DURKHEIM, E. (1915), *The Elementary Forms of the Religious Life*, Allen & Unwin.
DURKHEIM, E. (1961), *Moral Education*, Free Press, Chicago.
GERTH, H. H. and MILLS, C. W. (1948), *From Max Weber*, Routledge & Kegan Paul.
GLUCKMAN, M. (ed.) (1966), *Essays in Ritual of Social Relation*, Manchester University Press.
GOFFMAN, E. (1961), *Asylums*, New York, Anchor Books, Doubleday.
WALLER, W. (1961), *The Sociology of Teaching*, New York, Russell & Russell.

Chapter 3 Open schools — open society?

There has been much talk among sociologists concerned with education about the possibilities of analysing the school as a complex organization. The approach to current changes in the structure of the contemporary school system, which I attempt in this article, was initially set out by Durkheim over seventy years ago in his book, *The Divisions of Labour*. I shall interpret the changes in terms of a shift of emphasis in the principles of social integration—from 'mechanical' to 'organic' solidarity. Such changes in social integration within schools are linked to fundamental changes in the character of the British educational system: a change from education in depth to education in breadth. I shall raise throughout this article the question of the relationship between the belief and moral order of the school, its social organization and its forms of social integration.

The concepts, mechanical and organic solidarity, can be used to indicate the emphasis within a society of one form of social integration rather than another. Organic solidarity is emphasized wherever individuals relate to each other through a complex inter-dependence of specialized social functions. Therefore organic solidarity presupposes a society whose social integration arises out of *differences* between individuals. These differences between individuals find their expression becomes crystallized into *achieved* roles. Mechanical solidarity is emphasized wherever individuals share a common system of belief and common sentiments which produce a detailed regulation of conduct. If social roles are achieved under organic solidarity, they are *assigned* or 'ascribed' under mechanical solidarity.

Wherever we have mechanical solidarity, according to Durkheim,

67

punishment is necessary in order to revivify shared values and sentiments; i.e. punishment takes on a symbolic value over and beyond its specific utilitarian function. The belief system is made palpable in the symbolization of punishment. Durkheim took what he called repressive (criminal) law as an index of mechanical solidarity.

Under conditions of organic solidarity, the concern is less to punish but more to reconcile conflicting claims. Social control, in conditions of organic solidarity, is concerned with the relationships between *individuals* which have in some way been damaged. Durkheim took what he called restitutive law (civil) as his index of organic solidarity. Here the system of social control becomes restitutive or reparative in function. Whereas under mechanical solidarity, individuals confront one another indirectly, their confrontation being mediated by the belief system—under organic solidarity, in situations of social control, the belief system recedes into the background and the individuals confront one another directly.

Mechanical solidarity, according to Durkheim, arises in what he called a segmental society. He meant by this a type of society which could lose much of its personnel without damage to its continuity. Organic solidarity would correspond to the differentiated society, with diverse specialization of social roles; consequently the loss of a particular group of specialists might seriously impair the society. One can infer that segmental societies would make clear distinctions between inside and outside; whereas in differentiated societies the boundaries, as all symbolic boundaries, between inside and outside would become blurred.

Durkheim argued that a secondary cause of the division of labour arose out of the growing indeterminacy of the collective conscience (the value system). He said that sentiments would be aroused only by the infringement of highly general values, rather than by the minutiae of social actions. This, he said, would give rise to wider choice and so would facilitate individualism.

Organic solidarity refers to social integration at the level of individualized, specialized, interdependent social roles, whereas mechanical solidarity refers to social integration at the level of shared beliefs. Under mechanical solidarity, there would be little tension between private beliefs and role obligations. In organic solidarity, the tensions between private belief and role obligations could be severe. This tension might be felt particularly by those individuals in socializing roles—for example, parents, teachers, probation officers, psychiatrists.

This is the shift of emphasis in the principles of social integration in schools—from mechanical to organic solidarity—that I shall be talking about. I am not concerned whether all the relationships I refer to are factually present in all schools. Clearly, some schools will have shifted not at all, others more; the shift may be more pronounced in the education of special groups of pupils or within different subjects. I am interested only in the general movement which at the moment may exist at the ideological rather than the substantive level. However, the list of shifts in emphasis may form a measure or scale of the change in the principles of social integration.

Consider, first, the forms of social control. In secondary schools there has been a move away from the transmission of common values through a ritual order and control based upon position or status, to more personalized forms of control where teachers and taught confront each other as individuals. The forms of social control appeal less to shared values, group loyalties and involvements; they are based rather upon the recognition of differences between individuals. And with this there has been a weakening of the symbolic significance and ritualization of punishment.

Look now at the division of labour of the school staff. Irrespective of the pupil/teacher ratios, the staff is now much larger. The division of labour is more complex from the point of view of the range of subjects taught. Within the main subjects, the hierarchy of responsibility has become more differentiated. The teacher's role itself has fragmented to form a series of specialized roles (vocational, counselling, housemaster, social worker and so on). Still within the broad category of the division of labour consider—very briefly, for the moment—the organization of pupils. The pupils' position in the new schools in 'principle' is less likely to be fixed in terms of sex, age or IQ, for ideally their position, within limits, is achieved in terms of their individual qualities.

Thus we find (a) a movement towards a more complex division of labour among the staff and a greater differentiation of the teacher's role; and (b) at the same time, the pupils' relationships with other pupils in principle arise from their expression of their educational differences. This is good evidence of a shift towards organic solidarity.

Let us turn, next, to shifts in emphasis in the curriculum, pedagogy, the organization of teaching groups and teaching and pupil roles. Here we are at the heart of the instrumental order of the school: the transmission of skills and sensitivities.

Take the organization of teaching groups first. Here we can begin to see a shift from a situation where the teaching group is a fixed structural unit of the school's organization (the form or class), to secondary schools where the teaching group is a flexible or variable unit of the social organization. The teaching group can consist of one, five, twenty, forty or even 100 pupils and this number can vary from subject to subject. At the same time there has been an increase in the number of different teaching groups a pupil of a given age is in. The form or class tends to be weakened as a basis for relation and organization.

One can raise the level of abstraction and point out that space and time in the new schools—relative to the old—have (again within limits) ceased to have fixed references. Social spaces can be used for a variety of purposes and filled in a number of different ways. This potential is built into the very architecture.

Now for the changes in pedagogy. There is a shift—from a pedagogy which, for the majority of secondary school pupils, was concerned with the learning of standard operations tied to specific contexts—to a pedagogy which emphasizes the exploration of principles. From schools which emphasized the teacher as a solution-giver to schools which emphasize the teacher as a problem-poser or creator. Such a change in pedagogy (itself perhaps a response to changed concepts of skill in industry) alters the authority relationships between teacher and taught, and possibly changes the nature of the authority inherent in the subject. The pedagogy now emphasizes the *means* whereby knowledge is created and principles established, in a context of self-discovery by the pupils. The act of learning itself celebrates choice.

But what about the curriculum? I mean by curriculum the principles governing the selection of, and relation between, subjects. We are witnessing a shift in emphasis away from schools where the subject is a clear-cut definable unit of the curriculum, to schools where the unit of the curriculum is not so much a subject as an *idea*—say, topic-centred inter-disciplinary enquiry. Such a shift is already under way at the university level.

Now, when the basis of the curriculum is an idea which is supra subject, and which governs the relationship between subjects, a number of consequences may follow. The subject is no longer dominant, but subordinate to the idea which governs a particular form of integration. If the subject is no longer dominant, then this could affect the position of teacher as specialist. His reference point may no longer be his subject or discipline. His allegiance, his social point of gravity, may tend to switch from his commitment to his subject to the bearing his subject has upon the *idea* which is relating him to other teachers.

In the older schools, integration between subjects, when it existed, was determined by the public examination system, and this is one of the brakes on the shift I am describing. In the new schools, integration at the level of idea involves a new principle of social integration of staff: that of organic solidarity. This shift in the basis of the curriculum from subject to idea may point towards a fundamental change in the character of British education: a change from education in depth to education in breadth.

As a corollary of this, we are moving from secondary schools where the teaching roles were insulated from each other, where the teacher had an assigned area of authority and autonomy, to secondary schools where the teaching role is less autonomous and where it is a shared or co-operative role. There has been a shift from a teaching role which is, so to speak, 'given' (in the sense that one steps into assigned duties), to a role which has to be *achieved* in relation with other teachers. It is a role which is no longer made but *has to be made*. The teacher is no longer isolated from other teachers, as where the principle of integration is the relation of his subject to a public examination. The teacher is now in a complementary relation with other teachers at the level of his day-by-day teaching.

Under these conditions of co-operative, shared teaching roles, the loss of a teacher can be most damaging to the staff because of the interdependence of roles. Here we can begin to see the essence of organic solidarity as it affects the crucial role of teacher. The act of teaching itself expresses the organic articulation between subjects, teachers and taught. The form of social integration, in the central area of the school's function, is organic rather than mechanical.

How is the role of pupil affected? I said that, under mechanical solidarity, social roles were likely to be fixed and ascribed, aspirations would be limited, and individuals would relate to each other through common beliefs and shared sentiments. These beliefs and sentiments would regulate the details of social action. In the older secondary schools, individual choice was severely curtailed, aspirations were controlled through careful streaming, and streaming itself produced homogeneous groups according to an imputed similarity in ability. The learning process emphasized the teacher as solution-giver rather than problem-poser. The role of pupil was circumscribed and well defined.

Now there has been a move towards giving the pupil greater choice. Aspirations are likely to be raised in the new schools, partly because of changes in their social organization. The learning process creates greater autonomy for the pupil. The teaching group may be either a heterogeneous unit (unstreamed class) or a series of different homogeneous units (sets) or even both. The pupil's role is less clearly defined. Of equal significance, his role conception evolves out of a series of diverse contexts and relationships. The enacting of the role of pupil reveals less his similarity to others, but rather his difference from others.

I suggested earlier that, where the form of social integration was mechanical, the community would tend to become sealed off, self-enclosed, and its boundary relationship would be sharply defined. Inside and outside would be clearly differentiated. These notions can apply to changes both within the school and to its relation to the outside.

Schools' boundary relations, both within and without, are now more open. This can be seen at many levels. First of all, the very architecture of the new schools points up their openness compared with the old schools. The inside of the institution has become visible. Of more significance, the boundary relation between the home and school has changed, and parents (their beliefs and socializing styles) are incorporated within the school in a way unheard of in the older schools. The range and number of non-school adults who visit the school and talk to the pupils have increased. The barrier between the informal teenage subcultures and the culture of the school has weakened: often the non-school age group subculture becomes a content of a syllabus. The outside penetrates the new schools in other fundamental ways. The careful editing, specially for schools, of books, papers, films, is being replaced by a diverse representation of the outside both within the library and through films shown to the pupils.

Within the school, as we have seen, the insulation between forms and between teaching roles has weakened, and authority relationships are less formal. The diminishing of a one-to-one relation between a given activity, a given space and a given time—i.e. flexibility—must reduce the symbolic significance of particular spaces and particular times. The controls over flow in the new schools carry a different symbolic significance from the controls over flow in the old schools.

Let me summarize at a more general level the significance of these shifts of emphasis. There has been a shift from secondary schools whose symbolic orders point up or celebrate the idea of purity of categories—whether these categories be values, subjects in a curriculum, teaching groups or teachers—to secondary schools whose symbolic orders point up or celebrate the idea of mixture or diversity of categories. (These concepts have been developed by Mary Douglas in her book, *Purity and Danger*.) For example:

(1) The mixing of categories at the level of values. Changes in the boundary relationships between the inside and the outside of the school lead to a value system which is more ambiguous and more open to the influence of diverse values from outside.

(2) The mixing of categories at the level of curriculum. The move away from a curriculum where subjects are insulated and autonomous, to a curriculum which involves the subordination of subjects and their integration.

(3) The mixing of categories at the level of the teaching group. Heterogeneous rather than homogeneous teaching groups and differentiated sets of pupils rather than fixed forms or classes.

The secondary schools celebrate diversity, not purity. This may be symptomatic of basic changes in the culture of our society, particularly changes in the principles of social control. Until recently the British educational system epitomized the concept of purity of categories. At the apex of the system sat the lonely, specialized figure of the arts Ph.D., a dodo in terms of our current needs.

There was also the separation of the arts and the sciences, and within each the careful insulation between the 'pure' and the 'applied'. (Contrast all this with the United States.)

The concept of knowledge was one that partook of the 'sacred':

its organization and dissemination was intimately related to the principles of social control. Knowledge (on this view) is dangerous, it cannot be exchanged like money, it must be confined to special well-chosen persons and even divorced from practical concerns. The forms of knowledge must always be bounded and well insulated from each other; there must be no sparking across the forms with unpredictable outcomes. Specialization makes knowledge safe and protects the vital principles of social order. Preferably knowledge should be transmitted in a context where the teacher has maximum control or surveillance, as in hierarchical school relationships or the university tutorial relation. Knowledge and the principles of social order are made safe if knowledge is subdivided, well insulated and transmitted by authorities who themselves view their own knowledge or disciplines with the jealous eye of a threatened priesthood. (This applies much more to the arts than to the sciences.)

Education in breadth, with its implications of mixture of categories, arouses in educational guardians an abhorrence and disgust like the sentiments aroused by incest. This is understandable because education in breadth arouses fears of the dissolution of the principles of social order. Education in depth, the palpable expression of purity of categories, creates monolithic authority systems serving élitist functions; education in breadth weakens authority systems or renders them pluralistic, and it is apparently consensual in function. One origin of the purity and mixing of categories may be in the general social principles regulating the mixing of diverse groups in society. But monolithic societies are unlikely to develop education in breadth, in school systems with pronounced principles of organic solidarity. Such forms of social integration are inadequate to transmit collective beliefs and values.

It might now be helpful to drop the terms mechanical and organic solidarity and refer instead to 'closed' and 'open' schools.

Individuals, be they teachers or taught, may be able (under certain conditions) to make their own roles in a way never experienced before in the public sector of secondary education. But staff and students are likely to experience a sense of loss of structure and, with this, problems of boundary, continuity, order and ambivalence are likely to arise. This problem of the relationship between the transmission of belief and social organization is likely to be acute in largescale 'open' church schools. It may be that the open school with its organic modes of social integration, its personalized forms of social control, the indeterminacy of its belief and moral order (except at the level of very general values) will strengthen the adherence of the pupils to their age group as a major source of belief, relation and identity. Thus, is it possible that, as the open school moves further towards organic solidarity as its major principle of social integration, so the pupils may move further towards the 'closed' society of the age group? Are the educational dropouts of the fifties to be replaced by the moral dropouts of the seventies?

None of this should be taken in the spirit that yesterday there was order; today there is only flux. Neither should it be taken as a long sigh over the weakening of authority and its social basis. Rather we should be eager to explore changes in the forms of social integration in order to re-examine the basis for social control. This, as Durkheim pointed out decades ago, is a central concern of a sociology of education.

References

BERNSTEIN, B., ELVIN, H. L. and PETERS, R. S. (1966), 'Ritual in education', *Philosophical Transactions of the Royal Society of London*, Series B, 251, No. 772.

DOUGLAS, M. (1966), *Purity and Danger*, Routledge & Kegan Paul.

DURKHEIM, E. (1947), *The Division of Labour in Society*, Free Press, Chicago.

DURKHEIM, E. (1961), *Moral Education*, Free Press, Chicago.

Part II Changes in the coding of educational transmissions

Chapter 4   On the curriculum

To begin with, I am going to talk about the curriculum in a very abstract way.

In all educational institutions there is an organization of time into periods which may vary from fifteen minutes to three hours. I am going to call each such defined period of time a 'unit'. I shall use the word 'content' to describe how that period of time is filled. Now I shall start off by considering that all the units and their contents have equal status. And I shall define a curriculum in terms of the principle by which certain periods of time and their contents are brought into a special relationship with each other. I am thus opening up the question as to how it is that a certain curriculum emerges. I want to look more closely at the word 'relation' which I used in the definition.

First, we can examine the relationship between contents (that is, how a given period of time is filled) in terms of the amount of time accorded to a given content. Immediately we can see that more time is devoted to some contents than others.

Second, some of the contents may, from the point of view of the pupils, be compulsory or optional.

We can now talk about the relative status of a content in terms of the number of units given over to it and in terms of whether it is compulsory or optional.

We have so far looked at the word relation in terms of the relative status of a given content.

We can consider the relationship between contents from another point of view. We could ask about any given content whether the boundaries between it and another content were clear-cut or blurred. To what extent are the various contents insulated from each other?

If the various contents are well insulated from each other, I shall say that the contents stand in a closed relation to each other. If there is reduced insulation, I shall say that the contents stand in an open relation to each other.

So far then, I have suggested that we can go into any educational institution and examine the organization of time in terms of the relative status of contents and in terms of whether these contents stand in an open or closed relation to each other. I am deliberately using this very abstract language in order to emphasize that there is nothing intrinsic about how educational time is used, or the status of the various contents or the relation between the contents. I am emphasizing the social nature of the system of choices from which emerges a constellation called a curriculum.

I am now in a position to give a rather fuller definition of a curriculum. From this point of view any curriculum entails a principle or principles, whereby of all the possible contents of time some contents are given a special status and enter into an open or closed relation with each other.

I shall now distinguish between two broad types of curriculum; if those high status contents stand in a closed relation to each other, that is if the contents are clearly bounded and separated from each other, I shall call such a curriculum a *collection* type. Here the student has to collect a group of especially favoured contents in order to satisfy some external criteria; perhaps, but not always, a public examination. There may of course be some underlying concept to a collection, for example it may be that of the gentleman, the educated man, the skilled man, the non-vocational man.

Now I want to juxtapose against this notion of collection, a curriculum where the various contents do not go their separate ways, but where the favoured contents stand in an open relation to each other. Where we have a curriculum where the contents stand in an open relation to each other, I shall call such a curriculum an integrated type. Now these are extremes, for we can have degrees of integration. In a totally integrated curriculum there would be no fixed periods of time. In a total collection type, no contents would be open and all time-periods firmly fixed.

Where we have integration, the various contents are subordinate to some idea which reduces their isolation from each other. Where we have integration the various contents become part of a greater whole. And each content's function in that whole is made explicit.

Now, where we have collection, the underlying concept does not reduce the autonomy of the separate contents. For where we have collection, the syllabus of each content is in the hands of those who teach it and those who evaluate it. Where we have integration the syllabus for a given content is subordinate to a general idea which itself is subject to change. Where we have collection, it does permit considerable differences in teaching practice and forms of examining. Each teacher within *prescribed* limits can go his own way. Where we have integration, there is likely to be a move towards a common pedagogy, a common examining style, a common practice of teaching.

Now we can begin to see that if we are to discuss curriculum we have also to consider pedagogy and evaluation. In the sense I have treated it, Curriculum, Pedagogy and Evaluation form a whole and should be treated as a whole.

I have spent so much time on this introduction in order to go on to consider how the selective organization, transmission and evaluation of knowledge is intimately bound up with patterns of authority and control. The battle over curricula is also a conflict between different conceptions of social order and is therefore fundamentally moral.

On the whole, in Europe, the curriculum is of the collection type. England differs essentially in terms of the reduction in the number of closed contents with the length of the educational life. Now when we get such a decrease in the number of closed contents in a collection with the educational life, we have specialization. And such a form of a collection is referred to evaluatively as education in depth.

I am going to examine today the patterns of social relationships which arise out of the specialized form of collection, and those which are generated by curriculum of the integrated type.

With the specialized form of collection, as you get older you know more and more about less. Another more sociological way of putting this is to say, as you get older you become more different from others. Therefore specialization reveals differences from, rather than commonalty. It means that your educational identity and specific skills are clearly marked and bounded. Your educational category is pure.

The specialized form of collection, indeed any form of collection, involves a hierarchy whereby the ultimate mystery of the subject is revealed very late in the educational life. And education takes the form of a long initiation into this mystery. Knowledge partakes of the sacred, it is not ordinary or mundane. And this enhances the significance of the subject and those who profess it. A very powerful form of control. Now the receipt of this knowledge is not so much a right as something to be won, or earned. This is called discipline. The educational relationship tends to be hierarchical and ritualized, the educand seen as ignorant with little status and therefore few rights.

Specialized education, like any form of collection, is organized around subjects which stand in a closed relation to each other. Now in a society where knowledge is expanding and becoming more differential, it is not uncommon to find border disputes between subjects as to what does or does not belong. If knowledge is regarded as *sacred* under collection, it also appears to be very similar to *private property* with various kinds of symbolic fences, and the people who own the knowledge look rather like monopolists. Pupils and students are also carefully screened to see who belongs and who does not belong. And once such screening has taken place, it is very difficult, sometimes impossible, to change one's educational identity. With specialized education the sheep have to be very quickly separated from the goats and the goats are invested with attributes of pollution.

Your membership category is established relatively early and your particular status in a given collection is made clear by streaming, examining and a delicate system of grades. Subject loyalty is systematically developed in pupils and students, with the length of the educational life, and then transmitted by them as teachers and lecturers. The system is self-perpetuating. It is of interest that the hierarchic ordering of pupils is paralleled by a similar hierarchic ordering of staff, particularly at the university level. Under the specialized form of collection, knowledge tends to be transmitted in a context where the teacher has maximal control or surveillance, as in hierarchical secondary school relationships or small group university relationships. With increase in the educational life, under the specialist form of collection, we get a combination of the hierarchical *and* the inter-personal, which act to create a powerful agency of control.

The collection type of curriculum tends to be rigid, differentiating and hierarchical in character. How much so depends upon the general culture of the society. Yet for those beyond the novitiate stage it can provide order, identity and commitment. For those who do not pass beyond this stage it can often be wounding, and sometimes may even be seen as meaningless.

Now, where we have curricula of the integrated type, we will find a shift in emphasis from education in depth to education in breadth or, in less evaluative terms, from content closure to content openness. In order to accomplish integration the relational idea, the supra content concept, must focus much more upon general principles. This in turn is likely to affect the pedagogy: it will tend to emphasize ways of knowing rather than states of knowledge. If the underlying theory of pedagogy under collection is didactic, then under integration the underlying pedagogic theory is likely to be self-regulatory. Such a change in emphasis and pedagogy is likely to transform the teacher–pupil—lecturer–student authority relationships, and in particular increase the status and thus the rights of the pupil or student. We might also expect the organization of teaching groups to undergo a change and exhibit considerable flexibility compared with the rigidity of collection. Given all these changes, a pressure will be set up towards introducing forms of evaluation, forms of examining, which is appropriate to the curriculum and pedagogy.

Let us look briefly at staff relationships, where the organizing principle is integration. We have said that the boundaries between the contents are open. Now this will tend to weaken the separate hierarchies of specialized education. Further, teachers of different contents will enter into social relationships with each other which will arise not simply out of their leisure time activities but out of a shared co-operative educational task. Thus, instead of teachers or lecturers being divided and insulated by allegiance to small subject hierarchies, they will be more united by a common endeavour. These new horizontal relationships between teachers and between lecturers, especially at the lower staff levels, may alter the traditional power structure with educational institutions. And we might expect a similar situation to develop in students and even pupils.

Now we can begin to see that the tension between curriculum of the collection type and the integrated type is not simply a question of what is to be taught but a tension arising out of quite different patterns of authority, quite different concepts of order and of control.

Although it may seem that I have unwittingly been emphasizing the advantage of integrated curricula, I want to draw your attention briefly to the following:

(1) There must be some consensus about the integrating idea if it is to work at all.

(2) The idea must be made very explicit.

(3) The nature of the linkage between the idea and the several contents must be systematically and coherently worked out.

(4) A committee system of staff and pupils has to be set up in order to develop a sensitive control on the whole endeavour.

(5) Of greatest importance, very clear criteria of evaluation must be worked out.

Whereas under collection *order* arises out of the hierarchical nature of the authority relationships, the systematic ordering of the separate contents, an explicit, relatively objective examining system, under integration order is something that has to be developed and planned.

If the five conditions I gave earlier are not fulfilled, then the openness of learning under integration may well create an environment in which neither staff nor pupils have a sense of place, time or purpose.

I have implied that the British educational system is undergoing a change from curriculum of the collection type to curriculum of the integrated type. The social consequences of this shift will bring about disturbances in the traditional authority relationships in educational institutions. The move from collection to integration will radically alter the status and range of existing contents. It is likely to alter the relationship between teachers and between pupils. As we move from collection to integration, from close to open schools the outside will penetrate the schools in new ways. As we move from collection to integration the moral basis of our educational choices will become explicit and we must expect considerable conflict of values.

Reference

JEFFERY, G. B. (1950), *The Unity of Knowledge: Reflections on the Universities of Cambridge and London*, Cambridge Univ. Press.

Chapter 5   On the classification and framing of educational knowledge

Introduction

How a society selects, classifies, distributes, transmits and evaluates the educational knowledge it considers to be public, reflects both the distribution of power and the principles of social control. From this point of view, differences within, and change in, the organization, transmission and evaluation of educational knowledge should be a major area of sociological interest. (Bernstein, B., 1966, 1967; Davies, D. I., 1970a, 1970b; Musgrove, 1968; Hoyle, 1969; Young, M., 1970.) Indeed, such a study is a part of the larger question of the structure and changes in the structure of cultural transmission. For various reasons, British sociologists have fought shy of this question. As a result, the sociology of education has been reduced to a series of input-output problems; the school has been transformed into a complex organization or people-processing institution; the study of socialization has been trivialized.

Educational knowledge is a major regulator of the structure of experience. From this point of view, one can ask 'How are forms of experience, identity and relation evoked, maintained and changed by the formal transmission of educational knowledge and sensitivities?' Formal educational knowledge can be considered to be realized through three message systems: curriculum, pedagogy and evaluation. Curriculum defines what counts as valid knowledge, pedagogy defines what counts as a valid transmission of knowledge, and evaluation defines what counts as a valid realization of this knowledge on the part of the taught. The term, educational knowledge code, which will be introduced later, refers to the underlying principles which shape curriculum, pedagogy and evaluation. It will be argued that the form this code takes depends upon social principles which regulate the classification and framing of knowledge made public in educational institutions. Both Durkheim and Marx have shown us that the structure of society's classifications and frames reveals both the distribution of power and the principles of social control. I hope to show, *theoretically*, that educational codes provide excellent opportunities for the study of classification and frames through which experience is given a distinctive form. The paper is organized as follows:

(1) I shall first distinguish between two types of curricula: collection and integrated.
(2) I shall build upon the basis of this distinction in order to establish a more general set of concepts: classification and frame.
(3) A typology of educational codes will then be derived.
(4) Sociological aspects of two very different educational codes will then be explored.
(5) This will lead on to a discussion of educational codes and problems of social control.
(6) Finally, there will be a brief discussion of the reasons for a weakening of one code and a strengthening of the movement of the other.

Two types of curricula

Initially, I am going to talk about the curriculum in a very general way. In all educational institutions there is a formal punctuation of time into periods. These may vary from ten minutes to three hours or more. I am going to call each such formal period of time a 'unit'. I shall use the word 'content' to describe how the period of time is used. I shall define a curriculum initially in terms of the principle by which units of time and their contents are brought into a special relationship with each other. I now want to look more closely at the phrase 'special relationship'.

First, we can examine relationships between contents in terms of the amount of time accorded to a given content. Immediately, we can see that more time is devoted to some contents rather than others. Second, some of the contents may, from the point of view of the pupils, be compulsory or optional. We can now take a very crude measure of the relative status of a content in terms of the number of units given over to it, and whether it is compulsory or optional. This raises immediately the question of the relative status of a given content and its significance in a given educational career.

We can, however, consider the relationship between contents from another, perhaps more important, perspective. We can ask about any given content whether the boundary between it and another content is clear-cut or blurred. To what extent are the various contents well insulated from each other. If the various contents are well insulated from each other, I shall say that the contents stand in a *closed* relation to each other. If there is reduced insulation between contents, I shall say that the contents stand in an *open* relationship to each other. So far, then, I am suggesting that we can go into any educational institution and examine the organization of time in terms of the relative status of contents, and whether the contents stand in an open/closed relationship to each other. I am deliberately using this very abstract language in order to emphasize that there is nothing intrinsic to the relative status of various contents, there is nothing intrinsic to the relationships between contents. Irrespective of the question of the intrinsic logic of the various forms of public thought, the *forms* of their transmission, that is their classification and framing, are social facts. There are a number of alternative means of access to the public forms of thought, and so to the various realities which they make possible. I am therefore emphasizing the social nature of the system of alternatives from which emerges a constellation called a curriculum. From this point of view, any curriculum entails a principle or principles whereby of all the possible contents of time, some contents are accorded differential status and enter into open or closed relation to each other.

I shall now distinguish between two broad types of curricula. If contents stand in a closed relation to each other, that is if the contents are clearly bounded and insulated from each other, I shall call such a curriculum a *collection* type. Here, the learner has to collect a group of favoured contents in order to satisfy some criteria of evaluation. There may of course be some underlying concept to a collection: the gentleman, the educated man, the skilled man, the non-vocational man.

Now I want to juxtapose against the collection type, a curriculum where the various contents do not go their own separate ways, but where the contents stand in an open relation to each other. I shall call such a curriculum an integrated type. Now we can have various types of collection, and various degrees and types of integration.

Classification and frame

I shall now introduce the concepts, classification and frame, which will be used to analyse the underlying structure of the three message systems, curriculum, pedagogy and evaluation, which are realizations of the educational knowledge code. The basic idea is embodied in the principle used to distinguish the two types of curricula: collection and integrated. Strong insulation between contents pointed to a collection type, whereas reduced insulation pointed to an integrated type. The principle here is the strength of the *boundary* between contents. This notion of boundary strength underlies the concepts of classification and frame.

Classification, here, does not refer to *what* is classified, but to the *relationships* between contents. Classification refers to the nature of the differentiation between contents. Where classification is strong, contents are well insulated from each other by strong boundaries. Where classification is weak, there is reduced insulation between contents, for the boundaries between contents are weak or blurred. *Classification thus refers to the degree of boundary maintenance between contents.* Classification focuses our attention upon boundary strength as the critical distinguishing feature of the division of labour of educational knowledge. It gives us, as I hope to show, the basic structure of the message system, curriculum.

The concept, frame, is used to determine the structure of the message system, pedagogy. Frame refers to the form of the *context* in which knowledge is transmitted and received. Frame refers to the specific pedagogical relationship of teacher and taught. In the same way as classification does not refer to contents, so frame does not refer to the contents of the pedagogy. Frame refers to the strength of the boundary between what may be transmitted and what may not be transmitted, in the pedagogical relationship. Where framing is strong, there is a sharp boundary, where framing is weak, a blurred boundary, between what may and may not be transmitted. Frame refers us to the range of options available to teacher and taught in the *control* of what is transmitted and received in the context of the pedagogical relationship. Strong framing entails reduced options; weak framing entails a range of options. *Thus frame refers to the degree of control teacher and pupil possess over the selection, organization, pacing and timing of the knowledge transmitted and received in the pedagogical relationship.*[1]

There is another aspect of the boundary relationship between what may be taught and what may not be taught and, consequently, another aspect to framing. We can consider the relationship between the non-school everyday community knowledge of the teacher or taught, *and* the educational knowledge transmitted in the pedagogical relationship. We can raise the question of the strength of the boundary, the degree of insulation, between the everyday community knowledge of teacher and taught and educational knowledge. Thus, we can consider variations in the strength of frames as these refer to the strength of the boundary between educational knowledge and everyday community knowledge of teacher and taught.

From the perspective of this analysis, the basic structure of the message system, curriculum is given by variations in the strength of classification, and the basic structure of the message system pedagogy is given by variations in the strength of frames. It will be shown later that the structure of the message system, evaluation, is a function of the strength of classification and frames. It is important to realize that the strength of classification and the strength of frames can vary independently of each other. For example, it is possible to have weak classification and exceptionally strong framing. Consider programmed learning. Here the boundary between educational contents may be blurred (weak classification) but there is little control by the pupil (except for pacing) over *what* is learned (strong framing). This example also shows that frames may be examined at a number of levels and the strength can vary as between the levels of selection, organization, pacing and timing of the knowledge transmitted in the pedagogical relationship.

I should also like to bring out (this will be developed more fully later in the analysis) the power component of this analysis and what can be called the 'identity' component. Where classification is strong, the boundaries between the different contents are sharply drawn. If this is the case, then it pre-supposes strong boundary maintainers. Strong classification also creates a strong sense of membership in a particular class and so a specific identity. Strong frames reduce the power of the pupil over what, when and how he receives knowledge, and increases the teacher's power in the pedagogical relationship. However, strong *classification* reduces the power of the *teacher* over what he transmits, as he may not over-step the boundary between contents, *and* strong classification reduces the power of the teacher *vis-à-vis* the boundary maintainers.

It is now possible to make explicit the concept of educational knowledge codes. The code is fully given *at the most general level* by the relationship between classification and framing.

A typology of educational knowledge codes

In the light of the conceptual framework we have developed, I shall use the distinction between collection and integrated curricula in order to realize a typology of types and sub-types of educational codes. The *formal* basis of the typology is the strength of classification and frames. However, the sub-types will be distinguished, initially, in terms of substantive differences.

Any organization of educational knowledge which involves strong classification gives rise to what is here called a collection code. Any organization of educational knowledge which involves a marked attempt to reduce the strength of classification is here called an integrated code. Collection codes may give rise to a series of sub-types, each varying in the relative strength of their classification and frames. Integrated codes can also vary in terms of the strength of frames, as these refer to the *teacher/pupil/student* control over the knowledge that is transmitted.

Figure 5.1 sets out general features of the typology.

Collection codes

The first major distinction *within* collection codes is between specialized and non-specialized types. The extent of specialization can be measured in terms of the number of closed contents publicly examined at the end of the secondary educational stage.

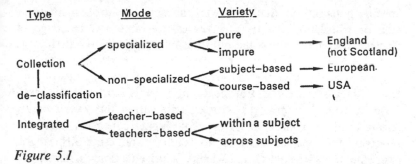

Figure 5.1

Thus in England, *although there is no formal limit,* the student usually sits for three 'A' level subjects, compared with the much greater range of subjects which make up the Abitur in Germany, the Baccalauréat in France, or the Studente Exam in Sweden.

Within the English specialized type, we can distinguish two varieties: a pure and an impure variety. The pure variety exists where 'A' level subjects are drawn from a common universe of knowledge, e.g. Chemistry, Physics, Mathematics. The impure variety exists where 'A' level subjects are drawn from different universes of knowledge, e.g. Religion, Physics, Economics. The latter combination, although formally possible, very rarely substantively exists, for pupils are not encouraged to offer—neither does timetabling usually permit—such a combination. It is a matter of interest that until very recently the pure variety at the university level received the higher status of an honours degree, whereas the impure variety tended to lead to the lower status of the general degree.[2] One can detect the beginnings of a shift in England from the pure to the impure variety, which appears to be trying to work towards the non-specialized type of collection.

Within the non-specialized collection code, we can distinguish two varieties, according to whether a subject or course is the basic knowledge unit. Thus the standard European form of the collection code is non-specialized, *subject*-based. The USA form of the collection is non-specialized, course-based.

I have so far described sub-types and varieties of the collection code in simple descriptive terms; as a consequence it is not easy to see how their distinctive features can be translated into sociological concepts in order to realize a specific sociological problem. Clearly, the conceptual language here developed has built into it a specific perspective: that of power and social control. In the process of translating the descriptive features into the language of classification and frames, the question must arise as to whether the hypotheses about their relative strength fits a particular case.

Here are the hypotheses, given for purposes of illustration:
(1) I suggest that the European, non-specialized, subject-based form of collection involves strong classification but *exceptionally* strong framing. That is, at levels *below* higher education, there are relatively few options available to teacher, and especially taught, over the transmission of knowledge. Curricula and syllabus are very explicit.

(2) The English version, I suggest, involves *exceptionally* strong classification, but relatively weaker framing than the European type. The fact that it is specialized determines what contents (subjects) may be put together. There is very strong insulation between the 'pure' and the 'applied' knowledge. Curricula are graded for particular ability groups. There can be high insulation between a subject and a class of pupils. 'D' stream secondary pupils will not have access to certain subjects, and 'A' stream students will also not have access to certain subjects. However, I suggest that framing, relative to Europe, is weaker. This can be seen particularly at the primary level. There is also, *relative* to Europe, less *central* control over what is transmitted, although, clearly, the various requirements of the university level exert a strong control over the secondary level.[3] I suggest that, although again this is *relative*, there is a weaker frame in England between educational knowledge and the everyday community knowledge for certain classes of students: the so-called less able. Finally, relative to Europe, I suggest that there are more options available to the pupil within the pedagogical relationships. The frame as it refers to pupils is weaker. Thus, I suggest that framing as it relates to teachers and pupils is relatively weaker, but that classification is relatively much stronger in the English than in the European system. Scotland is nearer to the European version of the collection.

(3) The course-based, non-specialized USA form of the collection, I suggest, has the weakest classification *and* framing of the collection code, especially at the secondary and university level. A far greater range of subjects can be taken at the secondary and university level, and are capable of combination; this indicates weak

classification. The insulation between educational knowledge and everyday community knowledge is weaker, as can be evidenced by community control over school; this indicates weak frames. The range of options available to pupils within the pedagogical relationship is, I suggest, greater. I would guess, then, that classification and framing in the USA is the weakest of the collection codes.

Integrated codes

It is important to be clear about the term 'integrated'. Because one subject uses the theories of another subject, this type of intellectual inter-relationship does not constitute integration. Such intellectual inter-relation may well be part of a collection code at some point in the history of the development of knowledge. Integration, as it is used here, refers minimally to the *subordination* of previously insulated subjects *or* courses to some *relational* idea, which blurs the boundaries between the subjects. We can distinguish two types. The first type is *teacher*-based. Here the teacher, as in the infant school, has an extended block of time with often the same group of children. The teacher may operate with a collection code and keep the various subjects distinct and insulated, or he can blur the boundaries between the different subjects. This type of integrated code is easier to introduce than the second type, which is *teachers*-based. Here, integration involves relationships with other teachers. In this way, we can have degrees of integration in terms of the number of teachers involved.

We can further distinguish two varieties according to whether the integration refers to a group of teachers *within* a common subject, or the extent to which integration involves teachers of different subjects. Whilst integrated codes, by definition, have the weakest classification, they may vary as to framing. During the initiating period, the frames the teachers enter will be weak, but other factors will effect the final frame strength. It is also possible that the frames the *pupils* enter can vary in strength.

Thus integrated codes may be confined to one subject or they can cross subjects. We can talk of code strength in terms of the range of different subjects co-ordinated by the code, or if this criterion cannot be applied, code strength can be measured in terms of the *number* of teachers co-ordinated through the code.

Integrated codes can also vary as to frame strength as this applies to teachers or pupils, or both.

Differences within, and between, educational knowledge codes from the perspective developed here, lie in variations in the strength and nature of the boundary maintaining procedures, as these are given by the classification and framing of the knowledge. It can be seen that the nature of classification and framing affects the authority/power structure which controls the dissemination of educational knowledge, and the *form* of the knowledge transmitted. In this way, principles of power and social control are realized through educational knowledge codes and, through the codes, enter into and shape consciousness. Thus, variations within and change of knowledge codes should be of critical concern to sociologists. The following problems arise out of this analysis:

(1) What are the antecedents of variations in the strength of classification and frames?[4]
(2) How does a given classification and framing structure perpetuate itself? What are the conditions of, and resistance to, change?
(3) What are the different socializing experiences realized through variations in the strength of classifications and frames?

I shall limit the application of this analysis to the consideration of aspects of the last two questions. I feel I ought to apologize to the reader for this rather long and perhaps tedious conceptual journey, before he has been given any notion of the view to which it leads.

Application

I shall examine the patterns of social relationship and their socializing consequences which are realized through the European, particularly English, version of the collection code, and those which are *expected* to arise out of integrated codes, *particularly those which develop weak framing*. I shall suggest that there is some movement towards forms of the integrated code and I shall examine the nature of the resistance towards such a change. I shall suggest some reasons for this movement.

Classification and framing of the European form of the collection code

There will be some difficulty in this analysis, as I shall at times switch from secondary to university level. Although the English system has the distinguishing feature of specialization, it does share certain features of the European system. This may lead to some blurring in the analysis. As this is the beginning of a limited sociological theory which explores the social organization and structuring of educational knowledge, it follows that all statements, including those which have the character of descriptive statements, are hypothetical. The descriptive statements have been selectively patterned according to their significance for the theory.

One of the major differences between the European and English versions of the collection code is that, with the specialized English type, a membership category is established early in an educational career, in terms of an early choice between the pure and the applied, between the sciences and the arts, between having and not having a specific educational identity. A particular status in a given collection is made clear by streaming and/or a delicate system of grading. One nearly always knows the social significance of where .one is and, in particular, *who* one is with each advance in the educational career. (Initially, I am doing science, or arts, pure or applied; or I am not doing anything; later I am becoming a physicist, economist, chemist, etc.). *Subject loyalty* is then systematically developed in pupils and finally students, with each increase in the educational life, and then transmitted by them as teachers and lecturers. The system is self-perpetuating through this form of socialization. With the specialized form of the collection it is banal to say that as you get older you learn more and more about less and less. Another, more sociological, way of putting this is to say that as you get older, you become increasingly *different* from others. Clearly, this will happen at some point in any educational career, but, with specialization, this happens much earlier. Therefore, specialization very soon reveals *difference from* rather than *communality with*. It creates relatively quickly an educational identity which is clear-cut and bounded. The educational category or identity is *pure*. Specialized versions of the collection code tend to abhor mixed categories and blurred identities, for they represent a potential openness, an ambiguity, which makes the consequences of previous socialization problematic. Mixed categories such as bio-physicist, psycho-linguist, are only permitted to develop after long socialization into a subject loyalty. Indeed, in order to change an identity, a previous one has to be weakened and a new one created. For example, in England, if a student has a first degree in psychology and he wishes to read for a higher degree in sociology, either he is not permitted to make the switch or he is expected to take a number of papers at first degree level in sociology. In the process of taking the papers, he usually enters into social relationships with accredited sociologists and students through whom he acquires the cognitive and social style particular to the sociological identity. Change of an educational identity is accomplished through a process of re-socialization into a *new* subject loyalty. A sense of the sacred, the 'otherness' of educational knowledge, I submit does not arise so much out of an ethic of knowledge for its own sake, but is more a function of socialization into subject loyalty; for it is the subject which becomes the linch-pin of the identity. Any attempt to weaken or *change* classification strength (or even frame strength) may be felt as a threat to one's identity and may be experienced as a pollution endangering the sacred. Here we have one source of the resistance to change of educational code.

The specialized version of the collection code will develop careful screening procedures to see who belongs and who does not belong, and once such screening has taken place, it is very difficult to change an educational identity. The various classes of knowledge are well insulated from each other. Selection and differentiation are early features of this particular code. Thus, the deep structure of the specialized type of collection code is *strong boundary maintenance creating control from within through the formation of specific identities.* An interesting aspect of the protestant spirit.

Strong boundary maintenance can be illustrated with reference to attempts to institutionalize new forms or attempts to change the strength of classification, within either the European or English type of collection. Because of the exceptional strength of classification in England, such difficulties may be greater here. Changes in classification strength and the institutionalizing of new forms of knowledge may become a matter of importance when there are changes in the structure of knowledge at the higher levels and/or changes in the economy. Critical problems arise with the question of new forms, as to their legitimacy, at what point they belong, when, where and by whom the form should be taught. I have referred to the 'sacred' in terms of an educational identity, but clearly there is the 'profane' aspect to knowledge. We can consider as the 'profane' the property aspect of knowledge. Any new form or weakening of classification clearly derives from past classifications. Such new forms or weakened classifications can be regarded as attempts to break or weaken existing monopolies. Knowledge under collection is private property with its own power structure and market situation. This affects the whole ambience surrounding the development and marketing of new knowledge. Children and pupils are early socialized into this concept of knowledge as private property. They are encouraged to work as isolated individuals with their arms around their work. This phenomenon, until recently, could be observed in any grammar school. It can be most clearly observed in examination halls. Pupils and students, particularly in the arts, appear, from this point of view, to be a type of entrepreneur.

There are, then, strong inbuilt controls on the institutionalizing of new knowledge forms, on the changing of strength of classification, on the production of new knowledge which derives from both 'sacred' and 'profane' sources.

So far, I have been considering the relationship between strong classification of knowledge, the concept of property and the creation of specific identities with particular reference to the specialized form of the collection code. I shall now move away from the classification of knowledge to its *framing* in the process of transmission.

Any collection code involves a hierarchical organization of knowledge, such that the ultimate mystery of the subject is revealed very late in the educational life. By the ultimate mystery of the subject, I mean its potential for creating new realities. It is also the case, and this is important, that the ultimate mystery of the subject is not coherence, but incoherence: not order, but disorder, not the known but the unknown. As this mystery, under collection codes, is revealed very late in the educational life—and then only to a select few who have shown the signs of successful socialization—then only the few *experience* in their bones the notion that knowledge is permeable, that its orderings are provisional, that the dialectic of knowledge is closure and openness. For the many, socialization into knowledge is socialization into order, the existing order, into the experience that the world's educational knowledge is impermeable. Do we have here another version of alienation?

Now, clearly, any history of any form of educational knowledge shows precisely the power of such knowledge to create endlessly new realities. However, socialization into the specific framing of knowledge in its transmission may make such a history experientially meaningless. The key concept of the European collection code is discipline. This means learning to work *within* a received frame. It means, in particular, *learning* what questions can be put at any particular time. Because of the hierarchical ordering of the knowledge in *time*, certain questions raised may not enter into a particular frame.

This is soon learned by both teachers and pupils. Discipline then means accepting a given selection, organization, pacing and timing of knowledge realized in the pedagogical frame. With increases in the educational life, there is a progressive weakening of the frame for both teacher and taught. Only the few who have shown the signs of successful socialization have access to these relaxed frames. For the mass of the population the framing is tight. In a sense, the European form of the collection code makes knowledge safe through the process of socialization into its frames. There is a tendency, which varies with the strength of specific frames, for the young to be socialized into assigned principles and routine operations and derivations. The evaluative system places an emphasis upon attaining *states* of knowledge rather than *ways* of knowing. A study of the examination questions and format, the symbolic structure of assessment, would be, from this point of view, a rewarding empirical study. Knowledge thus tends to be transmitted, particularly to élite pupils at the secondary level, through strong frames which control the selecting, organization, pacing[5] and timing of the knowledge. The receipt of the knowledge is not so much a right as something to be won or earned. The stronger the classification and the framing, the more the educational relationship tends to be hierarchical and ritualized, the educand seen as ignorant, with little status and few rights. These are things which one earns, rather like spurs, and are used for the purpose of encouraging and sustaining the motivation of pupils. Depending upon the strength of frames, knowledge is transmitted in a context where the teacher has maximal control or surveillance, as in hierarchical secondary school relationships.

We can look at the question of the framing of knowledge in the pedagogical relationship from another point of view. In a sense, educational knowledge is uncommonsense knowledge. It is knowledge freed from the particular, the local, through the various languages of the sciences or forms of reflexiveness of the arts which make possible either the creation or the discovery of new realities. Now this immediately raises the question of the relationship between the uncommonsense knowledge of the school and the *commonsense* knowledge, everyday community knowledge, of the pupil, his family and his peer group. This formulation invites us to ask how strong are the frames of educational knowledge in relation to experiential, community-based non-school knowledge? I suggest that the frames of the collection code, very early in the child's life, socialize him into knowledge frames which discourage connections with everyday realities, or that there is a highly selective screening of the connection. Through such socialization, the pupil soon learns what of the outside may be brought into the pedagogical frame. Such framing also makes of educational knowledge something not ordinary or mundane, but something esoteric, which gives a special significance to those who possess it. I suggest that when this frame is relaxed to include everyday realities, it is often, and sometimes validly, not simply for the transmission of educational knowledge, but for purposes of social control of forms of deviancy. The weakening of this frame occurs usually with the less 'able' children whom we have given up educating.

In general, then, and depending upon the specific strength of classification and frames, the European form of the collection code is rigidly differentiating and hierarchical in character; highly resistant to change particularly at the secondary level. With the English version, this resistance to change is assisted by the discretion which is available to headmasters and principals. In England, within the constraints of the public examination system, the heads of schools and colleges have a relatively wide range of discretion over the organization and transmission of knowledge. Central control over the educational code is relatively weak in England, although clearly the schools are subject to inspection from both central and local government levels. However, the relationship between the inspectorate and the schools in England is very ambiguous. To produce widespread change in England would require the co-operation of hundreds of individual schools. Thus, rigidity in educational knowledge codes may arise out of highly centralized *or* weak central control over the knowledge codes. Weak central control does permit a series of changes which have, initially, limited consequences for the system as a whole. On the other hand, there is much stronger central control over the organizational style of the school. This can lead to a situation where there can be a change in the organizational style *without* there being *any* marked change in the educational knowledge code, particularly where the educational code itself creates specific identities. This raises the question, which cannot be developed here, of the relationships between organizational change and change of educational knowledge code, i.e. change in the strength of classification and framing.

In general, then, the European and English form of the collection code may provide for those who go beyond the novitiate stage, order, identity and commitment. For those who do not pass beyond this stage, it can sometimes be wounding and seen as meaningless. What Bourdieu calls 'la violence symbolique'.

Integrated and collection codes

I shall now examine a form of the integrated code which is realized through very weak classification and frames. I shall, during this analysis, bring out further aspects of collection codes.

There are a number of attempts to institutionalize forms of the integrated code at different strengths, above the level of the infant school child. Nuffield Science is an attempt to do this with the physical sciences, and the Chelsea Centre for Science Education, Chelsea College of Technology, University of London, is concerned almost wholly in training students in this approach. Mrs Charity James, at Goldsmiths' College, University of London, is also producing training courses for forms of the integrated code. A number of comprehensive schools are experimenting with this approach at the middle school level. The SDS in Germany, and various radical student groups, are exploring this type of code in order to use the means of the university against the meaning. However, it is probably true to say that the code at the moment exists at the level of ideology and theory, with only a relatively small number of schools and educational agencies attempting to institutionalize it with any seriousness.

Now, as we said at the beginning of the paper, with the integrated code we have a shift from content closure to content openness, from strong to markedly reduced classification. Immediately, we can see that this disturbance in classification of knowledge will lead to a disturbance of existing authority structures, existing specific educational identities and concepts of property.

Where we have integration, the various contents are subordinate to some idea which reduces their isolation from each other. Thus integration reduces the authority of the separate contents, and this has implications for existing authority structures. Where we have collection, it does permit in principle considerable differences in pedagogy and evaluation, because of the high insulation between the different contents. However, the autonomy of the content is the other side of an authority structure which exerts jealous and zealous supervision. I suggest that the integrated code will not permit the variations in pedagogy and evaluation which are possible within collection codes. On the contrary, I suggest there will be a pronounced movement towards a common pedagogy and tendency towards a common system of evaluation. In other words, integrated codes will, at the level of the teachers, probably create homogeneity in teaching practice. Thus, collection codes increase the discretion of teachers (within, always, the limits of the existing classification and frames) whilst integrated codes will reduce the discretion of the teacher in direct relation to the strength of the integrated code (number of teachers—co-ordinated by the code). On the other hand, it is argued that the increased discretion of the teachers within collection codes is paralleled by *reduced* discretion of the pupils and that the reduced discretion of the teachers within integrated codes is paralleled by *increased* discretion of the pupils. In other words, there is a shift in the balance of power, in the pedagogical relationship between teacher and taught.

These points will now be developed. In order to accomplish any form of integration (as distinct from different subjects focusing upon a common problem, which gives rise to what could be called a *focused* curriculum) there must be some relational idea, a supra-content concept, which focuses upon general principles at a high level of abstraction. For example, if the relationships between sociology and biology are to be opened, then the relational idea (amongst many) might be the issue of problems of order and change examined through the concepts of genetic and cultural codes. Whatever the relational concepts are, they will act selectively upon the knowledge within each subject which is to be transmitted. The particulars of each subject are likely to have reduced significance. This will focus attention upon the *deep* structure of each subject, rather than upon its surface structure. I suggest this will lead to an emphasis upon, and the exploration of, *general* principles and the concepts through which these principles are obtained. In turn, this is likely to affect the orientation of the pedagogy, which will be less concerned to emphasize the need to acquire *states* of knowledge, but will be more concerned to emphasize *how* knowledge is created. In other words, the pedagogy of integrated codes is likely to emphasize various *ways* of knowing in the pedagogical relationships. With the collection code, the pedagogy tends to proceed from the surface structure of the knowledge to the deep structure, as we have seen, only the élite have access to the deep structure and therefore access to the realizing of new realities or access to the experiential knowledge that new realities are possible. *With integrated codes, the pedagogy is likely to proceed from the deep structure to the surface structure.* We can see this already at work in the new primary school mathematics. Thus, I suggest that integrated codes will make available from the beginning of the pupil's educational career, clearly in a way appropriate to a given age level, the deep structure of the knowledge, i.e. the principles for the generating of new knowledge. Such emphasis upon various *ways* of knowing, rather than upon the attaining of *states* of knowledge, is likely to affect, not only the emphasis of the pedagogy, but the underlying theory of learning. The underlying theory of learning of collection is likely to be didactic, whilst the underlying theory of learning of integrated codes may well be more group or self-regulated. This arises out of a different concept of what counts as having knowledge, which in turn leads to a different concept of how the knowledge is to be acquired. These changes in emphasis and orientation of the pedagogy are initially responsible for the relaxed frames, which teacher and taught enter. Relaxed frames not only change the nature of the authority relationships by increasing the rights of the taught, they can also weaken or blur the boundary between what may or may not be taught, and so *more* of the teacher and taught is likely to enter this pedagogical frame. The inherent logic of the integrated code is likely to create a change in the structure of teaching groups, which are likely to exhibit considerable flexibility. The concept of relatively weak boundary maintenance which is the core principle of integrated codes is realized both in the structuring of educational knowledge *and* in the organization of the social relationships.

I shall now introduce some organizational consequences of collection and integrated codes which will make explicit the difference in the distribution of power and the principles of control which inhere in these educational codes.

Where knowledge is regulated through a collection code, the knowledge is organized and distributed through a series of well insulated subject hierarchies. Such a structure points to oligarchic control of the institution, through formal and informal meetings of heads of department with the head or principal of the institution. Thus, senior staff will have strong horizontal work relationships (that is, with their peers in other subject hierarchies) and strong vertical work relationships within their own department. However, junior staff are likely to have only vertical (within the subject hierarchy) allegiances and work relationships.

The allegiances of junior staff are vertical rather than horizontal for the following reasons. First, staff have been socialized into strong subject loyalty and through this into specific identities. These specific identities are continuously strengthened through social interactions *within* the department *and* through the insulation between departments. Second, the departments are often in a competitive relationship for strategic teaching resources. Third, preferment within the subject hierarchy often rests with its expansion. Horizontal relationships of junior staff (particularly where there is no *effective* participatory administrative structure) are likely to be limited to *non-task-based* contacts. There may well be discussion of control problems ('X of 3b is a —— How do you deal with him?' or 'I can't get X to write a paper'). Thus the collection code within the framework of oligarchic control creates for *senior* staff strong horizontal and vertical based relationships, whereas the work relationships of junior staff are likely to be vertical and the horizontal relationships limited to non-work-based contacts. This is a type of organizational system which encourages gossip, intrigue and a conspiracy theory of the workings of the organization, for *both* the *administration* and the *acts of teaching* are *invisible* to the majority of staff. (See Figure 5.2.)

Now the integrated code will require teachers of different subjects to enter into social relationships with each other which will arise not simply out of non-task areas, but out of a shared, co-operative educational task. The centre of gravity of the relationships between teachers will undergo a radical shift. Thus, instead of teachers and lecturers being divided and insulated by allegiances to subject hierarchies, the conditions for their unification exist through a common work situation. I suggest that this changed basis of the relationships, between teachers or between lecturers, may tend to weaken the separate hierarchies of collection. These new work-based horizontal relationships between teachers and between lecturers may alter both the structure and distribution of power regulated by the collection code. Further, the administration and specific acts of teaching are likely to shift from the relative in-visibility to *visibility*.

We might expect similar developments at the level of students and even senior pupils. For pupils and students, with each increase in their educational life, are equally sub-divided and educationally insulated from each other. They are equally bound to subject hierarchies and, for similar reasons, to staff; their identities and their future is shaped by the department. Their vertical allegiances and work-based relationships are strong, whilst their horizontal relationships will tend to be limited to non-task areas (student/pupil societies and sport) or peripheral non-task based administration. Here again, we can see another example of the strength of boundary maintenance of collection codes; this time between task and non-task areas. Integrated codes may well provide the conditions for strong horizontal relationships and allegiances in students and pupils, based upon a common work task (the receiving and offering of knowledge).[6] In this situation, we might expect a weakening of the boundary between staff, especially junior staff, and students/pupils.

Thus, a move from collection to integrated codes may well bring about a disturbance in the structure and distribution of power, in property relationships and in existing educational identities. This change of educational code involves a fundamental change in the nature and strength of boundaries. It involves a change in what counts as having knowledge, in what counts as a valid transmission of knowledge, in what counts as a valid realization of knowledge, *and* a change in the organizational context. At the cultural level, it involves a shift from the keeping of categories pure to the mixing of categories; whilst at the level of socialization the outcomes of

Ideal typical organizational structures

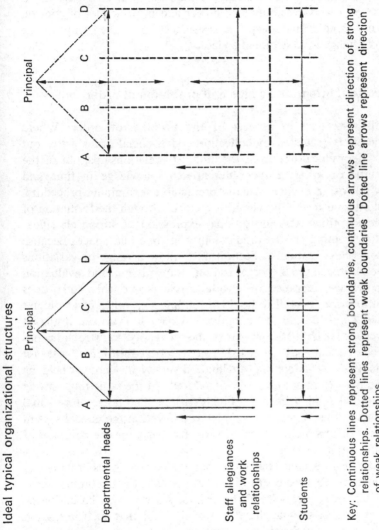

Key: Continuous lines represent strong boundaries, continuous arrows represent direction of strong relationships. Dotted lines represent weak boundaries. Dotted line arrows represent direction of weak relationships

Collection code type = Strong classification: strong frames

Integrated code type = Weak classification: weak frames

Figure 5.2

integrated codes *could* be less predictable than the outcomes of collection codes. This change of code involves fundamental changes in the classification and framing of knowledge and so changes in the structure and distribution of power and in principles of control. It is no wonder that deep-felt resistances are called out by the issue of change in educational codes.

Collection, integrated codes and problems of order

I shall now turn to aspects of the problem of order. Where knowledge is regulated by collection codes, social order arises out of the hierarchical nature of the authority relationships, out of the systematic ordering of the differentiated knowledge in time and space, out of an explicit, usually predictable, examining procedure. Order internal to the individual is created through the formation of specific identities. The institutional expression of strong classification and framing creates predictability in time and space. Because of strong classification, collection does allow a range of variations between subjects in the organization, transmission and evaluation of knowledge. Because of strong classification, this code does permit *in principle* staff to hold (within limits) a range of ideologies because conflicts can be contained *within* its various insulated hierarchies. At levels below that of the university, the strong frames between educational knowledge and non-educational relevant knowledge *in principle* may facilitate diversity in ideology held by staff because it cannot be explicitly offered. At the same time, strong framing makes such intrusion highly visible. The range of personal freedoms at the *university* level are symbolized in the ethical system of some collection codes and so form the basis for the cohesion of the differentiated whole.

Whilst it is usually the case that collection codes, relative to integrated codes, create strong frames between the uncommonsense knowledge of the school and the everyday community-based knowledge of teacher and taught, it is also the case that such insulation creates areas of privacy. For, inasmuch as community-based experience is irrelevant to the pedagogical frame, these aspects of the self informed by such experiences are also irrelevant. These areas of privacy reduce the penetration of the socializing process, for it is possible to distance oneself from it. This still means, however, that the socialization can be deeply wounding, either for those who wish for, but do not achieve, an identity, or for the majority for whom the pursuit of an identity is early made irrelevant.

Order created by integrated codes may well be problematic. I suggest that if four conditions are not satisfied, then the openness of learning under integration may produce a culture in which neither staff nor pupils have a sense of time, place or purpose. I shall comment briefly on these four conditions as I give them.

(1) There must be consensus about the integrating idea and it must be very explicit. (It is ironic that the movement towards integration is going on in those countries where there is a low level of moral consensus.) It may be that integrated codes will only work[7] when there is a *high* level of ideological consensus among the staff. We have already seen that, in comparison with collection, integrated codes call for greater homogeneity in pedagogy and evaluation, and therefore reduce differences between teachers in the form of the transmission and assessment of knowledge. Whereas the teaching process under collection is likely to be invisible to other teachers, unless special conditions prevail, it is likely that the teaching process regulated through integrated codes may well become visible as a result of developments in the pedagogy in the direction of flexibility in the structure of teaching groups. It is also the case that the weak classification and relaxed frames of integrated codes permit greater expressions of differences between teachers, and possibly between pupils, in the selection of what is taught. The moral basis of educational choices is then likely to be explicit at the initial planning stage. Integrated codes also weaken specific identities. For the above reasons, integrated codes may require a high level of ideological consensus, and this may affect the recruitment of staff. Integrated codes at the surface level create weak or blurred boundaries, but at bottom they may rest upon closed explicit ideologies. Where such ideologies are not shared, the consequences will become visible and threaten the whole at every point.

(2) The nature of the linkage between the integrating idea and the knowledge to be co-ordinated must also be coherently spelled out. It is this linkage which will be the basic element in bringing teachers *and* pupils into their working relationship. *The development of such a co-ordinating framework will be the process of socialization of teachers into the code. During this process, the*

teachers will internalize, as in all processes of socialization, the interpretative procedures of the code so that these become implicit guides which regulate and co-ordinate the behaviour of the individual teachers in the relaxed frames and weakened classification. This brings us to a major distinction between collection and integrated codes. With a collection code, the period of socialization is facilitated by strong boundary maintenance both at the level of *role* and at the level of knowledge. Such socialization is likely to be continuous with the teacher's own educational socialization. With integrated codes both the role and the form of the knowledge have to be *achieved* in relation to a range of different others, and this may involve re-socialization if the teacher's previous educational experience has been formed by the collection code. The collection code is capable of working when staffed by mediocre teachers, whereas integrated codes call for much greater powers of synthesis, analogy and for more ability to both tolerate and enjoy ambiguity at the level of knowledge *and* social relationships.

(3) A committee system of staff may have to be set up to create a sensitive feed-back system and which will also provide a further agency of socialization into the code. It is likely that evaluative criteria are likely to be relatively weak, in the sense that the criteria are less likely to be as explicit and measurable as in the case of collection. As a result, it may be necessary to develop committees for both teachers, students, and, where appropriate, pupils, which will perform monitoring functions.

(4) One of the major difficulties which inhere in integrated codes arises over what is to be assessed, and the form of assessment: also the place of specific competencies in such assessment. It is likely that integrated codes will give rise to multiple criteria of assessment compared with collection codes. In the case of collection codes, because the knowledge moves from the surface to the deep structure, then this progression creates ordered principles of evaluation in time. The form of temporal cohesion of the knowledge regulated through the integrated code has yet to be determined, and made explicit. Without clear criteria of evaluation, neither teacher nor taught have any means to consider the significance of what is learned, nor any means to judge the pedagogy. In the case of collection codes, evaluation at the secondary level often consists of the fit between a narrow range of specific competencies and states of knowledge, and previously established criteria (varying in explicit-

ness) of what constitutes a right or appropriate or convincing answer. The previously established criteria together with the specific social context of assessment create a relatively objective procedure. I do not want to suggest that this necessarily gives rise to a form of assessment which entirely disregards distinctive and original features of the pupil's performance. In the case of the integrated code under discussion (weak frames for teacher and taught), this form of assessment may well be inappropriate. The weak frames enable a greater range of the student's behaviour to be made public, and they make possible considerable diversity (at least in principle) between students. It is possible that this might lead to a situation where assessment takes more into account 'inner' attributes of the student. Thus if he has the 'right' attitudes, then this will result later in the attainment of various specific competencies. The 'right' attitude may be assessed in terms of the fit between the pupil's attitudes and the current ideology. It is possible, then, that the evaluative criteria of integrated codes with weak frames may be weak as these refer to specific cognitive attributes but strong as these refer to dispositional attributes. If this is so, then a new range of pupil attributes become candidates for labels. It is also likely that the weakened classification and framing will encourage more of the pupil/student to be made public; more of his thoughts, feelings and values. In this way more of the pupil is available for control. As a result the socialization could be more intensive and perhaps more penetrating. In the same way as pupils/students defend themselves against the wounds of collection, or distance themselves from its overt code, so they may produce new defences against the potential intrusiveness of the integrated code and its open learning contexts.

We can summarize this question of the problem of order as follows. Collection codes have explicit and strong boundary maintaining features and they rest upon a tacit ideological basis. Integrated codes have implicit and weak boundary maintaining features and they rest upon an explicit and closed ideological basis. The ideological basis of the collection code is a condensed symbolic system communicated through its explicit boundary maintaining features. Its covert structure is that of mechanical solidarity. The ideological basis of integrated codes is *not* a condensed symbolic system, it is verbally elaborated and explicit. It is an *overt* realization of organic solidarity and made substantive through weak forms of boundary maintenance (low insulations). Yet the covert structure of mechanical solidarity of collection codes creates through its specialized outputs *organic* solidarity. On the other hand the overt structure of organic solidarity of integrated codes creates through its *less* specialized outputs *mechanical* solidarity. And it will do this to the extent to which its ideology is explicit, elaborated and closed *and* effectively and *implicitly* transmitted through its low insulations. Inasmuch as integrated codes do not accomplish this, then order is highly problematic at the level of social organization and at the level of the person. Inasmuch as integrated codes do accomplish such socialization, then we have the covert deep closure of mechanical solidarity. This is the fundamental paradox which has to be faced and explored.

Change of educational code

I have tried to make explicit the relationships between educational codes and the structure of power and principles of social control. Attempts to change or modify educational codes will meet with resistance at a number of different levels, irrespective of the intrinsic educational merit of a particular code. I shall now briefly discuss some reasons for a movement towards the institutionalizing of integrated codes *of the weak classification and weak framing (teacher and taught) type*,[8] above the level of the primary school.[9]

(1) The growing differentiation of knowledge at the higher levels of thought, together with the integration of previously discrete areas, may set up requirements for a form of socialization appropriate to these changes in the structure of knowledge.

(2) Changes in the division of labour are creating a different concept of skill. The in-built obsolescence of whole varieties of skills reduces the significance of context-tied operations and increases the significance of general principles from which a range of diverse operations may be derived. In crude terms, it could be said that the nineteenth century required submissive and inflexible man, whereas the late twentieth century requires conforming but flexible man.

(3) The less rigid social structure of the integrated code makes it a potential code for egalitarian education.

(4) In advanced industrial societies which permit, within limits, a range of legitimizing beliefs and ideologies, there is a major problem of control. There is the problem of making sense of the differentiated, weakly co-ordinated and changing symbolic systems and the problem of inner regulation of the person. Integrated codes, with their stress on the underlying unity of knowledge, through their emphasis upon analogy and synthesis, could be seen as a response to the first problem of 'making sense'. The *inter-personal* rather than *inter-positional* control of the integrated code may set up a penetrating, intrusive form of socialization under conditions of ambiguity in the system of beliefs and the moral order.

If these reasons operate, we could consider the movement towards integrated codes as stemming from a technological source. However, it is possible that there is another and deeper source of the movement away from collection. I suggest that the movement away from collection to integrated codes symbolizes that there is a crisis in society's basic classifications and frames, and therefore a crisis in its structures of power and principles of control. The movement from this point of view represents an attempt to de-classify and so alter power structures and principles of control; in so doing to unfreeze the structuring of knowledge and to change the boundaries of consciousness. From this point of view integrated codes are symptoms of a moral crisis rather than the terminal state of an educational system.

Conclusion

In this paper, I have tried to explore the concept of boundary in such a way that it is possible to see *both* the power and control components. The analysis focuses directly upon the structuring of transmitted educational knowledge.

Although the concept, 'classification', appears to operate on a single dimension, i.e. differences in degrees of insulation between content (subjects/courses, etc.) it explicitly points to power and control components. In the same way, the concept, 'frame', appears to operate in a single dimension; what may or may not be taught in the pedagogical relationship. Yet the exploration of the concept again points to power and control components. Through defining educational codes in terms of the relationship between classification and framing, these two components are built into the analysis at all levels. It then becomes possible in one framework to derive a typology of educational codes, to show the inter-relationships between organizational and knowledge properties, to move from macro- to micro-levels of analysis, to relate the patterns internal to educational institutions to the external social antecedents of such patterns, and to consider questions of maintenance and change. At the same time, it is hoped that the analysis makes explicit tacit assumptions underlying various educational codes. It attempts to show at a *theoretical* level, the relationships between a particular symbolic order and the structuring of experience. I believe that it offers an approach which is well capable of exploration by diverse methods at the empirical level.

It should be quite clear that the specific application of the concepts requires at every point empirical evidence. I have not attempted to bolster the argument with references, because in many cases the evidence which is required does not exist in a *form* which bears directly upon the chain of inferences, and therefore would offer perhaps spurious support. We have, for example, little *first*-hand knowledge which bears upon aspects of framing as this concept is used in the paper. We also have next to no *first*-hand knowledge of the day-by-day encounters realized by various types of integrated codes.

I hope that the kinds of questions raised by this approach will encourage sociologists of education to explore both theoretically and empirically the structure of educational knowledge which I take to be the distinctive feature of this field.

Acknowledgments

I am most grateful to Professor Wolfgang Klafki, and particularly to Mr Hubertus Huppauf of the University of Marburg, for many valuable suggestions and constructive criticisms. I should also like to acknowledge many hours of discussion with my colleague Mr Michael Young. I have also learned much from Mr David Adelstein, graduate student in the Department of the Sociology of Education, University of London Institute of Education. I am particularly grateful to Mr W. Brandis, research officer in the Department's

Research Unit. I have also benefited from the stringent criticisms of Professor R. Peters, and Mr Lionel Elvin, of the University of London Institute of Education. My greatest debt is to Professor Mary Douglas, University College, London.

I should like to thank the Director of the Chaucer Publishing Company, Mr L. G. Grossman, for a small but vital grant.

Notes

1   It follows that frame strength for teacher and taught can be assessed at the different levels of selection, organization, pacing and timing of the knowledge.
2   Consider the recent acrimonious debate over the attempt to obtain permission at Oxford to develop a degree in anthropology, sociology, psychology and biology—a relatively 'pure' combination.
3   The content of public examinations between the secondary and the tertiary level is controlled by the tertiary level directly or indirectly, through control over the various syllabuses. Thus, if there is to be any major shift in secondary schools' syllabuses and curricula, then this will require changes in the tertiary level's policy, as this affects the acceptance of students. Such a change in policy would involve changes in the selection, organization, pacing and timing of knowledge at the tertiary level. Thus, the conditions for a major shift in the knowledge code at the secondary level is a major shift in the knowledge code at the tertiary level. Changes in the knowledge code at the secondary level are likely to be of a somewhat limited nature without similar changes at the tertiary level. There clearly are other interest groups (industry) which may affect a given curriculum and syllabus.
4   Such variations may well be linked to variations in the development of class structure, see chapter 6.
5   What is often overlooked is that the pacing of the knowledge (i.e. the rate of expected learning) is implicitly based upon the middle-class socialization of the child. Middle-class family socialization of the child is a hidden subsidy, in the sense that it provides both a physical and psychological environment which immensely facilitates, in diverse ways, school learning. The middle-class child is oriented to learning almost anything. Because of this hidden subsidy, there has been little incentive to change curriculum and pedagogy, for the middle-class child is geared to learn; he may not like, or indeed approve of, what he learns, but he learns. Where the school system is not subsidized by the home, the pupil often fails. In this way, even the *pacing* of educational knowledge is class based. It may well be that frame strength, as this refers to pacing, is a critical variable in the study of educability. It is possible that the weak frame strength (as this refers to *pacing*) of integrated

codes indicates that integrated codes pre-suppose a longer average educational life. Middle-class children may have been potential pupils for progressive schools because of their longer educational life.

6   It is possible that the weak boundary maintaining procedures of integrated codes at the level of the organizational structure, knowledge structure and identity structure may increase the pupils/students informal age group affiliations as a source of identity, relation and organization.

7   In the sense of creating order.

8   In the paper, I suggested that integrated codes rest upon a closed explicit ideology. It should then follow that this code would stand a better chance of successful institutionalization in societies where (1) there were strong and effective constraints upon the development of a range of ideologies and (2) where the educational system was a major agency of political socialization. Further, the weak boundary maintaining procedures of the integrated code would (1) increase the penetration of the socialization as more of the self of the taught is made public through the relaxed frames and (2) deviancy would be more visible. On the other hand, integrated codes carry a potential for change in power structures and principles of control. I would therefore guess that in such societies integrated codes would possess weak classification, but the frames for teacher and taught would be strong.

9   It is a matter of interest that, in England, it is only in the infant school that there is relatively widespread introduction of this form of integrated code. This raises the general question of how this level of the educational system was open to such change. Historically, the primary school developed distinct concepts of infant and junior stages, and distinct heads for these two stages. Given the relative autonomy over the transmission of knowledge which characterizes the British system of education, it was in principle possible to have change. Although only a ceiling may separate infant from junior departments, two quite distinct and often incompatible educational codes can develop. We can regard this as a necessary, but not sufficient, condition for the emergence of integrated codes at the infant school level. It was also the case, until very recently, that the selection function started in the junior department, because that department was the gateway to the grammar school. This left the infant school relatively free of control by levels higher than itself. The form of integration in the infant school, again until recently, was *teacher*-based, and therefore did not set up the problems which arise out of *teachers*-based integration. Finally, infant school teachers are not socialized into strong educational identities. Thus the English educational system, until recently, had two potential points of openness—the period between the ages of five to seven years, before selection began, and the period post-eighteen years of age, when selection is

virtually completed. The major control on the structuring of knowledge at the secondary level is the structuring of knowledge at the tertiary level, specifically the university. Only if there is a major change in the structuring of knowledge at this level can there be effective code change at lower levels; although in any one school there may be a variety of knowledge codes.

References

BERNSTEIN, B. (1967), 'Open schools, open society?' *New Society*, 14 September. Reprinted as Chapter 3 of the present volume.

BERNSTEIN, B., ELVIN, L. and PETERS, R. (1966), 'Ritual in education', *Philosophical Transactions of the Royal Society of London*, Series B, 251, No. 772.

DAVIES, D. I. (1970a), 'The management of knowledge: a critique of the use of typologies in educational sociology', *Sociology* 4, No. 1.

DAVIES, D. I. (1970b), 'Knowledge, education and power', paper presented to the British Sociological Association Annual Conference, Durham.

DOUGLAS, M. (1966), *Purity and Danger*, Routledge & Kegan Paul.

DOUGLAS, M. (1970), *Natural Symbols*, Barrie & Rockliff, The Cresset Press.

DURKHEIM, E. (1947), *The Division of Labour in Society*, Free Press, Chicago.

DURKHEIM, E. (1961), *Moral Education*, Free Press, Chicago.

DURKHEIM, E. and MAUSS, M. (1963), *Primitive Classification* (translated by R. Needham), Cohen & West.

HOYLE, E. (1969), 'How does the curriculum change? (1) A proposal for enquiries (2) Systems and Strategies', *Journal of Curriculum Studies*, Vol. 1, Nos 2 and 3.

JEFFREY, G. B. (1950), *The Unity of Knowledge: Reflections on the Universities of Cambridge and London*, Cambridge University Press.

KEDDIE, N. G. (1970), 'The social basis of classroom knowledge', MA dissertation, University of London Institute of Education.

MUSGROVE, F. (1968), 'The contribution of sociology to the study of the curriculum', in *Changing the Curriculum*, ed. J. F. Kerr, University of London Press.

YOUNG, M. (1970), 'Curricula as socially organised knowledge', in *Knowledge and Control*, ed. M. Young, Collier-Macmillan.

Chapter 6 Class and pedagogies: visible and invisible

I shall examine some of the assumptions and the cultural context of a particular form of pre-school/infant school pedagogy. A form which has at least the following characteristics:

(1) Where the control of the teacher over the child is implicit rather than explicit.

(2) Where, ideally, the teacher arranges the *context* which the child is expected to re-arrange and explore.

(3) Where within this arranged context, the child apparently has wide powers over what he selects, over how he structures, and over the time-scale of his activities.

(4) Where the child apparently regulates his own movements and social relationships.

(5) Where there is a reduced emphasis upon the transmission and acquisition of specific skills.[1]

(6) Where the criteria for evaluating the pedagogy are multiple and diffuse and so not easily measured.

Invisible pedagogy and infant education

One can characterize this pedagogy as an invisible pedagogy. In terms of the concepts of classification and frame, the pedagogy is realized through weak classification and weak frames. Visible pedagogies are realized through strong classification and strong frames. The basic difference between visible and invisible pedagogies is in the *manner* in which criteria are transmitted and in the degree of specificity of the criteria. The more implicit the manner of transmission and the more diffuse the criteria, the more invisible the

116

pedagogy, the more specific the criteria, the more explicit the manner of their transmission, the more visible the pedagogy. These definitions are extended below.

Formal definitions of visible and invisible pedagogies

We shall propose that the crucial social relationship of cultural reproduction is that between transmitter(s) and acquirer(s). We shall suggest three basic features regulate this relationship.

(1) *Hierarchy* There must be rules, formal and/or informal, whereby the social relationship is initially constituted. These rules regulate what it is to be a transmitter and what it is to be an acquirer. The acquirer is expected to learn how to be a particular type of acquirer, as much as the transmitter has learned to be a particular type of transmitter. These rules determine the hierarchical form of the transmission. They establish its rules of conduct.

(2) *Sequencing rules* Any transmission extends in time. As a consequence, something occurs before and something comes later. There must be rules regulating the progression of the transmission in time, and which establish sequences. We shall call the principle regulating the transmission, the sequencing rules.

(3) *Criteria* Any relationship of transmission/acquisition entails, necessarily, the transfer of criteria which the acquirer is expected to take over and explore and to evaluate the behaviour of himself/herself and relevant others.

We are arguing that hierarchy, sequencing rules and criteria are basic features of any relationship of transmission and acquisition, and so crucial to education. We shall further argue that the *form* taken by the hierarchical relation affects both the sequencing rules and the criteria. On the basis of these three features, we can make sharper definitions of visible and invisible pedagogies or transmissions.

(1) Hierarchy

The hierarchical rules may be explicit or implicit. If the rules are explicit, then the relationships between transmitter and acquirer are relationships of unambiguous super- and subordination. However, the hierarchical rules may be implicit rather than explicit. In this case, the relationship is not one of clearly marked super-subordination. The acquirer appears to have greater control over the regulation of his/her movements, activities, communication. Essentially, implicit hierarchy masks the power relationships. Where the hierarchy is implicit, the acquirer is likely to be subject to the regulation of his/her peers. Consider the illustrations to the Plowden Report. The teacher is rarely obvious; the children are in the foreground.

(2) Sequencing rules

The sequencing rules regulating the transmission may be *explicit* or *implicit*. If the sequencing rules are explicit, then (if we are considering a school) those rules *publicly* regulate what a child of five, six, seven, etc. should be able to do. These sequencing rules regulate the unfolding of a syllabus, the curricula, the system of assessment. Where sequencing rules are explicit, there is an explicit concept of the progression of a child so that the child is in some sense aware of, has knowledge of, his/her future expected state of consciousness. He/she may or may not identify with what is expected. Sequencing rules may, however, be implicit. If sequencing rules are implicit, the acquirer (the child) can never know the principles of his own progression. Only the transmitter will know. Where sequencing rules are implicit, then syllabus and curriculum are less clearly defined. Where sequencing rules are implicit, then the sex and chronological age of the child do not become strong marking features of the sequencing rules. Finally, where sequencing rules are implicit, only the transmitter knows them. For when such rules are implicit, they will be drawn from different areas and special theories of child developmental psychology. The transmitter will interpret the behaviour of the child in the light of these theories. The transmitter will look for signs of the child's developmental stage, whether these be linguistic, social, intellectual or affective, and respond to the child and arrange contexts and contents according to how the signs are interpreted. Thus, implicit sequencing rules should create theories of signs. In this case, the meaning of the sign of the child's progression can be known only to the teacher, not to the acquirer. Where the sequencing rules are explicit, the child is aware of the signs which indicate his/her progression. He/she can read the meaning of his/her signs. Also entailed in the sequencing rules is the pacing of the transmission. In general, but not always, explicit sequencing rules = strong pacing (rate of expected acquisition); implicit sequencing rules = weak pacing of the transmission. Thus the sequencing rules of the transmission may be explicit or implicit.

(3) Criteria

In the same way that the hierarchical and sequencing rules may be explicit or implicit, so the criteria transferred may be explicit and specific *or* implicit, multiple and diffuse. Where the transmission realizes explicit criteria, then the transmitter is continuously making the acquirer aware either in oral or written form what is *not* in his/her production. Consider an infant school, fifty years ago, with the children sitting on their individual small chairs and working at small desks arranged in rows. The children have a small piece of paper and a small box of paints with three colours in the top and three in the bottom layer. Beside the paints is one small, thin brush. What are the children doing? They are making facsimiles of the outside. They are learning a reproductive aesthetic code. They may be drawing or painting figures, houses, etc. The teacher looks at the product of one child and says, 'That's a very good house, but *where* is the chimney?', or 'There are no windows in your house', or 'That man has got only three fingers', etc. Here the child is made aware of what is *missing* in the production, and what is missing is made explicit and specific, and subject to finely graded assessment.

In some infant schools today, the children have a large sheet of paper, and not a small box of paints but an assembly of media whereby their unique visual imagination may be momentarily revealed. This is allegedly not a reproductive aesthetic code, but a productive aesthetic code. The teacher here is less likely to say, 'What's that?'; is less likely explicitly to create in the child a consciousness of what is missing in the product: the teacher is more likely to do this indirectly, in a context of general, diffuse support. Where the transmission realizes implicit criteria, it is *as if* the acquirer is the source of the criteria.

We can now formally define visible or invisible pedagogies or transmissions. (Visible and invisible refer to the transmission from the point of view of the acquirer, *not* that of the transmitter.)

A visible pedagogy is created by: (1) explicit hierarchy;

                                                 (2) explicit sequencing rules;

                                                 (3) explicit and specific criteria.

The underlying rule is: 'Things must be kept apart.' The question is, why, and for what purpose? Strong classification is generally realized through visible pedagogies (strong framing).

An invisible pedagogy is created by:

(1) implicit hierarchy;
(2) implicit sequencing rules;
(3) implicit criteria.

The underlying rule is: 'Things must be put together.' The question is, what things, for what purpose? Weak classification is realized through invisible pedagogies (weak framing) but it does not necessarily follow that weak classification always gives rise to weak framing. Finally, in order to avoid confusion, it is important to be absolutely clear that although there are many implications to the concept of invisible pedagogy, it is being used here in the context of the *early years of the child's life either in the home or in the school*. Integrated codes are structurally equivalent at the secondary levels and above.

Discussion

If the pedagogy is invisible, what aspects of the child have high visibility for the teacher? I suggest two aspects. The first arises out of an inference the teacher makes from the child's ongoing behaviour about the *developmental* stage of the child. This inference is then referred to a concept of *readiness*. The second aspect of the child refers to his external behaviour and is conceptualized by the teacher as busyness. The child should be busy doing things. These inner (readiness) and outer (busyness) aspects of the child can be transformed into one concept of 'ready to do'. The teacher infers from the 'doing' the state of 'readiness' of the child as it is revealed in his present activity and as this state adumbrates future 'doing'.

We can briefly note in passing a point which will be developed later. In the same way as the child's reading releases the child from the teacher and socializes him into the privatized, solitary learning of an explicit anonymous past (i.e. the textbook), so busy children (children doing) releases the child from the teacher but socializes him into an ongoing inter-actional present in which the past is invisible and so implicit (i.e. the teacher's pedagogical theory). Thus a non-doing child in the invisible pedagogy is the equivalent of a non-reading child in the visible pedagogy. (However, a non-reading child may be at a greater disadvantage and experience greater difficulty than a 'non-doing' child.)

The concept basic to the invisible pedagogy is that of play. This is not the place to submit this concept to logical analysis, but a few points may be noted:

(1)   Play is the means by which the child exteriorizes himself to the teacher. Thus the more he plays and the greater the range of his activities, the more of him is made available to the teacher's screening. Thus, play is the fundamental concept with 'readiness' and 'doing' as subordinate concepts. Although not all forms of doing are considered as play (hitting another child, for example) most forms can be so characterized.

(2)   Play does not merely describe an activity, it also contains an evaluation of that activity. Thus, there is productive and less productive play, obsessional and free-ranging play, solitary and social play. Play is not only an activity, it entails a theory from which interpretation, evaluation and diagnosis are derived and which also indicates a progression: a theory which the child can never know in the way a child can know the criteria which are realized in visible pedagogy. Play implies a potentially all-embracing theory, for it covers nearly all if not all the child's doing and not doing. As a consequence, a very long chain of inference has to be set up to connect the theory with any one exemplar ('a doing' or a 'not doing'). The theory gives rise to a total—but invisible—surveillance of the child, because it relates his inner dispositions to all his external acts. The 'spontaneity' of the child is filtered through this surveillance and then implicitly shaped according to interpretation, evaluation and diagnosis.

(3)   Both the means and ends of play are multiple and change with time. Because of this, the stimuli must be, on the whole, highly abstract, available to be contextualized by the child, and so the unique doing of each child is facilitated. Indeed, play encourages each child to make his own mark. Sometimes, however, the stimulus may be very palpable when the child is invited to feel a leaf, or piece of velour, but what is *expected* is a *unique* response of the child to his own sensation. What is the code for reading the marks; a code the child can never know, but implicitly acquires. How does he do this?

(4)   The social basis of this theory of play is not an individualized

act, but a personalized act; not strongly framed, but weakly framed encounters. Its social structure may be characterized as one of *overt* personalized organic solidarity, but covert mechanical solidarity. Visible pedagogies create social structures which may be characterized as *covert* individualized organic solidarity and *overt* mechanical solidarity.[2] (See later discussion.)

(5) In essence, play is work and work is play. We can begin to see here the class origins of the theory. For the working class, work and play are very strongly classified and framed; for certain sub-groups of the middle class, work and play are weakly classified and weakly framed. For these sub-groups, no strict line may be drawn between work and play. Work carries what is often called 'intrinsic' satisfactions, and therefore is not confined to *one* context. However, from another point of view, work offers the opportunity of symbolic narcissism which combines inner pleasure and outer prestige. Work for certain sub-groups of the middle class is a personalized act in a privatized social structure. These points will be developed later.

Theories of learning and invisible pedagogy

We are now in a position to analyse the principles underlying the selection of theories of learning which invisible pre-school/infant school pedagogies will adopt. Such pedagogies will adopt any theory of learning which has the following characteristics:

(1) The theories in general will be seeking universals and thus are likely to be developmental and concerned with sequence. A particular context of learning is only of interest inasmuch as it throws light on a sequence. Such theories are likely to have a strong biological bias.

(2) Learning is a tacit, invisible act, its progression is not facilitated by explicit public control.

(3) The theories will tend to abstract the child's personal biography and local context from his cultural biography and institutional context.

(4) In a sense, the theories see socializers as potentially, if not actually, dangerous, as they embody an adult-focused, therefore reified, concept of the socialized. Exemplary models are relatively unimportant and so the various theories in different ways point

towards *implicit* rather than explicit hierarchical social relationships. Indeed, the imposing exemplar is transformed into a *facilitator*. (5) Thus the theories can be seen as interrupters of cultural reproduction and therefore have been considered by some as progressive or even revolutionary. Notions of child's time replace notions of adult's time, notions of child's space replace notions of adult's space; facilitation replaces imposition and accommodation replaces domination.

We now give a group of theories, which, despite many differences, fulfil at a most abstract level all or nearly all of the five conditions given previously:

Piaget	1	2	3	4	5
Freud	1	2	3	4	5
Chomsky	1	2	3	4	5
Ethological theories					
of critical learning	1	2	3		
Gestalt		2	3	4	5

What is of interest is that these theories form rather a strange, if not contradictory group. They are often selected to justify a specific element of the pedagogy. They form in a way the theology of the infant school. We can see how the crucial concept of play and the subordinate concepts of readiness and doing fit well with the above theories. We can also note how the invisibility of the pedagogy fits with the invisible tacit act of learning. We can also see that the pre-school/infant school movement from one point of view is a progressive, revolutionary, colonizing movement in its relationships to parents, and in its relationship to educational levels above itself. It is antagonistic for different reasons to middle-class and working-class families, for both create a deformation of the child. It is antagonistic to educational levels above itself, because of its fundamental opposition to their concepts of learning and social relationships. We can note here that as a result the child is abstracted from his family and his future educational contexts.

Of central importance is that this pedagogy brings together two groups of educationists who are at the extremes of the educational hierarchy, infant school teachers and university teachers and researchers. The consequence has been to professionalize and raise the status of the pre-school/infant school teacher; a status not based upon a specific competence, a status based upon a weak educational identity (no subject). The status of the teachers from this point of view is based upon a diffuse, tacit, symbolic control which is legitimized by a closed explicit ideology, the essence of weak classification and weak frames.

Class and the invisible pedagogy

From our previous discussion, we can abstract the following:

(1)   The invisible pedagogy is an interrupter system, both in relation to the family and in its relation to other levels of the educational hierarchy.

(2)   It transforms the privatized social structures and cultural contexts of visible pedagogies into a personalized social structure and personalized cultural contexts.

(3)   Implicit nurture reveals unique nature.

The question is what is it interrupting? The invisible pedagogy was first institutionalized in the private sector for a fraction of the middle class—the new middle class. If the ideologies of the old middle class were institutionalized in the public schools and through them into the grammar schools, so the ideology of the new middle class was first institutionalized in private pre-schools then private/ public secondary schools, and finally into the state system, at the level of the infant school. Thus the conflict between visible and invisible pedagogies, from this point of view, between strong and weak classification and frames, is an ideological conflict within the middle class. The ideologies of education are still the ideologies of class. The old middle class were domesticated through the strong classification and frames of the family and public schools, which attempted, often very successfully, cultural reproduction. But what social type was reproduced?

We know that every industrialized society produces organic solidarity. Now Durkheim, it seems to me, was concerned with only *one* form of such solidarity—the form which created individualism. Durkheim was interested in the vicissitudes of the types as their classification and framing were no longer, or only weakly, morally integrated, or when the individual's relation to the classification and frames underwent a change. His analysis is based upon the old middle class. He did not foresee, although his conceptual procedures make this possible, a form of organic solidarity based upon weak classification and weak frames; that is, a form of solidarity developed by the new middle class. Durkheim's organic solidarity refers to *individuals* in privatized class relationships; the second form of organic solidarity refers to persons in privatized class relationships.[3] The second form of organic solidarity celebrates the apparent release, not of the individual, but of the persons and *new* forms of social control.[4] Thus, we can distinguish *individualized* and *personalized* forms of organic solidarity *within* the middle class, each with their own distinctive and conflicting ideologies and each with their own distinctive and conflicting forms of socialization and symbolic reality. These two forms arise out of developments of the division of labour within class societies. Durkheim's individualized organic solidarity developed out of the increasing complexity of the economic division of labour; personalized organic solidarity, it is suggested, develops out of increases in the complexity of the division of labour of cultural or symbolic control which the new middle class have appropriated. The new middle class is an interrupter system, clearly not of class relationships, but of the *form* of their reproduction. In Bourdieu's terms, there has been a change in habitus, but not in function. This change in habitus has had far-reaching effects on the selective institutionalization of symbolic codes and codings in the areas of sex and aesthetics, and upon preparing and repairing agencies, such as the family, school, and mental hospitals. In all these areas there has been a shift towards weak classification and frames.[5]

This conflict within the middle class is realized sharply in different patterns of the socialization of the young. In the old middle class, socialization is into strong classification and strong framing, where the boundaries convey, tacitly, critical condensed messages. In the new middle class, socialization is into weak classification and weak frames, which promote, through the explicitness of the communication code, far greater ambiguity, and drives this class to make visible the ideology of its socialization; crucial to this ideology is the concept of the *person* not of the *individual*. Whereas the concept of the *individual* leads to specific, unambiguous role identities and relatively inflexible role performances, the *concept* of the person leads to ambiguous personal identity and flexible role performances. Both the old and the new middle class draw upon biological theories, but of very different types. The old middle class held theories which generated biologically fixed types, where variety of the type constituted a threat to cultural reproduction. The new middle class also hold theories which emphasize a fixed biological type, but they also hold that the type is capable of great variety. This, in essence, is a theory which points towards social mobility—towards a meritocracy. For the old middle class, variety must be severely reduced in order to ensure cultural reproduction; for the new middle class, the variety must be encouraged in order to ensure interruption. Reproduction and interruption are created by variations in the strength of classifications and frames.[6] As these weaken, so the socialization encourages more of the socialized to become visible, his uniqueness to be made manifest. Such socialization is deeply penetrating, more total as the surveillance becomes more invisible. This is the basis of control which creates personalized organic solidarity. Thus the forms of socialization within these two conflicting factions of the middle class are the origins of the visible and invisible pedagogies of the school. We have a homologue between the interruption of the new middle class of the reproduction of the old and the interruption of the new educational pedagogy of the reproduction of the old; between the conflict within the middle class and the conflict between the two pedagogies: yet it is the conflict between the interruption of *forms* of transmission of class relationships. This point we will now develop. The new middle class, like the proponents of the invisible pedagogy, are caught in a contradiction; for their theories are at variance with their objective class relationship. A deep-rooted ambivalence is the ambience of this group. On the one hand, they stand for variety against inflexibility, expression against repression, the inter-personal against the inter-positional; on the other hand, there is the grim obduracy of the division of labour and of the narrow pathways to its positions of power and prestige. Under individualized organic solidarity, property has an essentially physical nature; however, with the development of personalized organic solidarity, although property in the physical sense remains crucial, it has been partly psychologized and appears in the form of ownership of valued skills made available in educational institutions. Thus, if the new middle class is to repeat its position in the class structure, then appropriate secondary socialization into privileged education becomes crucial. But as the relation between education and occupation becomes more direct and closer in time, then the classifications and frames increase in strength. Thus the new middle class take up some ambivalent enthusiasm for the invisible pedagogy for the early socialization of the child, but settle for the *visible* pedagogy of the secondary school. And they will continue to do this until the university moves to a weaker classification and a weaker framing of its principles of transmission and selection. On the other hand, they are among the leaders of the movement to institutionalize the invisible pedagogy in state preschools and often for its colonization of the primary school and further extension into the secondary school. And this can be done with confidence for the secondary school is likely to provide both visible and invisible pedagogies. The former for the middle class and the latter for the working class.

Symbolic control[7] and the identification of the new middle class

However a ruling class is defined, it has a relatively direct relationship to the means and forms of production, but a relatively *indirect* relationship to the means and forms of cultural reproduction. It is the various strata of the middle class which have a direct relationship to the means and forms of cultural reproduction, but only an indirect relationship to the means and forms of production. What we call here the old middle class (essentially nineteenth century) based itself on the ideology of radical individualism (a form of integration referred to as individualized organic solidarity), whether its functions were entrepreneurial or professional. The ideology of radical individualism presupposes explicit and unambiguous values. It is this clarity in values which is fundamental to the transmission and reproduction of visible pedagogies. The explicit hierarchies of visible pedagogies require legitimation based upon explicit and unambiguous values. The new middle class, as a structure, is a middle/late-twentieth-century formation, arising out of the scientific organization of work and corporate capitalism. The new middle class is both a product and a sponsor of the related expansion of education and fields of symbolic control. It is ambiguously located in the class structure. The ambiguity of the location is probably related to an ambiguity in its values and purpose. Such ambiguity shifts the modality of social control. Invisible pedagogies rest upon implicit hierarchies, which do not require legitimation by explicit and unambiguous values. The form of integration of this faction shifts to personalized organic solidarity. This fraction of the middle class can be regarded as the *disseminators* of new forms of social control. The opposition between fractions of the middle class is not an opposition about radical change in class structure, but an opposition based upon conflicting forms of social control.

We shall offer a classification of the agencies/agents of symbolic control.

(1) Regulators: Members of the legal system, police, prison service, church.

(2) Repairers: Members of the medical/psychiatric services and its derivatives; social services.

(3) Diffusers: Teachers at all levels and in all areas. Mass and specialized media.

(4) Shapers: Creators of what count as developments within or change of symbolic forms in the arts and sciences.

(5) Executors: Civil service and bureaucrats.

Whilst it is true that category (1)—Regulators—might well be classified as *maintainers*, we want to emphasize that they play an important legal rôle in regulating the flow of people, acts, ideas. In the same way, some repairers may well have more of the function of regulators (in the above sense) than repairers. Further, each category has both its own hierarchy and its own internal ideological conflicts. In the same way, there may well be ideological conflicts *between* the categories which unite agents occupying dissimilar or similar positions in the respective hierarchies. Whilst we can distinguish the structure of integration, social control and processes of transmission which characterize the new middle class, the *agents* will be found in different proportions in different levels of the hierarchy in each category. This is a subject of continuing research. It is a matter of some importance (following Bourdieu) to consider the underlying structure of the field of cultural reproduction constituted by the agents and agencies of symbolic control, the underlying structure of the interrelationships of agents and agencies and the *forms* of symbolic control. Agents may be strongly or weakly classified in terms of the extent of their activity in more than one category and they may employ strong or weak framing procedures. The classification and framing analysis may be applied *within* a category *or between* categories. *The analysis in this paper is focused upon changes in the form of transmission.*

A brief discussion of the classification

(1) Regulators: These are the agencies and agents whose *function* is to define, monitor and maintain the limits of persons and activities. Why place the official religious agencies with regulators? These agencies at one time both informed and legitimized the features of the legal system. Today the relationship between official religious agencies and the legal system is more complex. The rôle of official religious agencies as moral regulators has been considerably weakened, although, in certain societies, official religious agencies have been active in supporting those who wish to change the system of regulation (e.g. the Roman Catholic church in Latin America). Official religious agencies have been grouped with the structure of legal agencies because of their *function* as regulating agencies of symbolic control.

(2) Repairers: These are the agencies and agents whose *function* is to prevent, or repair, or isolate, what count as breakdowns in the body, mind, social relationships. As we have mentioned in the text, at different times and in different societies some repairers may well act as regulators, at other times sub-groups may well be in conflict with regulators.

(3) Diffusers: These are the agencies and agents whose *function* is to disseminate certain principles, practices, activities, symbolic forms, or to appropriate principles and practices, symbolic forms for the purpose of inducing consumption of symbolic forms, goods, services or activities.

(4) Shapers: These are the agencies and agents whose *function* is the developing of what count as changing, crucial symbolic codes in the arts or sciences. The problem here is that at certain levels there is an overlap with diffusers. We would argue that film producers, gallery-owners, theatre-owners, publishers, are an *important sub-set* of diffusers on the ground that they operate specialized media. However, what do we do with performers (actors, musicians, dancers) and specialized critics? I think we would argue that performers should be classified as diffusers and specialized critics should be classified as shapers.

(5) Executors: These are the agencies and agents whose *function*

is administrative. The crucial agency here is the civil service and local government, although it is important to point out that they exist as agents in the above agencies.

We have left out the whole area of sport, which is undoubtedly a crucial agency in its own right, for the following reason. The classification has been set up in order to examine changes in the *form* of symbolic control *crucial* to the problem of the relationship between class and cultural reproduction. From this point of view, and from this point of view only, sport is not a crucial agency.

Class assumptions of invisible pedagogies

Women as agents of cultural reproduction in the middle class

The shift from individualized to personalized organic solidarity in the middle class changes the structure of family relationships, and in particular the role of the woman in socializing the child. Historically, under individualized organic solidarity, the mother is not important as a transmitter of either physical or symbolic property. She is almost totally abstracted from the means of reproduction of either physical or symbolic property. The caring for, and preparation of, the children is delegated to others—nanny, governess, tutor. She is essentially a domestic administrator and it follows she can be only a model for her daughter. The woman was capable of cultural reproduction, for often she possessed a more sensitive awareness and understanding than her husband of the general literature of the period. This concept of the abstracted maternal function perhaps reappears in the concept of the pre-school assistant as a baby-minder and the governess as the teacher of elementary competencies. Thus individualized organic solidarity might generate two models for the early formal education by women of the child (see Figure 6.1).

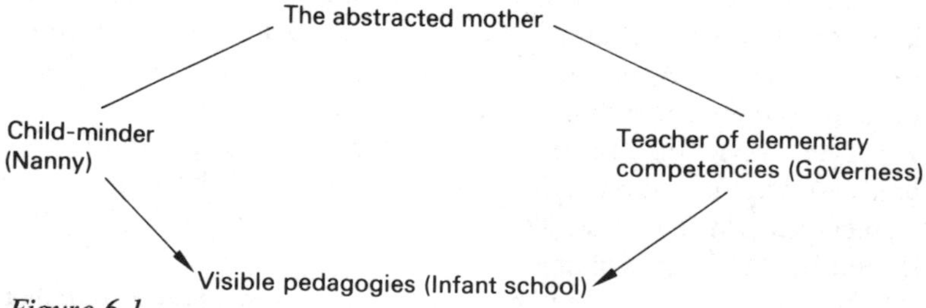

Figure 6.1

Initially, with individualized organic solidarity, property has a physical basis which exists in forms of capital where ownership and control are combined. Access to, and reproduction of, class position here is related to access to and ownership of capital. Although there is clearly a link between class and forms of education, education in itself plays a relatively minor rôle in creating access to and reproduction of class position. However, with developed forms of capitalism, not only do management functions become divorced from ownership, but there is an expansion of social control positions which have their basis in specialized forms of communication, which are more and more available from the expanding system of education. With this extension and differentiation of control functions, the basis of property becomes partly psychologized, and its basis is located in ownership of specialized forms of communication. These in turn have their origin in specialized *forms of interaction* initiated, developed and focused very early in the child's life. The rôle of the mother in the rearing of her children undergoes a qualitative change. The mother is transformed into a crucial preparing agent of cultural reproduction who provides access to symbolic forms and shapes the dispositions of her children so that they are better able to exploit the possibilities of public education. We can see an integration of maternal functions, as the basis of class position becomes psychologized. *Delegated* maternal caring and preparation *becomes* maternal caring and preparation. What is of interest here is the *form* of the caring and the form of the preparation. According to the thesis, the form may be constituted by either a visible or an invisible pedagogy. The old middle class perpetuated itself through a visible pedagogy, whereas the new middle class, the bearers of the structures of personalized organic solidarity, developed invisible pedagogies.

Women played an active rôle in initiating (Montessori), shaping and disseminating invisible pedagogies. Consider:

(1) The application of Freudian theory by Anna Freud to child analysis. The modification of Freudian theory by Melanie Klein and her followers, Hannah Segal, Joan Rivière and Marion Milner, and the development of the interpretation of play as phantasy content in child analysis.

(2) The extension of psycho-analytic theory into education and the training of teachers (post 1945) through Susan Isaacs at the University of London Institute of Education, and its

further development by Dolly Garner. Parallel work with a Piagetian basis was carried out by Molly Brierley, Principal of the Froebel College of Education.

(3)   A number of women in a much earlier period were active in the education and training of teachers, e.g. Philippa Fawcett, Rachel McMillan.

It is possible that women were crucial agents in the last quarter (and perhaps even before) of the nineteenth century. For inasmuch as the concept of the child was changed, so was the hierarchy to which women were subordinate. At the same time, the pedagogy provided the basis of a professional identity. From this point of view, women transformed maternal caring and preparing into a *scientific* activity.

With the shift from individualized to personalized organic solidarity within fractions of the middle class, the woman is transformed into a crucial preparing agent of cultural reproduction. There is, however, a contradiction in her structural relationships. Unlike the mother in a context of individualized solidarity (visible pedagogy), she is unable to get away from her child. The weak classification and framing of her child-rearing firmly anchor her to her child (see (3) below). For such a mother, interaction and surveillance are totally demanding, whilst at the same time her own socialization into both a personal and an occupational identity points her away from the family. These tensions may be partly resolved by placing the child early in a pre-school, which faithfully reproduces the ambience of her own child-rearing. The infant school, however, may amplify the messages and wish to extend them into the junior school. Here we can see a second contradiction, for such an amplification brings the middle-class mother and the school into conflict. The public examination system is based upon a visible pedagogy realized through strong classification and relatively strong framing. It is this pedagogy which generates symbolic property: the means whereby class position is reproduced. If access to a visible pedagogy is delayed too long, then examination success may be in danger.

The argument here is that an invisible pedagogy is based upon a concept of the woman as a *particular* preparing agent of cultural reproduction—an agent having its origins in a particular fraction of the middle class.

We will now turn to more specific class assumptions of invisible pedagogy.

(1) Concept of time

In the first place, invisible pedagogies are based upon a middle-class concept of time because they presuppose a long educational life. If all children left school at fourteen, there would be no visible pedagogies. Visible pedagogies are regulated by *explicit* sequencing rules: that is, the progression of the transmission is ordered in time by explicit rules. In a school, the syllabus regulates the progression of a subject and the curriculum regulates the relationships between subjects *and* those selected as appropriate for given ages. The sequencing rules, when they are explicit, define the future expected states of the child's consciousness and behaviours. However, in the case of invisible pedagogies, the sequencing rules are not explicit, but *implicit*. The progression of the transmission is based upon theories of the child's inner development (cognitive, moral, emotional, etc.). The sequencing rules are derived from particular theories of child development. In the case of invisible pedagogies, it is totally impossible for the child to know or be aware of the principles of the progression. He/she cannot know the principles of his/her own development as these are expressed in the regulating theories. Only the transmitter knows the principles, the sequencing rules. The sequencing rules are *implicit* in the transmission, rather than explicit. We can generalize and say that the sequencing rules of a transmission define its time dimension. However, they do more than this. Inasmuch as they regulate future expected states of consciousness and behaviours, they define what the child is expected *to be* at different points of time. In which case they define the concept of child. It follows that because visible and invisible pedagogies are regulated by different, indeed from one point of view, opposing, sequencing rules, then they entail different concepts of time and they are also based upon different concepts of child. Visible and invisible pedagogies are based upon different concepts of childhood and its progressive transformation, which have their origin in different factions of the middle class.

(2) Concept of space

In the first place, invisible pedagogies require for their transmission a different material structure from the material structure upon which a visible pedagogy is based. A visible pedagogy requires only a very small fixed space; essentially a table, a book and a chair. Its material structure is remarkably cheap. However in order for the material base to be exploited, it still requires a form of acquisition regulated by an elaborated code. However, in the case of an invisible pedagogy, its material basis is a very much larger surface. Consider the large sheets of paper, the space demands of its technology, bricks and kits for doing the creativity thing, an assembly of media whereby the child's consciousness may be uniquely revealed. The technology requires a relatively large space for the child. In this sense the production of an invisible pedagogy in the home cannot be effected in an overcrowded, materially inadequate home. However, invisible pedagogies are based upon a concept of space which is more fundamental. Visible pedagogies are realized through strongly classified space; that is, there are very strong boundaries between one space and another *and* the control of the spaces is equally strongly classified. Rooms in the house have specialized functions: seating arrangements, for example at meals, are specific to classes of person— mother, father, children; there are explicit, strongly marked boundaries regulating the movement in space of persons at different times. Further, the contents of different spaces are not interchangeable: e.g. dining-spaces are dining-spaces, children's areas and contents are children's areas and contents, the kitchen is the kitchen, etc. The explicit hierarchy of a visible pedagogy creates spaces and relationships between spaces which carry a specific set of symbolic messages which all illustrate the principle that things must be kept apart.

However, in the case of invisible pedagogies, space has a different symbolic significance, for here spaces and their contents are relatively weakly classified. The controls over flow of persons and objects between spaces are much weaker. This means that the *potential space available to the child is very much greater.* The privacy embodied in space regulated by visible pedagogies is considerably reduced. Architects tend to call the spatial organization of invisible pedagogies 'open-plan living'. *The child learns to understand the possibilities of such weakly classified spaces and the rules upon which such learning is based.* We can point out, in passing, the irony of, on the one hand, an invisible pedagogy, but, on the other, the fact of the continuous *visibility* of persons and their behaviour: the possibility of continuous surveillance. Invisible pedagogies are based upon concepts of space derived from a fraction of the middle class.

(3)   Concept of social control

Where the pedagogy is visible, the hierarchy is explicit, space and time are regulated by explicit principles, there are strong boundaries between spaces, times, acts, communications. The power realized by the hierarchy maintains the strong boundaries, the apartness of things. As the child learns these rules, he acquires the classification. An infringement of the classification is immediately visible, for any infringement signals *something is out of place*—communication, act, person or object. The task is to get the child to accept (not necessarily to understand) the ordering principles. This can be accomplished (not always necessarily) by linking infringements with an explicit calculus of punishment and relatively simple announcements of proscribing and prescribing rules. Motivation is increased by a gradual widening of privileges through age. The hierarchy is manifest in the classifications, in the strong boundaries, within the insulations. *The language of social control is relatively restricted, and the relationships of control, explicitly hierarchical.*

However, where the pedagogy is invisible, the hierarchy is *implicit*, space and time are weakly classified. This social structure does not create in its symbolic arrangements strong boundaries which carry critical messages of control. Because the hierarchy is implicit (*which does not mean it is not there, only that the form of its realization is different*), there is a relative absence of *strongly marked* regulation of the child's acts, communication, objects, spaces, times and progression. In what lies the control? We will suggest that control inheres in *elaborated interpersonal communication* in a context where maximum surveillance is possible. *In other words, control is vested in the process of interpersonal communication.* A particular function of language is of special significance, and its realization is of an elaborated form in contrast to the more restricted form of communication where the pedagogy is visible. The form of transmission of an invisible pedagogy encourages more of the child to be made public and so more of the child is available for direct and indirect surveillance and control. Thus invisible pedagogies realize specific modalities of social control which have their origins in a particular fraction of the middle class.

We have attempted to make explicit four class assumptions underlying the transmission of an invisible pedagogy.

(1)   It presupposes a particular concept of the mother as a crucial

preparing agent of cultural reproduction.
(2) It presupposes a particular concept of time.
(3) It presupposes a particular concept of space.
(4) It presupposes a particular form of social control—which inheres in interpersonal communication (elaborated code— person-focused).

The educational consequences of an invisible pedagogy will be, according to this thesis, crucially different depending upon the social class position of the child.

We started this section by abstracting the following points from our initial discussion of the invisible pedagogy.
(1) The invisible pedagogy is an interrupter system, both in relation to the home and in relation to other levels of the educational hierarchy.
(2) It transforms the privatized social structure and cultural contents of visible pedagogies into a personalized social structure and personalized cultural contents.
(3) It believes that implicit nurture reveals unique nature.

We have argued that this pedagogy is one of the realizations of the conflict between the old and the new middle class, which in turn has its social basis in the two different forms of organic solidarity, individualized and personalized; that these two forms of solidarity arise out of differences in the relation to, and the expansion of, the division of labour within the middle class; that the movement from individualized to personalized interrupts the *form* of the reproduction of class relationships; that such an interruption gives rise to different forms of *primary* socialization within the middle class; that the form of primary socialization within the middle class is the model for primary socialization into the school; that there are contradictions within personalized organic solidarity which create deeply felt ambiguities, as a consequence, the outcomes of the form of the socialization are less certain. The contemporary new middle class is unique, for in the socialization of its young is a sharp and penetrating contradiction between a subjective personal identity and an objective privatized identity; between the release of the person and the hierarchy of class. The above can be represented as in Figure 6.2.

Whereas it is possible for school and university to change the basis of its solidarity from individualistic to personalized: i.e. to relax its classification and frames, it is more difficult for those agencies to change their privatizing function: i.e. the creation of knowledge as

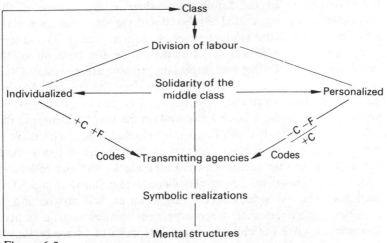

Figure 6.2

private property. It by no means follows that a shift to personalized organic solidarity will change the privatizing function. Indeed, even the shift in this form of solidarity is more likely to occur in that part of the educational system which creates no private property, as in either the education of the lower working class, or the education of the very young. We are then left with the conclusion that the major effects of this change in solidarity will be in the areas of condensed communication (sex, art, style) and in the form of social control (from explicit to implicit).

Transition to school

(a)   Class culture, power and conflict

The shift from visible to invisible pedagogies at the pre- and primary levels of education changes the relationships between the family and the school. We have already noted the ambiguous attitude of the middle class to such a shift. In the case of the working class, the change is more radical. The weak classification and the weak framing of the invisible pedagogy potentially makes possible the inclusion of the culture of the family and the community. Thus the experience of the child and his everyday world could be psychologically active in the classroom, and if this were to be the case, then the school would legitimize rather than reject the class-culture of the family. Inasmuch as the pacing of the knowledge to be transmitted is relaxed and the emphasis upon early attainment of specific competencies is reduced, the progression is less marked by middle-class assumptions. In the case of visible pedagogies early reading and, especially, writing are essential. Once the child can read and write, such acts free the teacher, but, of more importance, once the child can read he can be given a book, and once he is given a book he is well on the way to managing the role of the solitary privatized educational relationship. The book is the preparation for receiving the past realized in the textbook. And the textbook in turn tacitly transmits the ideology of the collection code: for it epitomizes strong classification and strong frames. The textbook orders knowledge according to an explicit progression, it provides explicit criteria, it removes uncertainties and announces hierarchy. It gives the child an immediate index of where he stands in relation to others in the progression. It is therefore a silent medium for creating competitive relationships. Thus socialization into the textbook is a critical step towards socialization into the collection code. The stronger the collection code, that is the stronger classification and frames, the greater the emphasis on early reading and writing. The middle-class child is prepared for this emphasis, but this is not so in the case of the working-class child. The weakening of classification and frames reduces the significance of the textbook and transforms the impersonal past into a personalized present. It would appear that the invisible pedagogy carries a beneficial potential for working-class children. However, because the form we are discussing has its origins in a fraction of the middle class, this potential may not be actualized.

This point we will now develop. From the point of view of working-class parents, the visible pedagogy of the collection code at the primary level is immediately understandable. The basic competencies which it is transmitting of reading, writing, and counting, in an ordered explicit sequence, make sense. The failures of the children are the children's failures not the school's for the school is apparently carrying out impersonally its function. The school's form of social control does not interfere with the social control of the family. The infant school teacher will not necessarily have high status, as the competencies she is transmitting are, in principle, possible also for the mother. In this sense, there is symbolic continuity (or rather extension) between the working-class home and the school. However, in the case of the invisible pedagogy, there is possibly a sharp discontinuity. The competencies and their progression disappear, the form of social control may well be at variance with the home. The theory of the invisible pedagogy may not be known by the mother or be imperfectly understood. The lack of stress on competencies may render the child a less effective (useful) member of the family, e.g. running errands, etc. However, there is a more fundamental source of tension. The invisible pedagogy contains a different theory of transmission and a new technology, which views the mother's own informal teaching, where it occurs, or the mother's pedagogical values, irrelevant if not downright harmful. There are new reading schemes, new mathematics replace arithmetic, an expressive aesthetic style replaces one which aims at facsimile. If the mother is to be helpful, she must be re-socialized or kept out of the way. If it is the former or the latter, then the power relationships have changed between home and school: for the teacher has the power and the mother is as much a pupil as the pupil. This in turn may disturb the authority relationships within the home: this disturbance is further facilitated by the use of implicit forms of social control of the school. Even if the pedagogy draws its contents from the class culture, basic forms of discontinuity still exist. If the mother wishes to understand the theory of the invisible pedagogy, then she may well find herself at the mercy of complex theories of child development. Indeed, whichever way the working-class mother turns, the teacher has the power: although the mother may well be deeply suspicious of the whole ambience.[8]

Where, as in the case of the visible pedagogy there are, for the working class, relative to the middle class, implicit forms of discontinuity and explicit forms of inequality in the shape of the holding power of the school over its teachers, the size of class and possibly streaming: in the case of the invisible pedagogy, there is also an *explicit* symbolic discontinuity which may well go with inequalities in provision and quality of teaching staff. The teacher also has difficulties, because the invisible pedagogy presupposes a particular form of maternal primary socialization *and* a small class of pupils *and* a particular architecture. Where these are absent, the teacher may well find great difficulty. Ideally, the invisible pedagogy frees the teacher so that time is available for ameliorating the difficulties of any one child, but if the class is large, the socialization, from the point of view of the school, inadequate, the architecture inappropriate, then such individual assistance becomes infrequent and problematic. Here again we can see that such a pedagogy, if it is to be successfully implemented in its own terms, necessarily requires minimally the same physical conditions of the middle-class school. It is an *expensive* pedagogy because it is derived from an expensive class: the middle class.

From the point of view of the middle class, there is at least an intellectual understanding of the invisible pedagogy, if not always an acceptance of its values and practice. Further, if the middle-class child is not obtaining the basic competencies at the rate the mother expects, an educational support system can be organized through private coaching or through the mother's own efforts. The power relationships between the middle-class mother and the teacher are less tipped in favour of the teacher. Finally, the middle-class mother always has the choice of the private school or of moving near a state school of her choice. However, because of the middle-class mother's concept of the function of secondary education, she is likely to be anxious about the acquisition of basic competencies, and this will bring her into conflict with the school at some point.

Finally, inasmuch as age and sex statuses within the family are strongly classified and ritualized, it is likely that the acquisition, progression and evaluation of competencies obtained within the school will become part of the markers of age and sex status within the family. For example, there is a radical change in the status and concept of the child when he is transformed into a pupil. Now, to the extent that the infant/primary school fails to utilize age and sex as allocating categories *either* for the acquisition and progression of competencies *or* for the allocation of pupils to groups and spaces, the school is weakening the function of these categories in the family and community. Visible pedagogies not only reinforce age and sex classification, they also provide markers for progression within them. Invisible pedagogies are likely to weaken such classifications and inasmuch as they do this they transform the concept of the child and the concepts of age and sex status.

(b) Class, pedagogy and evaluation

Interesting questions arise over the system of evaluating the pupils.

Where the pedagogy is visible, an 'objective' grid exists for the evaluation of the pupils in the form of (*a*) clear criteria and (*b*) a delicate measurement procedure. The child receives a grade or its equivalent for any valued performance. Further, where the pedagogy is visible, it is likely to be standardized and so schools are directly comparable as to their successes and failures. The profile of the pupil may be obtained by looking across his grades. The pupil knows where he is, the teacher knows where he is, and so do the parents. The parents have a yardstick for comparing schools. When children change schools they can be slotted into place according to their academic profile. Further, it is difficult for the parent to argue about the profile for it is 'objective'. Clearly, there are subjective elements in the grading of the children, but these are masked by the apparent objectivity of the grid. In the case of invisible pedagogies, no such grid exists. The evaluation procedures are multiple, diffuse and not easily subject to apparently precise measurement. This makes comparison between pupils complex, and also comparisons between schools.[9] First, the invisible pedagogy does not give rise to progression of a *group*, but is based upon progression of a person. Second, there is likely to be considerable variation between infant/pre-school groups *within* the general form of the pedagogy. There is less difficulty in slotting a child into a new school because there is no explicit slot for him. Thus the mother is less able to diagnose the child's progress and as a consequence she cannot *provide specific educational support*.[10] She would be forced into providing a general educational milieu in the home and this she might only be able to do if she had fully internalized the invisible pedagogy's theoretical basis. As we have previously argued, this is less likely to be the case where the parents are working-class. Thus these parents are cut off from the evaluation of their child's progress. More, they are forced to accept what the teacher counts as progress.

Because an apparently objective grid exists for the evaluation of the visible pedagogies, this grid acts selectively on those dispositions of the child which become candidates for labelling by the teacher. Clearly motivation and interest are probably relevant to any pedagogy, but their significance will vary with the pedagogy, and certainly their consequences. In the case of visible pedagogies, the behaviour of the child is focused on the teacher so that, in this case, attentiveness to, co-operation with, the teacher becomes relevant: persistence and carefulness are also valued by the teacher. Further, it is possible for there to be a conflict between the child's academic profile *and* the teacher's evaluation of his attitudes and motivation. These objective and subjective criteria may have different consequences for different class groups of pupils. Either criteria, irrespective of their validity, are likely to be *understood* by working-class parents. In the case of invisible pedagogy, as more of the child is made available, and, because of the theory which guides interpretation, diagnosis and evaluation, a different class of acts and dispositions of the child become relevant. In the case of visible pedagogies we have argued that the attention of the child is focused on the teacher; however, in the case of invisible pedagogies the attention of the teacher is focused on the *whole* child: in its total doing and 'not doing'. This can lead to discrepancies between the teacher's and the parents' view of the child unless the parents share the teacher's theory. Indeed, it is possible that the dispositions and acts which are subject to evaluation by the teacher may be considered by some parents as irrelevant or intrusive or inaccurate or all three. Where this occurs the child's behaviour is being shaped by conflicting criteria. From the point of view of the teacher, the child becomes an *innovating* message to the home. The invisible pedagogy is not only an interrupter system in the context of educational practice, but it also transforms the child, under certain conditions, into an innovating message to the family.

This pedagogy is likely to lead to a change in the school's procedures of evaluation, both objective and subjective. Where the pedagogy is visible, there is a profile which consists of the grading of specific competencies and a profile which consists of the grading of the child's motivation and work attitudes. It is likely that the latter will consist of rather short, somewhat stereotyped unexplicated judgments. In the case of invisible pedagogies, these highly condensed, unexplicated but *public* judgments are likely to be replaced by something resembling a dossier which will range across a wide variety of the child's internal processes and states *and* his external acts. Further, the connection between inner and outer is likely to be made *explicit*. In other words, there is likely to be an explicit elaborated account of the relationships between the child's internal states and his acts. It is now possible that the school will have a problem of secrecy. How much is to go into the dossier, where is it to be kept, how much of and in what way are its contents to be made available to parents or to others in the school and outside of it? Thus invisible pedagogies may also generate *covert* and *overt* forms and contents of evaluation. Such a system of evaluation increases the power of the teacher to the extent that its underlying theory is not shared by parents *and* even when it is shared.

Finally, the major analysis in this section has been of idealized pedagogies. If, however, the argument is correct, that there may be a disjunction in the forms of socialization between primary and secondary stages, *or* between secondary and tertiary stages, then behind weak classification and weak frames may well be strong classification and strong frames. Thus we can have a situation where strong Cs and Fs follow weak Cs and Fs, *or* where weak Cs and Fs follow strong Cs and Fs, as, possibly, in the case of the training of infant school teachers in England. It is important not only to understand continuity in the strength of classification and frames, but also *disjunction* and *when* the disjunction occurs. It is more than likely that if we examine empirically invisible pedagogies we shall find to different degrees a stress on the transmission of *specific* isolated competencies. Thus the 'hidden curriculum' of invisible pedagogies may well be, embryonically, strong classification, albeit with relatively weak frames. It becomes a matter of some importance to find out which children or groups of children are particularly responsive to this 'hidden curriculum'. For some children may come to see or ·be led to see that there are two transmissions, one overt, the other covert, which stand in a figure–ground relation to each other. We need to know for which teachers, and for which children, what is the figure and what is the ground. Specifically, will middle-class children respond to the latent visible pedagogy, or are they more likely to be selected as receivers? Will lower working-class children respond more to the invisible pedagogy or receive a weaker form of the transmission of visible pedagogy? The 'hidden curriculum' of invisible pedagogies may well be a visible pedagogy. However, the outcomes of the imbedding of one pedagogy in the other are likely to be different than they are in the case of the transmission of any *one* pedagogy. From a more theoretical standpoint, the crucial component of visible pedagogy is the strength of its *classification*, for in the last analysis it is this which creates what counts as valued property, and also, in so doing, regulates mental structures. Frame strength regulates the modality of the socialization into the classification. In the microcosm of the nursery or infant class, we can see embryonically the new forms of transmission of class relationships.

Let us take a concrete example to illustrate the above speculation. An infant school teacher in England may experience the following conjunctions or disjunctions in her socialization:

    (1)   Between socialization in the family and between primary and secondary school.

    (2)   Between secondary school and teacher training. The higher the qualifications required by the college of education, the more likely that the socialization in the later years of the secondary school will be through strong classification and frames. On the other hand, the socialization into the college of education may well be into classification and frames of varying strengths.

Transition between stages of education

We have examined aspects of the transition to school; there is also the question of transition between stages of education, from preschool to primary, from primary to secondary. These transitions between stages are marked by three inter-related features:

    (1)   An increase in the strength of classification and frames (initiation into the collective code).

    (2)   An increase in the range of different teachers; that is, the pupil is made aware of the insulations within the division of labour. He also learns that the principle of authority transcends the individuals who hold it, for, as teachers/subjects change, his role remains the same.

    (3)   The weak classification and frames of the invisible pedagogy emphasize the importance of *ways* of knowing, of constructing problems, whereas the strong classification and frames of visible pedagogies emphasize states of knowledge and received problems.

Thus there is a crucial change in what counts as having knowledge, in what counts as a legitimate realization of that knowledge *and* in the social context.

Thus the shift from invisible to visible pedagogies in one phrase is a change in code; a change in the principles of relation and evaluation whether these are principles of knowledge, of social relationships, of practices, of property, of identity.

It is likely that this change of code will be more effectively made (despite the difficulties) by the new middle-class children, as their own socialization within the family contains *both* codes—the code which creates the manifestation of the person and the code which creates private property. Further, as we have argued elsewhere, it is more likely that the working-class children will experience continuity in code between stages of education. The class bias of the collection code (which creates a visible pedagogy) may make such a transmission difficult for them to receive and exploit. As a consequence, the continuation of the invisible pedagogy in the form of an integrated code is likely for working-class children, and its later institutionalization for the same children at the secondary level.

We can now begin to see that the conditions for continuity of educational code for *all* children, irrespective of class, is the type of code transmitted by the university. Simply expanding the university, increasing differentiation within the tertiary level, equalizing opportunity of access and outcome, will not fundamentally change the situation at levels below. We will only have expanded the size of the cohort at the tertiary level. From another point of view, although we may have changed the organizational structure we have *not* changed the code controlling transmission; the process of reproduction will not be fundamentally affected. To change the code controlling transmission involves changing the culture and its basis in privatized class relationships. Thus if we accept, for the sake of argument, the greater educational value of invisible pedagogies, of weak classification and frames, the condition for their effective and total institutionalization at the secondary level is a fundamental change of code at the tertiary level. If this does not occur then codes and class will remain firmly linked in schools.

Finally, we can raise a basic question. The movement to invisible pedagogies realized through integrated codes may be seen as a superficial solution to a more obdurate problem. Integrated codes are integrated at the level of ideas, they do *not* involve integration at the level of institutions, i.e. between school and work. Yet the crucial integration is precisely between the principles of education and the principles of work. There can be no such integration in Western societies (to mention only one group) because the work epitomizes class relationships. Work can only be brought into the school in terms of the function of the school as a selective mechanism or in terms of social/psychological adustment to work. Indeed, the abstracting of education from work, the hallmark of the liberal tradition, or the linkage of education to leisure, masks the brutal fact that work and education cannot be integrated at the level of social principles in class societies. They can either be separated or they can *fit* with each other. Durkheim wrote that changes in pedagogy were indicators of a moral crisis; they can also disguise it and change its form. However, inasmuch as the move to weak classification and frames has the *potential* of reducing insulations in mental structures and social structures, has the potential of making explicit the implicit and so creating *greater* ambiguity but less disguise, such a code has the potential of making visible fundamental social contradictions.

Acknowledgments

This paper was written on the suggestion of Henri Nathan for a meeting on the effects of scholarization, itself a part of the International Learning Sciences Programme, CERI, OECD. I am grateful to Henri Nathan for his insistence on the need to understand the artefacts of learning.

    The basis of this paper was written whilst I was a visitor to the École Pratique des Hautes Études (Centre de Sociologie Européenne under the direction of Pierre Bourdieu). I am very grateful to Peter Corbishley, graduate student in the Department of the Sociology of Education for his help in the explication of the concept of an 'interrupter system'. The definition used in this paper owes much to his clarification. Finally I would like to thank Gerald Elliot, Professor of Physics, Open University) who, whilst in no way ultimately responsible, assisted in the formal expression of an 'object code'.

Notes

1   This raises a number of questions. We cannot consider skills abstracted from the context of their transmission, from their

relationships to each other and their function in creating, maintaining, modifying or changing a culture. Skills and their relationship to each other are culturally specific competencies. The manner of their transmission and acquisition socializes the child into their contextual usages. Thus, the unit of analysis cannot simply be an abstracted specific competence like reading, writing, counting, but the *structure* of social relationships which produces these specialized competencies. The formulation 'where there is a reduced emphasis upon transmission and acquisition of specific skills' could be misleading, as it suggests that in the context under discussion there are few specialized repertoires of the culture. It may be better to interpret the formulation as indicating an emphasis upon the inter-relationships between skills which are relatively weakly classified and weakly framed. In this way any skill or sets of skills are referred to the *general features of the socialization.*

2 This can be seen very clearly if we look at a school class; visible pedagogies create *homogeneous* learning contexts; invisible pedagogies create *differentiated* learning contexts.

3 A shift from the production of differentiated types of individuals to a type of person.

4 It is a matter of some interest to consider changes in emphasis of research methodologies over recent decades. There has been a shift from the standardized closed questionnaire or experimental context to more unstructured contexts and relationships. It is argued that the former methodology renders irrelevant the subjective meanings of those who are the object of study. In so doing, the researched offer their experience through the media of the researchers' imposed strong classification and strong frames. Further, it is argued that such a method of studying people is derived from a method for the study of objects, and therefore it is an outrage to the subjectivity of man for him to be transformed into an object. These arguments go on to link positivist methods with the political control of man through the use of the technology of social science. The new methodology employs apparently weak classification and weak frames, but it uses techniques (participant observation, tape-recordings, video tapes, etc.) which enable more of the researched to be visible, and its techniques allow a range of others to witness the spontaneous behaviour of the observed. Even if these public records of natural behaviour are treated as a means of dialogue between the recorded and the recorder, this dialogue is, itself, subject to the disjunction between intellectual perspectives which will shape the communication. The self-editing of the researcher's communication is different from that of the researched, and this is the *invisible* control. On the other hand, paradoxically, in the case of a closed questionnaire the privacy of the subject is safeguarded, for all that can be made public is a pencil mark which is transformed into an impersonal score.

Further, the methods of this transformation must be made public so that its assumptions may be criticized. In the case of the new methodology, the principles used to restrict the vast amount of information and the number of channels are often implicit. One might say that we could distinguish research methodologies in terms of whether they created invisible or visible pedagogies. Thus the former give rise to a total surveillance of the person who, relative to the latter, makes public more of his inside (e.g. his subjectivity), which is evaluated through the use of diffuse, implicit criteria. We are suggesting that the structural origins of changes in the classification and framing of forms of socialization may perhaps also influence the selection of research methodologies. The morality of the research relationship transcends the dilemmas of a particular researcher. Research methodologies in social science are themselves elements of culture.

5   It is interesting to see, for example, where the invisible pedagogy first entered the secondary-school curriculum. In England we would suggest that it first penetrated the *non-verbal* area of *unselective* secondary schools; the area which is considered to be the least relevant (in the sense of not producing symbolic property) and the most strongly classified: the area of the art room. Indeed, it might be said that, until very recently, the greatest symbolic continuity of pedagogies between primary and secondary stages lay in the non-verbal areas of the curriculum. The art room is often viewed by the rest of the staff as an area of relaxation or even therapy, rather than a space of crucial production. Because of its strong classification and irrelevance (except at school 'show-off' periods) this space is potentially open to change. Art teachers are trained in institutions (at least in recent times) which are very sensitive to innovation, and therefore new styles are likely to be rapidly institutionalized in schools, given the strong classification of art in the secondary-school curriculum, and also the belief that the less able child can at least do something with his hands even if he finds difficulty with a pen. We might also anticipate that with the interest in such musical forms as pop on the one hand and Cage and Stockhausen on the other, music departments might move towards the invisible pedagogy. To complete the direction in the non-verbal area, it is possible that the transformation of physical training into physical education might also extend to movement. If this development took place, then the non-verbal areas would be realized through the invisible pedagogy. We might then expect a drive to integrate the three areas of sight, sound and movement; *three* modalities would then be linked through a common code.

6   We can clarify the issues raised in this paper in the following way. Any socializing context must consist of a transmitter and an acquirer. These two form a matrix in the sense that the communication is regulated by a structural principle. We have suggested that the underlying principle of a socializing matrix is realized in

classification and frames. The relationship between the two and the strengths show us the structure of the control and the form of communication. We can, of course, analyse this matrix in a number of ways: (1) we can focus upon the transmitter; (2) we can focus upon the acquirer; (3) we can focus upon the principles underlying the matrix; (4) we can focus upon a given matrix and ignore its relationship to other matrices; (5) we can consider the relationships between critical matrices, e.g. family, peer group, school, work.

We can go on to ask questions about the function of a matrix and questions about the change in the form of its realization, i.e. changes in the strength of its classification and frames. We believe that the unit of analysis must always be the matrix and the matrix will always include the theories and methods of its analysis (see note 4 on research methodology). Now any one matrix can be regarded as a reproducer, an interrupter, or a change matrix. A reproduction matrix will attempt to create strong classification and strong frames. An interrupter matrix changes the *form* of transmission, but not the critical relationship *between* matrices. A change matrix leads to a fundamental change in the structural relationship *between* matrices. This will require a major change in the institutional structure. For example, we have argued that within the middle class there is a conflict which has generated two distinct socializing matrices, one a reproducer, the other an interrupter. And these matrices are at work within education for similar groups of children up to possibly the primary stage, and different groups of pupils at the secondary stage. However, inasmuch as the structural relationship between school and work is unchanged (i.e. there has been no change in the basic principles of their relationship), then we cannot by this argument see current differences in educational pedagogy as representing a change matrix. In other words, the form of the reproduction of class relationships in education has been *interrupted* but not changed. We might speculate that ideological conflict within the middle class takes the form of a conflict between the symbolic outcomes of reproduction and interruption matrices. If one takes the argument one stage further, we have to consider the reproduction of the *change* in the form of class relationships. In this case, the reproduction of an interrupter matrix is through weak classification and weak frames. However, it is possible that such a form of reproduction may at some point evoke its own interrupter, i.e. an increase in either classification or frame strength, or both.

7   Symbolic control is the means of cultural reproduction, in the terms of Bourdieu. What is reproduced is a function of the degree of integration within *or* conflict between the transmitting agents *and* the response of those who are subject to the transmission. What must be explored is the complex relationship between changes in the

150 CHANGES IN THE CODING OF EDUCATIONAL TRANSMISSIONS

forms of production and changes in the forms of symbolic control.
8 This does *not* mean *all* teachers wish to have the power or use it.
9 Paradoxically, this situation carries a potential for increasing competitiveness.
10 She can offer, of course, elements of a visible pedagogy.

References

BERNSTEIN, B. (1967), 'Open schools, open society?' *New Society*, 14 September. Reprinted as Chapter 3 of the present volume.
BERNSTEIN, B. (1971), *Class, Codes and Control*, Vol. 1, Part III, Routledge & Kegan Paul.
BERNSTEIN, B., ELVIN, L. and PETERS, R. (1966), 'Ritual in education', *Philosophical Transactions of the Royal Society of London*, Series B, 251, No. 772.
BLYTH, W. A. L. (1965), *English Primary Education*, Vols. 1 and 2, Routledge & Kegan Paul.
BOLTANSKY, L. (1969), *Prime Éducation et morale de classe*, Paris and The Hague: Mouton.
BOURDIEU, P. and PASSERON, J. C. (1970), *La Reproduction: éléments pour une théorie du système d'enseignement*, Paris: Les Éditions de Minuit.
BRANDIS, W. and BERNSTEIN, B. (1973), *Selection and Control: A Study of Teachers' Ratings of Infant School Children*, Appendix, Routledge & Kegan Paul.
CHAMBOREDON, J-C. and PREVOT, J. Y. (1973), 'Le Métier d'enfant', Définition sociale de la prime enfance et fonctions différentielles de l'école maternelle. Centre de Sociologie Européenne (basic paper).
CREMIN, L. (1961), *The Transformation of the School*, New York: Knopf.
DOUGLAS, M. (1973), *Natural Symbols*, revised edition, Allen Lane.
DURKHEIM, E. (1933), *The Division of Labour in Society* (translated by G. Simpson), New York: Macmillan.
DURKHEIM, E. (1938), *L'Évolution pédagogique en France*, Paris: Alcan.
DURKHEIM, E. (1956), *Education and Sociology* (translated by D. F. Pocock), Cohen & West, (chapters 2 and 3).
GARDNER, B. (1973), *The Public Schools*, Hamish Hamilton.
GOLDTHORPE, J. and LOCKWOOD, D. (1962), 'Affluence and the Class Structure', *Sociological Review*, vol. XI.
GREEN, A.G. (1972), 'Theory and practice in infant education, a sociological approach and case study', M.Sc. dissertation, University of London Institute of Education Library (for discussion of 'busyness').
HALLIDAY, M. A. K. (1973), *Exploration in the Function of Language*, Edward Arnold.
HOUDLE, L. (1968), *An Enquiry into the Social Factors affecting the*

Orientation of English Infant Education since the early Nineteenth Century, M.A. dissertation, University of London Institute of Education Library, (excellent bibliography).

PLOWDEN REPORT (1967), *Children and their Primary Schools*, a report of the Central Advisory Council for Education (England), HMSO, Vol. 1.

SHULMAN, L. S. and KREISLAR, E. R. (eds.) (1966), *Learning by Discovery; a critical appraisal*, Chicago: Rand McNally.

SIMON, B. (ed.) (1972), *The Radical Tradition in Education in Britain*, Lawrence & Wishart.

STEWART, W. A. C. and MCCANN, W. P. (1967), *The Educational Innovators*, Macmillan.

ZOLDANY, M. (1935), *Die Entstehungstheorie des Geistes*, Budapest: Donau.

Appendix: A note on the coding of objects and modalities of control

The coding of objects

The concepts of classification and frame can be used to interpret communication between objects. In other words, objects and their relationships to each other constitute a message system whose code can be stated in terms of the relationship between classification and frames of different strengths.

We can consider:

(1) The strength of the rules of exclusion which control the array of objects in a space. Thus the stronger the rules of exclusion the more distinctive the array of objects in the space; that is, the greater the difference between object arrays in different spaces.

(2) The extent to which objects in the array can enter into different relationships to each other.

Now the stronger the rules of exclusion the stronger the *classification* of objects in that space and the greater the difference between object arrays in different spaces. In the same way in which we discussed relationships between subjects we can discuss the relationships between object arrays in different spaces. Thus the stronger the classification the more the object arrays resemble a collection code; the weaker the classification the more the object arrays resemble an integrated code. The greater the number of different relationships objects in the array can enter into with each other the weaker their framing. The fewer the number of different relationships objects in the array can enter into with each other the stronger their framing. (If the objects in the array can be called lexical items, then the syntax is their relationships to each other. A restricted code is a syntax with few choices: an elaborated code a syntax which generates a large number of choices.)

We would expect the social distribution of power and the principles of control to be reflected in the coding of objects. This code may be made more delicate if we take into account:

(1) The number of objects in the array;
(2) The rate of change of the array.

We can have strong classification with a large *or* a small number of objects. We can have strong classification of large or small arrays where the array is fixed across time *or* where the array varies across time. Consider, for example, two arrays which are strongly classified: a late-Victorian, middle-class living-room and a mid-twentieth-century, trendy, middle-class 'space' in Hampstead. The Victorian room is likely to contain a very large number of objects, whereas the middle-class room is likely to contain a small number of objects. In one case the object array is foreground and the space background, whereas in the second case the space is a vital component of the array. The Victorian room represents both strong classification and strong framing. Further, whilst objects may be added to the array, its fundamental characteristics would remain constant over a relatively long time-period. The Hampstead room is likely to contain a small array which would indicate strong classification (strong rules of exclusion) but the objects are likely to enter into a variety of relationships with each other; this would indicate weak framing. Further, it is possible that the array would be changed across time, according to fashion.

We can now see that if we are to consider classification (C) we need to know:

(1) Whether it is strong or weak;
(2) Whether the array is small or large (x);
(3) Whether the array is fixed or variable (y).

At the level of frame (F) we need to know: Whether it is strong or weak (p); that is, whether the coding is restricted or elaborated.

It is also important to indicate in the specification of the code the context (c) to which it applies. We should also indicate the nature of the array by adding the concept realization (r). Thus, the most abstract formulation of the object code would be as follows:

$$f\,(c,r,\,C\,(x,y),\,F\,(p))$$

The code is some unspecified function of the variables enclosed in the brackets.

It is important to note that because the classification is weak it does not mean that there is less control. Indeed, from this point of view it is not possible to talk about amount of control, only of its modality. This point we will now develop.

Classification, frames and modalities of control

Imagine four lavatories. The first is stark, bare, pristine, the walls are painted a sharp white; the washbowl is like the apparatus, a gleaming white. A square block of soap sits cleanly in an indentation in the sink. A white towel (or perhaps pink) is folded neatly on a chrome rail or hangs from a chrome ring. The lavatory paper is hidden in a cover and peeps through its slit. In the second lavatory there are books on a shelf and some relaxing of the rigours of the first. In the third lavatory there are books on the shelf, pictures on the wall and perhaps a scattering of tiny objects. In the fourth lavatory the rigour is *totally relaxed*. The walls are covered with a motley array of postcards, there is a varied assortment of reading matter and curio. The lavatory roll is likely to be uncovered and the holder may well fall apart in use.

We can say that as we move from the first to the fourth lavatory we are moving from a strongly classified to a weakly classified space: from a space regulated by strong rules of exclusion to a space regulated by weak rules of exclusion. Now if the rules of exclusion are strong, then the space is strongly marked off from other spaces in the house or flat. The *boundary* between the spaces or rooms is sharp. If the rules of exclusion are strong, the boundaries well-marked, then it follows that there must be strong boundary maintainers (authority). If things are to be kept apart, then there must be some strong hierarchy to ensure the apartness of things. Further, the first lavatory constructs a space where pollution is highly visible. Inasmuch as a user leaves a personal mark (a failure to replace the towel in its original position, a messy bar of soap, scum in the washbowl, lavatory paper floating in the bowl, etc.), this constitutes pollution and such pollution is quickly perceived. Thus the criteria for competent usage of the space are both *explicit* and *specific*. So far we have been discussing aspects of classification; we shall now consider framing.

Whereas classification tells us about the structure of relationships in *space*, framing tells us about the structure of relationships in *time*. Framing refers us to inter-action, to the power relationships of inter-action; that is, framing refers us to communication. Now in the case of our lavatories, framing *here* would refer to the communication between the occupants of the space and those outside of the space. Such communication is normally strongly framed by a door usually equipped with a lock. We suggest that as we move from the strongly classified to the weakly classified lavatory, despite the potential insulation between inside and outside, there will occur a reduction in frame strength. In the case of the first lavatory we suggest that the door will always be closed and after entry will be locked. Ideally, no effects on the inside should be heard on the outside. Indeed, a practised user of this lavatory will acquire certain competencies in order to meet this requirement. However, in the case of the most weakly classified lavatory, we suggest that the door will normally be open; it may even be that the lock will not function. It would not be considered untoward for a conversation to develop or even be continued either side of the door. A practised user of this most weakly classified and weakly framed lavatory will acquire certain communicative competencies rather different from those required for correct use of the strongly classified one.

We have already noted that lavatory one creates a space where pollution is highly visible, where criteria for behaviour are explicit and specific, where the social basis of the authority maintaining the strong classification and frames is hierarchical. Yet it is also the case that such classification and frames create a *private* although impersonal space. *For providing that the classification and framing is not violated, the user of the space is beyond surveillance.*

However, when we consider lavatory four, which has the weakest classification and weakest frames, it seems at first sight that such a structure celebrates weak control. There appear to be few rules regulating what goes into a space and few rules regulating communication between spaces. Therefore it is difficult to consider what counts as a violation or pollution. Indeed, it would appear that such a classification and framing relationship facilitates the development of spontaneous behaviour. Let us consider this possibility.

Lavatory one is predicated on the rule 'things must be kept apart', be they persons, acts, objects, communication; and the stronger the classification and frames the greater the insulation, the stronger the boundaries between classes of persons, acts, objects, communications. Lavatory four is predicated on the rule that approximates to 'things must be put together'. As a consequence, we would find objects in the space that could be found in other spaces. Further, there is a more relaxed marking off of the space, and communication is possible between inside and outside. We have as yet not discovered the fundamental principles of violation.

Imagine one user, who, seeing the motley array and being sensitive to what he or she takes to be a potential of the space, decides to add to the array and places an additional postcard on the wall. It is possible that a little later a significant adult might say 'Darling, that's beautiful but it doesn't quite fit' or 'How lovely, but wouldn't it be better a little higher up?' In other words, we are suggesting that the array has a principle, that the apparently motley collection is ordered but that the principle is implicit, and although it is not easily discoverable it is capable of being violated. Indeed, it might take our user a very long time to infer the *tacit* principle, and generate choices in accordance with it. Without knowledge of the principle our user is unlikely to make appropriate choices and such choices may require a long period of socialization. In the case of lavatory one, no principle is required; all that is needed is the following of the command 'Leave the space as you found it.'

Now let us examine the weak framing in more detail. We suggest that locking the door, avoiding or ignoring communication, would count as violation; indeed anything which would offend the principle of *things must be put together*. However, inasmuch as the framing between inside and outside is weak, then it is also the case that the user is potentially or indirectly under continuous surveillance, in which case there is no privacy. Here we have a social context which at first sight appears to be very relaxed, which promotes and provokes the expression of the person, 'a do your own thing' space where highly personal choices may be offered, where hierarchy is not explicit, yet on analysis we find that it is based upon a form of implicit control which carries the potential of total surveillance. Such a form of implicit control encourages more of the person to be made manifest, yet such manifestations are subject to continuous screening and general rather than specific criteria. *At the level of classification the pollution is 'keeping things apart'; at the level of framing the violation is 'withholding'; that is, not offering, not making visible the self.*

If things are to be put together which were once set apart, then there must be some principle of the new relationships, but this principle cannot be mechanically applied and therefore cannot be mechanically learned. In the case of the rule 'things must be kept apart', then the apartness of things is something which is clearly marked and taken for granted in the process of initial socialization. The social basis of the categories of apartness is implicit, but the social basis of the authority is explicit. In the process of such socialization the insulation between things is a condensed message about the all-pervasiveness of the authority. It may require many years before the social basis of the principles underlying the category system is made fully explicit, and by that time the mental structure is well-initiated into the classification and frames. Strong classification and frames celebrate the *reproduction* of the past.

When the rule is 'things must be put together' we have an *interruption* of a previous order, and what is of issue is the authority (power relationships) which underpins it. Therefore the rule 'things must be put together' celebrates the present over the past, the subjective over the objective, the personal over the positional. Indeed, when everything is put together we have a total organic principle which covers all aspects of life *but* which admits of a vast range of combinations and re-combinations. This points to a very abstract or general principle from which a vast range of possibilities may be derived, so that individuals can both register personal choices *and* have knowledge when a combination is not in accordance with the principle. What is taken for granted when the rule is 'things must be kept apart' is *relationships* which themselves are made explicit by when the rule is 'things must be put together'. They are made explicit by the weak classification and frames. But the latter creates a form of implicit but potentially continuous surveillance and at the same time promotes the making public of the self in a variety of ways. We arrive finally at the conclusion that the conditions for the release of the person are the absence of explicit hierarchy but the presence of a more intensified form of social interaction which creates continuous but invisible screening. From the point of view of the socialized they would be offering novel, spontaneous combinations.

Empirical note

It is possible to examine the coding of objects from two perspectives. We can analyse the coding of overt or visible arrays and we can compare the code with the codings of covert or invisible arrays (e.g. drawers, cupboards, refrigerators, basements, closets, handbags, etc.). We can also compare the coding of verbal messages with the coding of non-verbal messages. It would be interesting to carry out an empirical study of standardized spaces, e.g. LEA housing estate, middle-class suburban 'town house' estate, modern blocks of flats, formal educational spaces which vary in their architecture and in the pedagogy.

I am well aware that the lavatory may not be seen as a space to be *specially contrived* and so subject to *special regulation* in the sense discussed. Some lavatories are not subject to the principles I have outlined. Indeed some may be casually treated spaces where pieces of newspaper may be stuffed behind a convenient pipe, where the door does not close or lock, where apparatus has low efficiency and where sound effects are taken-for-granted events.

Chapter 7 The sociology of education: a brief account

Sociology is carried out in an historical context, and its approaches and problems are an expression of that context. Contemporary sociology offers a weakly co-ordinated body of thought and practices, but it is extraordinarily prolific in approaches. The sociological imagination should make visible what is rendered invisible through the society's institutional procedures, and through the daily practices of its members. The 'news' the sociologist brings is about the nature of constraint, of control, of the ways in which man's symbolic arrangements at one and the same time shape his innermost experience and yet create the potential for change. However, the 'news' of much contemporary sociology appears to be news about the conditions necessary for creating acceptable news. Theories are less to be examined and explored at conceptual and empirical levels, but are to be assessed in terms of their underlying models of man and of society. It follows that students are to be made aware of the values underlying theories, and to learn how to place them in the perspective of an approach; students are socialized into approaches rather than encouraged to create news. On the other hand, such socialization into the various 'approach paradigms' ensures that the dilemmas and contradictions of society are continuously being made explicit. Whilst the tensions between approach paradigms may well ensure the possibility of continuous questioning, they do not necessarily guarantee any answers. Indeed, the very form such questioning may take may obscure our understanding. For example, the attack of Douglas (amongst others) on Durkheim is based almost wholly upon *Suicide* and *The Rules of the Sociological Method*. Douglas ignores almost completely *The Division of Labour in Society*, *Primitive Classification* and *The Elementary Forms of the Religious Life;*

books which have had a vital influence upon French anthropology and contemporary sociology. If Douglas had asked how it was that *Suicide* had had such a powerful influence on American sociology, and so little influence in France, then we might have obtained a rather more general understanding of the development of sociology in two cultures within which he could have developed his critique. The dangers of 'approach paradigms' are that they may tend to witch-hunting and heresy-spotting; at the same time, they do provide a social basis for the creation of new—or the invigorating of old—sociological identities. It might be useful to outline in a dichotomous form four such approaches. I have drawn upon the work of Horton (1966) and Dawe (1970) who have shown some of the schisms in contemporary sociological thinking. I have added to this list of schisms. I shall, then, discuss somewhat briefly the relationships between these approaches and their social basis.

The tension between these approaches—

(1) Those who place the emphasis upon the problem of order as against those who place the emphasis upon the problem of control;

(2) Those who place the emphasis upon interdependence and dependence, as against those who place the emphasis upon conflict and voluntarism;

(3) Those who place the emphasis upon how social reality is constructed out of negotiated encounters with others, and those who place the emphasis upon structural relationships;

(4) Those who emphasize the need to understand the everyday practices of members and the assumptions which make the daily practices work, and those who set up observers' categories and observers' procedures of measurement by means of which they reconstruct the constructions of members;

reflects the dilemmas and contradictions of contemporary society and, in particular, the enduring crisis in the USA. There, bureaucracy, technology and social cleavage, are in their most advanced Western forms. It is no accident that structural-functional approaches, with their assumptions of shared values, have been attacked and that the Americans should have revived their own tradition of symbolic interactionism, introduced various forms of phenomenology and re-developed Marxist theory. It is no accident that these approaches which emphasize man as both a product and a creator of meanings, man as an active and experiencing subject, rather than an orientating receiver, should be playing such an important part in current sociological thought. Parallel to the making visible of the assumptions underlying hierarchical arrangements, whether these are realized in economic, sexual or educational contexts, is the questioning of the assumptions underlying the distinction between (and strong classification of) uncommonsense knowledge and commonsense knowledge.

There is also an ambivalence underlying sociological thought as to its methods and objects. All would agree that an exciting sociological account should be comparative and historical and should reveal the relationships between structural features and interactional practices in a context of change. But how do we obtain such an account? What is the relationship between the *means* sociologists use to gain knowledge of others and the nature of the knowledge obtained? How does the sociologist make his knowledge public and plausible? In what sense is sociology an empirical discipline? What is the relationship between observer categories and the categories used by members to create order and change meanings? None of these are new questions. What is of significance is that they are being put today with a new vigour and intensity. The methods of the natural sciences (which include both the form of the theory and the manner of its empirical exploration) are considered by some to be either inappropriate or dehumanizing, or both, when applied to the study of man. It is argued that man reflecting upon man is qualitatively a different relationship from man reflecting upon objects. How can man, then, reflect upon man in such a way that he is not transformed into an object through the means of his reflection?

These debates are fierce because they are fundamentally political. They are about what view of social phenomena the sociologist *ought* to have *and* the relationship between the sociologist and his society. They reveal the dilemma of being a sociologist. Whom do we serve? Which side are we on?

Sociologists of education are today caught up in the larger debate. The basic inter-actional unit of their study is an inter-generational relationship. The basic content of their study is the social origins and consequences of variations in the *formal* structuring of consciousness. The basic institutions which they attempt to understand are cultural repeaters. The formal or planned educational relationship is a crucial repeater of whatever it is to be repeated, even if it is the unlikely. The inter-actional context, its contents and its institutional expression realize in condensed and explicit forms, in visible and invisible ways, the constraints and possibilities of a given society. Alive in the context, contents and institutional embodiment of education is the distribution of power and principles of social control. As a consequence, educational arrangements are only comprehensible when they are viewed from the perspective of the total society.

It might be instructive to analyse changes in the approaches of sociologists to education in England since the Second World War.

On the whole, our knowledge of schools is almost wholly confined to the surface features of their selective principles. This is partly because such knowledge is relatively easily acquired, partly because of its policy and educational implications, partly because of the interests and training of sociologists, and partly because of the relatively low *per capita* cost of such research. However, it is important to add that because such features are surface, it does not mean to say that they are not of considerable significance. Such research enables us to map the incidence and variation of the problem which these selective principles create. This research does not (nor is such research designed to do this) give us any specific understanding of *how* the selective principles give rise to the behaviour with which they are correlated. It is also true that these studies did not focus upon the knowledge properties of the school in terms of its form, content and manner of transmission. This was because these studies took as their problem stratification features within and between schools. Because the knowledge properties of the school were not treated as problematic, but as an invariant, the research emphasized continuities and discontinuities between the knowledge properties of the home and those of the school. This in turn gave rise to a view of the school as an agency of unsuccessful assimilation, and the view of the family as a primary source of educational pathology.

The debates of the 1950s focused upon the organizational structure of the schools, the social origins of measured intelligence and its relation to attainment, within the wider issues of manpower requirements and social equality. The basic concern was the *demonstration*, not explanation, of institutional sources of inequality in education. The poverty surveys of the early twentieth century were replaced by the surveys of educational 'wastage' in the mid-twentieth century. Apart from London and Leicester, there were few universities of this period which possessed viable departments of sociology. During this period, there were only *two* major sociologists engaged in research or systematic teaching in the sociology of education. The sociology of education in the 1950s did not exist as an established examined subject in the colleges and departments of education, nor in undergraduate degrees in sociology. The first taught master's degree in this area was established at the University of London Institute of Education only in 1964, and the first degrees were awarded in 1966. It is very important for the student to realize that the interest of sociologists in the social basis of symbolic systems, the forms of their legitimation, the interpretative procedures to which they give rise, the manner of their transmission, is of very recent origin.

The first teaching approach or paradigm was developed essentially by Floud and Halsey, who were the two major sociologists active in educational research in the mid-1950s, or early 1960s.

Their research was essentially a development of the enquiry into social mobility carried out by Professor D. Glass of the London School of Economics. The book which reported his extensive investigation contained five chapters on education (Glass, 1954). Jean Floud taught at the London School of Economics before taking up a position at the University of London Institute of Education, and A. H. Halsey obtained his degree at the London School of Economics. Jean Floud was faced with the problem of constructing advanced courses in the sociology of education, and with the supervision of students who wished to read for higher degrees in this area. Both Floud and Halsey were active in creating the sociology of education as a field of study (1958, 1961).

One of the major problems in the transformation of a specialized field of research into a subject to be taught is what is to be selected from the parent subject which can be used to legitimize the specialized field as a *subject*. This is particularly important when the new subject is to be created out of a low status field of research, such as education. In the case of the sociology of education, the legitimizing institution might be said to have been the London School of Economics, and the legitimizing area was the problems and process of industrialization. This was partly because this area of sociology at both theoretical and empirical levels was well documented, partly because it reflected the then current LSE interests in stratification and mobility and industrialization, and partly because it could be fitted into a *weak* structural-functional approach in the context of problems of social policy and educational planning. This approach did not call for any major rethinking of classical and contemporary sociology in terms of its potential application to a sociology of education. Once the approach was established as a taught course, with the development of a university syllabus, reading lists, examination papers and finally textbooks, it became difficult for some to think outside of what became the legitimate contents. The approach, once institutionalized, reinforced the existing research and defined future problems. The approach bore the hallmarks of British applied sociology; atheoretical, pragmatic, descriptive, and policy-focused. Yet if we look back to the mid-1950s, it is not easy to see how there could have been an alternative. There was little work available at theoretical or empirical levels to form the basis for comparative studies of education; studies of organizations were few, and they were limited to industrial, administrative and custodian institutions; studies of professional groups and the professionalizing process were in their infancy; there was little interest, either here or in the USA, in the study of cultural transmission, and the major theoretical approach was that of structural-functionalism. It is important to emphasize that the number of active workers in the field of the sociology of education at that time in England could be counted on the fingers of one hand! Indeed, it is amazing that the approach was so successfully institutionalized. It happened, perhaps, because it coincided with the expansion of educational departments in the colleges of education at a time when the focus of interest was on the relationships between the home and the school. If educational psychology had not been so preoccupied with the diagnosis and measurement of skills, child development and personality, but instead had developed a social psychology relevant to education, the story might have been different.

From the mid-1960s onwards, there was a massive expansion of sociology in Britain, and in the same period sociology became established in the colleges and departments and institutes of education. The rationale for the establishment of sociology in the education of teachers was given by the first approach. However, during this period, new sociological perspectives were attaining influence in the USA. From different sources, Marxist, Phenomenological, Symbolic-

Interactionist and Ethnomethodological viewpoints began to assert themselves. Although there are major differences between these approaches, they share certain common features:

(1) A view of man as a creator of meanings.
(2) An opposition to macro-functional sociology.
(3) A focus upon the assumptions underlying social order, together with the treatment of social categories as themselves problematic.
(4) A distrust of forms of quantification and the use of objective categories.
(5) A focus upon the *transmission* and acquisition of interpretative procedures.

The movements arose in the USA at a period of political economic and educational crisis in an overall social context of advanced technological control. During this period, students in the West, particularly in Germany and in the USA, were turning their attention to the authority and knowledge properties of the university. This brought into sharp focus the social organization of knowledge, the manner of its transmission and the power relationships upon which it rested. Fundamental questions were raised about the existing classification and framing of educational knowledge as to its significance for the structuring of experience and as a repeater of society's hierarchical arrangements. At the same time, the ineffectiveness of USA schools to educate, even in their own terms, Black, Puerto-Rican, Mexican and Indian minority groups, gave rise to a tidal wave of educational research. This research was mainly carried out by psychologists and it was based upon a deficit model of the child, family and community, rather than upon a deficit model of the school. The reaction against this definition of the problem, itself associated with the rise of Black Power, led to a reconsideration of the power relationships between the school and the community it served; it led to a major questioning of the administration of school systems; it led to a major questioning of the organizational forms of education, and in particular to a major questioning of the transmission and contents of school knowledge. The impact of these intellectual movements, and of the political context in the USA, upon the sociology of education in England, led to a broadening of its concerns and almost to an identification of the field with the sociology of knowledge.

We should also bear in mind that the belief in the 1950s and 1960s in England that the development of the comprehensive school would reduce educational problems was shown to have an inadequate foundation in the 1970s onwards. The Newsom Report raised fundamental questions about the content of education for the 'average' child. The proposal to raise the school leaving age created a 'crisis' of the curriculum. The development of the Schools Council led to an increase of interest in curriculum development. A number of new chairs in Curriculum Studies were established. Research continued to reveal class differences in educational attainment. It would not be too much to say that the emphasis was shifting from the organizational structure of schools to an emphasis upon what was to be taught. It would also not be entirely wrong to suggest that the incentive to change curricula arose out of the difficulties secondary schools were experiencing in the education of the non-élite children. We can thus trace a number of influences, in both the USA and here, which lead to a rather different approach to the sociology of education. We have only to compare the textbooks by Ottaway and Musgrove and Banks, and the reader edited by Halsey, Floud and Anderson, with Young's collection of essays and the Open University reader *School and Society* to see the impact. We now have a second approach to the sociology of education which is, itself, partly a response of the new generation of sociologists to intellectual movements in sociology and to their personal and political context.

I shall briefly compare the two approaches. Both approaches share a common concern with the inter-relationships between class, selection and equality. However, the first approach placed its emphasis upon macro-structural relationships, as these controlled the relationships between levels of the educational system, the organizational features of schools and their selective principles, and the inter-relationships with the division of labour, social stratification and social mobility. The basic unit of this approach tended to be an element of a structure, e.g. a role, or a structure examined in its relation to another structure. The basic unit of the second approach is a situated activity and it focuses upon inter-actional contexts and their contents. The second approach focuses upon the knowledge properties of schools and is therefore concerned to study the social basis of what is defined as educational knowledge. Whereas the first approach made explicit how social class entered into, maintained and repeated itself in the organizational structure of education, the second approach carries out a similar analysis on the contents of education. As a result, curricula, pedagogy and forms of assessment are brought sharply into focus, and their ideological assumptions and forms of legitimation are explored. This switch in focus has enabled the sociology of education to draw upon the sociology of knowledge and to take advantage of the approaches mentioned earlier. Whereas the major technique of enquiry of the first approach was the social survey or enquiries based upon large populations by means of the closed questionnaire, the second approach favours case studies of ongoing activities in which participant observation, the tape recorder and video machines play an important role in the construction of close ethnographic descriptions which as yet have not been made in this country.

It is customary to characterize the first approach as structural-functional, but if one reads Floud and Halsey carefully, they specifically point out the limitations of this perspective:

> The structural-functionalist is preoccupied with social integration based on shared values—that is, with consensus—and he conducts his analysis solely in terms of motivated action of individuals to behave in ways appropriate to maintain society in a state of equilibrium. But this is a difficult notion to apply to developed industrialized societies, even if the notion of equilibrium is interpreted dynamically. They are dominated by social change, and 'consensus' and 'integration' can be only very loosely conceived in regard to them (Floud and Halsey, 1958).

They did, however, accept the thesis of increasing subordination of the educational system to the economy in advanced industrial societies. They saw the development and structural differentiation of the educational system very much as a response to the needs of the technological society, and they saw education as active essentially in its role of creating new knowledge. Their basic view was that education was contained by the rigidities of an out-moded class structure which deeply penetrated its organizational forms. *It is important to realize that Floud and Halsey used a manpower and equality argument as a double-barrelled weapon to bring about change in the procedures of selection and the organizational structure of schools.* They were aware of the need to study the contents of schools and universities, and explicitly and repeatedly used a Weberian approach to the issue. Halsey's most recent book (1971) is an elaborate analysis, within a Weberian framework, of the British universities, focused on the distinctive role of British university teachers as creators and transmitters of knowledge. But it is now fashionable to belittle the earlier work of Floud and Halsey and to consider that their treatment of education paid little regard to its problematics. This is quite untrue. For them, the existing organization structure was certainly something not to be taken for granted—nor were the procedures of selection. Halsey (1958) wrote a major piece on genetics and social structure. They were both considerably involved in attacking the assumptions underlying the measurement of intelligence. Taylor, a student of Floud, wrote a book showing clearly the dubious assumptions underlying the creation of the secondary modern school (Taylor, 1963).

Whereas the first approach tended to assume a normative system, and the problems of its acquisition, the second approach takes as problematic the normative system and its acquisition, but it, itself, pre-supposes a complex structural arrangement which provides, at least initially, and often finally, the terms of local situated activities. Negotiated meanings pre-suppose a structure *of* meanings (and their history) wider than the area of negotiation. Situated activities pre-suppose a situation; they pre-suppose relationships between situations; they pre-suppose sets of situations.

Part of the difficulty arises out of the confusion of the term structure with structural functionalism. Structural relationships do not necessarily imply a static social theory, nor do they imply features which are empirically unchanging. At the level of the individual, they exist in the form of interpretative procedures. For example, the relationship between subjects is a structural relationship, and specific identities are created by the nature of the relationship. Whether these structural relationships are repeated, and how they are repeated, depends upon a range of factors. The structural relationships, implicitly and explicitly, carry the power and control messages *and* shape, in part, the form of the response to them at the level of inter-action. Because relationships are structural, it does not mean that the initially received objective reality is without contradiction, or a seamless fabric, nor that there is a uniform shared subjective meaning.

What is of interest is that the new approach is not an approach, but is made up of a variety of approaches (some of which are in opposition to each other) which have been outlined earlier. As a result, there has been a refreshing increase in the range and type of questions we can ask. Of equal significance, there is now the possibility of a wider-based connection between sociology and the sociology of education, which in turn provides a much stronger source of legitimation of this field. However, major questions still remain unanswered, or answered only at a highly formal level. For example, there is the issue of how we relate macro and micro levels of explanation. Berger (1966) argues that this can be done by relating his phenomenological approach to the sociology of knowledge to symbolic interactionism. This does not show us *how*, it simply indicates a *direction*. Others have suggested relating symbolic interactionism with forms of Marxist analysis. However, this again misses the question of how theories which are based on very *different* assumptions are to be related. There is also the very perplexing issue of what happens when we move from raising questions or writing highly speculative essays to the giving of answers. It is not at all clear how we obtain reliable knowledge, which can be made public and plausible.

Whilst we are told of the sins of empiricism, of the abstracted fictions created by observer's categories and arithmetic, of the importance of close ethnographic study of situated activities, we are not told precisely what the new criteria are by means of which we can both create and judge the accounts of others. We are told and socialized into what to reject, but rarely told how to create.

In the same way as the first approach to the sociology of education defined research problems, so the recent approaches carry research directions. It is therefore important to consider where the emphasis is falling in order to ensure that our range of questions are not always coincident with whatever appears to be the approach.

And this takes us to the heart of the matter. In a subject where theories and methods are weak, intellectual shifts are likely to arise out of conflict between *approaches* rather than conflict between explanations, for, by definition, most explanations will be weak and often non-comparable, because they are approach-specific. The weakness of the explanation is likely to be attributed to the approach, which is analysed in terms of its ideological stance. Once the ideological stance is exposed, then all the work may be written off. Every new approach becomes a social movement or sect which immediately defines the nature of the subject by re-defining what is to be admitted, and what is beyond the pale, so that with every new approach the subject almost starts from scratch. Old bibliographies are scrapped, the new references become more and more contemporary, new legitimations are 'socially constructed' and courses take on a different focus. What may be talked about and how it is to be talked about has changed. Readers typifying and, more importantly, reifying, the *concept* of *approach* are published. A power struggle develops over the need to institutionalize the new approach by obtaining control over the means of transmission and evaluation. This power struggle takes the form of the rituals of the generation, as the guardians of the old approaches (usually the successfully established) fight a rear-guard action against the new. Eventually the new approach becomes institutionalized, and every sociology department has a representative. A new option is created, and the collection which is sociology has expanded to include a few more specialized identities: ethnomethodologist, symbolic interactionist, phenomenologist, structuralist. People begin to say the subject is alive, our range of questions has expanded; the sociological imagination has been re-vitalized! The dust finally settles and students have a few more approaches to learn, which are then suitably regurgitated in examinations in the form of the dichotomies given in the early part of this article. What is a little remarkable is that our forms of teaching sociology in England do not even give rise to *either* new explanations or even new approaches. We appear to be almost wholly parasitic on the Americans, who provide for some of us a constant source of the emperor's new clothes.[1]

We shall now raise issues of a very general nature, which at first sight may seem far removed from the everyday activities of schools, and yet these everyday activities carry within themselves the processes and practices crucial for the understanding of more general questions. It is a matter of some importance that we develop forms of analysis that can provide a dynamic relationship between 'situated activities of negotiated meanings' and the 'structural' relationships which the former pre-suppose. Indeed, it is precisely what is taken as given in social action approaches which allows the analysis to proceed in the first place. Nor can the relationships between structural and inter-actional aspects be created by meta-sociological arguments, as in the case of Berger, when he shows how his phenomenological approach can be linked to symbolic interactionism. The levels, if they are to be usefully linked, must be linked at the *substantive* level by an explanation whose conceptual structure directs empirical exploration of the relationship between the levels.[2] In a way, the concepts of classification and frame which I have developed attempt to do this. The concept 'classification' is a structural concept. It points to that which is to be repeated. However, whether it is or not depends upon the strength of 'frames' at the inter-actional levels. As both concepts have built into them both power and control elements, we can see how different forms of constraint emerge as the relationship between these concepts changes.

If we are to consider the relationships between schooling and society, a crucial question becomes that of accounting for the constraints which limit the style educational knowledge takes for groups of pupils and students. For example, in England until recently the style for élite pupils was specialized. Compare the number of 'A' level subjects offered with the number of subjects offered by European students. Now this specialized style for élite pupils has a number of consequences. The first is that we cannot possibly understand the form and content of education in England unless we take this into account. It is quite remarkable that no sociologist has concerned himself with this question, nor for that matter have historians. Now in order to come to terms with such a question, we need to consider the relationship between culture and social structure, between power and control from an historical and comparative perspective.

There is also a tendency to view the structuring of knowledge in schools in isolation from other symbolic arrangements of society. We might ask if there were any relationships between the attempts to de-classify and weaken educational frames (particularly for the non-élite children) and the musical forms of a Cage or a Stockhausen. Even within schools, the emphasis upon the stratification of knowledge may promote interest in certain subjects or groupings at the expense of others. Witkin at Exeter and John Hayes at King's College, London, are almost alone among British sociologists interested in education who are concerned (albeit from different perspectives) to understand the educational shaping of aesthetic experience. (The first group of students in England to protest against the form and content of education were art students.) We have in education also a remarkable opportunity to study changes in the forms of socialization which control the body as a message system. From this point of view the transformation, over the past decade or so, of physical training into physical education and movement is of some interest. It might be of interest to examine if there are any relationships between the latter shift and the shift of emphasis in English from the strong framing and classification of aestheic experience to weak framing and classification of such experience; from the *word* abstracted from the pupil's experience to the *word* as a critical realization of the pupil's experience. Latent in the teaching of English is a crucial sociological history of the class structure and *one* means of the latter's cultural control. If we are to take shifts in the content of education seriously, then we need to relate such shifts to institutions and symbolic arrangements external to the school.

In the same way as we discussed the importance of examining the range, variation and change in what we have called knowledge styles at both the societal and school levels, it is equally as important to consider range variation and change in what we can call organizational styles.

In England, over the past decade, there has developed a variety of secondary school structures, and within any one such structure there are often considerable differences in the internal organization between schools. It is also possible that, cutting across this diversity, there may well be for certain groups of pupils a similarity in the organizational and knowledge features of schools which affects the ongoing relationships between teachers, between pupils, between teachers and pupils. To what extent do the controls of higher education and the economy in combination with the focusing of the initial class socialization of pupils create a context of *plus ça change, plus c'est la même chose*? Finally, we need to ask what are the social controls which monitor and change the range of organizational styles within and between levels of the educational system? And all these questions must be examined from both an historical and a comparative perspective. (We could of course extend the form of this general question to the professional socialization of the teacher.)[8]

Sociologists are creatures of their time, and the range of approaches to their subject is in part a realization of the political context and the sociologist's relation to it. As I have attempted to argue, sociologists of education are particularly sensitive to this political context, because the areas of cleavage, dilemma and contradiction in the wider society are particularly transparent and are most visible in the educational arrangements. Thus, there is a resonance between the value positions underlying the various approaches and the problems of educational arrangements, because these problems are the problems of society, which in turn calls out the sociological approaches. Thus, depending upon who is counting, we may have two, three or even four sociologies from which, given time, there will be derived a similar number of sociologies of education, each with their own legitimators, readers, references and special forms of examination questions. The research of one will not be acceptable to the other, because of disputes over the methods of enquiry and/or our disparate ideological assumptions. However, because these approaches attempt to make explicit the assumptions underlying socialization and their categorical expressions, they temporarily lift the weight of these categories, so that we can see a little how we are, what we are, and inasmuch as they do this, they restore to us a sense of choice and create a notion that it can be different: whether the 'it' refers to sociology or society, for in the end the two are the same.

Yet it is a matter of doubt as to whether this sense of the possible, that is, the construction and analysis of the alternative forms social relationships can take, is developed more by socialization into an approach, into the sect which is its social basis, or by openness to the variety of social experience. This does not mean that our stance is aesthetic, or one of spurious objectivity, or that we are insensitive to the violations in our political context. Rather, it means we need to explore the ambiguities and contradictions upon which our symbolic arrangements ultimately rest; for in these ambiguities are both the seeds of change and man's creative acts. In order to do this, we must be able to show how the distribution of power and the principles of control shape the structure of these symbolic arrangements, how they enter into our experience as interpretative procedures *and* the conditions of their repetition and change. This may require a widening of the focus of the sociology of education, less an allegiance to an approach, and more a dedication to a problem.

Notes

1 We are often made aware of continental thought through the writings of American sociologists.
2 It may be unwise to formulate the issue as one of levels. It is more a question of formulating the problem in such a way that one is not denied access to a variety of viewpoints. It is possible that 'approaches' sometimes function as sociological mechanisms of denial.
3 Clearly, these questions about the range and variations in organizational and knowledge styles, their social antecedents and consequences, would lead on towards fundamental questions.

References

BANKS, O. (1968), *Sociology of Education*, Batsford.
BERGER, P. (1966), 'Identity as a problem in the sociology of knowledge', *Archives Européennes de Sociologie*, 7, pp. 10–115.
BERNSTEIN, B. (1971), 'On the classification and framing of educational knowledge', in *Class, Codes and Control*, Volume 1, Routledge & Kegan Paul.
BOURDIEU, P. and PASSERON, J. C. (1970), *La Reproduction: éléments pour une théorie du système d'enseignement*, Paris: Les Éditions de Minuit.
DAWE, A. (1970), 'The two sociologies', *Br. J. Soc.*, *21*, No. 2, pp. 207–18.
DOUGLAS, J. D. (1967), *The Social Meanings of Suicide*, Princeton University Press.
DURKHEIM, E. (1915), *The Elementary Forms of the Religious Life* (translated by J. W. Swain), Allen & Unwin.
DURKHEIM, E. (1933), *The Division of Labour in Society* (translated by G. Simpson), New York: Macmillan.
DURKHEIM, E. (1938), *The Rules of the Sociological Method* (translated by S. A. Solovay and J. H. Mueller), University of Chicago Press.
DURKHEIM, E. (1938), *L'Évolution pédagogique en France*, Paris: Alcan.
DURKHEIM, E. (1951), *Suicide: A Study in Sociology* (translated by J. A. Spoulding and G. Simpson), Free Press.
DURKHEIM, E. and MAUSS, M. (1963), *Primitive Classification* (translated by R. Needham), Cohen & West.
FLOUD, J. and HALSEY, A. H. (1958), 'The sociology of education: a trend report and bibliography' *Current Sociology*, 7, 3.
GLASS, D .V. (ed.) (1954), *Social Mobility*, Routledge & Kegan Paul.
HALSEY, A. H. (1958), 'Genetics, social structure and intelligence', *Br. J. Soc.*, *10*, pp. 15–28.
HALSEY, A. H., FLOUD, J. and ANDERSON, C. A. (1961), *Education, Economy and Society: A Reader in the Sociology of Education*, Collier-Macmillan.

HALSEY, A. H. and TROW, M. A. (1971), *The British Academics*, Faber & Faber.
HORTON, J. (1966), 'Order and Conflict Theories of Social Problems', *Amer. J. Soc.*, *11*, pp. 701–13.
MUSGROVE, P. W. (1965), *Sociology of Education*, Methuen.
OPEN UNIVERSITY SCHOOL AND SOCIETY COURSE TEAM : COSIN, B. R., DALE, I. R., ESLAND, G. M., and SWIFT, D. F. (1971), *School and Society: A Sociological Reader*, Routledge & Kegan Paul, in association with the Open University Press.
OTTAWAY, A. K. C. (1953), *Education and Society: An Introduction to the Sociology of Education*, Routledge & Kegan Paul.
STONE, G. P. and FARBERMAN, H. A. (1967), 'On the edge of rapprochement; was Durkheim moving towards the perspective of symbolic interactionism?', *Sociological Quarterly*, *8*, pp. 149–64.
TAYLOR, W. (1963), *The Secondary Modern School*, Faber & Faber.
YOUNG, M. F. D. (ed.) (1971), *Knowledge and Control: New Directions for the Sociology of Education*, Collier-Macmillan.

Chapter 8 Aspects of the relations between education and production

Introduction

The primary intention of this concluding chapter is to apply the concepts which have been developed earlier in the book, to consider the relationships between education and production, school and work. Writings in the sociology of education tend to neglect this crucial relationship. Sometimes those (Bowles and Gintis) who focus their analysis on the educational consequences of the mode of production regard the educational system as a producer of types of personality relevant to production. That is, they regard education as creating, and changing, psychological dispositions appropriate to changes in the organization of production. Althusser analyses education essentially as the crucial means of ideological control, transmission and reproduction. Bourdieu, the major theorist in this area, emphasizes education as a distributor and legitimator of cultural capital, the ideological significance of the structure, contents and processes of educational transmissions, the formation of a class-regulated habitus within a general theory of cultural reproduction. Bourdieu indicates the curious position of education as being both dependent and relatively independent, or autonomous of a material base. His analysis is mainly concerned with the relatively autonomous relationship of education. On the other hand, Bowles and Gintis are concerned more with the dependent relationship of education on the mode of production. These writers do not give much space in their theorizing to change, conflict and contradiction. This is possibly because they would regard such movements as relatively superficial phenomena which do not disturb fundamentally the relationships they are positing. Is it always *plus ça change, plus c'est la même chose*?

We will commence with an analysis of educational codes which are determined by the relationship and values of classification and framing. The reader should notice that the definitions of classification and framing have become more abstract and the link between power and classification and framing and control has become more explicit. It is also important to note the relationship between class and codes. Class is conceived as the fundamental *dominant cultural category*, created and maintained by the mode of production. It is the basic classification which creates the social relationships of production. However, the realizations of this dominant cultural category vary in time. That is, the *form* taken by the social relationships of production and the *form* taken by the social relationships of education has changed over time.

In the account to follow, we shall be using the concepts of *classification* and *framing* to determine the codes of education and the codes of production. Thus *variations* in the codes of education and production are different historical realizations of the dominant cultural category. These variations represent different means of its reproduction. Having determined the codes of education and production (which is a different statement from the determining power of the codes), we shall inquire into their relationship with each other. We shall then examine both the dependent and relative autonomous features of the relationship between education and production. We shall argue that, where there is a strong classification between education and production, this creates the condition for the relative autonomy of education, and thus a division of labour between those who are located in production and those who are located in cultural reproduction (education): that is, between power and control. We shall argue that a fraction of the middle class has become the producers and disseminators of theories of social control which are institutionalized in agencies of cultural reproduction and which are incorporated at different historical periods into the social relationships of production. We shall be concerned to examine the relationships between the relative autonomy of education and the formation and reproduction of the consciousness of the middle class.

The codes of education

Any social phenomenon is fundamentally a structure of contextualized meanings. From this point of view, a school creates a particular structure of meanings. At one level, we have groupings of teachers, ancillary staff and pupils. These inter-actions take place in a context —a building, or complex of buildings. Communication of diverse kinds goes on between teachers, between pupils, between teachers and pupils. When we look more closely, we find rules which underlie the diverse sets of *specialized* meanings which regulate the inter-actions and practices. These rules regulate the flow of persons, acts, communications at different times and in different contexts. These rules create criteria, standards whereby persons, acts, communications are evaluated, compared and grouped. Pupils possess criteria whereby they evaluate, compare and group the meanings they receive *and* create. There may be potential or actual conflict within and between the intentions and communications of the staff and those of the pupils. If we call this level the level of everyday activity, we can ask what are the fundamental principles which create the everyday activity? In answering this question, we may find that these everyday activities, everyday practices, take on quite another significance. We can talk about the division of labour of staff and pupils. This division of labour is expressed essentially in the relationships between subjects and in the relationships between pupils. Now we can use the concept classification to refer to the relationships between categories whether these categories are agencies (schools of various levels), agents (teachers) or acquirers (pupils). The concept classification refers to the *principle* of the relationships between categories. Now there must be some *form* of power in order to maintain and reproduce the particular relationships between the various categories. Further, the teachers and pupils are involved in a relationship of transmission and acquisition, whether this is unilateral or, in some part, reciprocal. The concept *framing* refers to the *principle* underlying this relationship. It refers to the *principle* which regulates the process of transmission and acquisition. Framing refers to the controls on what is made available, how it is made available, when it is made available *and* the social relationships. In other words, framing refers to the *principles of control* underlying pedagogic communication. As the principle varies, so do the form and content of the social relationship. Different principles of framing regulate the *experience* of pupils which is realized in the pedagogic relationship. So—different principles of framing, different forms of experience.

We can now say that classification tells us something fundamental about the relationships between categories which create the *context* of the school, and framing tells us something fundamental about the *form* of the content in *the process of its transmission*. Now, apparently, we are a long way from the everyday activities and practices of the school and its surface rules. What we are trying to do is to extract the principles which generate activities, practices and rules. Or perhaps, more accurately, we are trying to analyse the principles of which the everyday experiences, activities and practices are *realizations*. From this point of view the basic message structures of the school, the *codes* which the acquirer tacitly infers, are given by the principle of the relationships between classification and framing. We have argued that the principles of the power relationships are made manifest in the principle of the classification (the relationships between the categories), *and* the form of control is realized in the principles which create the framing (pedagogical practice). As the acquirer tacitly acquires these principles, he/she acquires the underlying code. In this way, classification and framing regulate meanings, and, more importantly, the *principle* which creates and maintains what count as legitimate meanings. From this point of view, power and control are made substantive in the classification and framing procedures which, in *turn*, create *particular* contexts and forms of educational practice which constitute the particular acts of social relationships of the school. We can say that from *this point of view*, in its social relationships, activities and practices, the school *symbolizes* power and control. It becomes a further crucial question to enquire into the social origins and consequences of the form(s) of power and control, overt and covert, in the school in different historical periods and in different societies.

In previous papers we have used the concepts 'classification' and 'framing' to specify and analyse different transmission codes. We shall here take that analysis for granted and spell out in more detail the relationships of power to classification and control to framing in the analysis of education, in the analysis of production and in the relationships between education and production. We should point out that these concepts are being used not for the purposes of description, but for the purpose of analysis (see Figure 8.1).

The positional structure of a school refers to the relationships between the school's fundamental categories. It refers to the relationships between teachers and between acquirers. We are here concerned *only* with the structural relationships between teachers and between acquirers. We are not concerned with the *form of communication* or transmission. The positional structure tells us the form of relationship

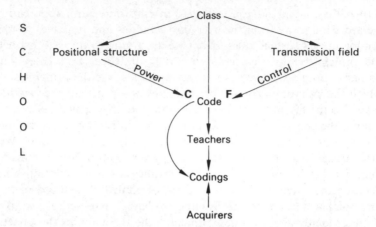

Figure 8.1 (*Positional structure and transmission field are based on concepts created by L. Vlasceanu*)

between teachers: that is, whether teachers are grouped into discrete units on the basis of their subject (strong classification) or whether the grouping of teachers is defined not by their subject, but by some principle which integrates and so subordinates subjects (weak classification). In the same way, we can consider the grouping of pupils. In all schools there is a fundamental separation of pupils in terms of their age. Thus we can say that the *temporal progression* of pupils is strongly classified. However, if we consider any age structure (first, second, third year) we can ask what is the principle regulating the relationships between pupils in any one year? How are they grouped? What are the principles of exclusion, principles of separation? For example, are the groupings based upon sex, upon 'ability', upon separate curricula? The stronger the rules of exclusion, the stronger the classification of pupils; the weaker the rules of exclusion, the weaker the classification of pupils.

In principle, we can have at least:

(1)   +C of teachers (subjects) +C of pupils
(2)   +C of teachers (subjects) −C of pupils

or

(3)   −C of teachers (subjects) +C of pupils
(4)   −C of teachers (subjects) −C of pupils.

In fact, we are not likely to find (3) because, as we have argued elsewhere, the move to weaken the classification of teachers is part of a more general movement to de-classify; that is, to weaken classification.

So far, we have been concerned only with the structural relationships between the fundamental categories of the social division of labour which create the positional structure. The *principle* of this division of labour, the *principle* of the positional structure, the *principle* of the relationships between the categories is given by the strength of classification. Now we shall consider the *regulation* on the realizations of the categories. The realization of the categories, teachers (subject matter) and pupils refers to the process of transmission of the categories: what is usually called the pedagogic practice. It is the pedagogic practice that *directly* constitutes the experience of the pupil.[1] The pedagogic practice makes the *power-relations* which constitute, maintain and reproduce the relationships between categories substantive at the level of everyday interactions between teachers and pupils. The pedagogical practices create what we call the transmission field. We can now ask what are the fundamental principles of the transmission field? To ask this question is to ask what is the regulation on what may be communicated, when can it be communicated, how must it be communicated. *In other words, the principle of transmission is the regulation on communication.* We use the concept, framing, to define the transmission field created .by the pedagogical practices. Framing refers to the controls on the selection, organization (sequencing) and pacing (rate of expected acquisition) of the transmission (knowledge) to be acquired.[2] Where framing is strong, then the acquirer has little control over the selection, organization and pacing of the transmission. Where framing is weak, then alternatives (options) are made available so that the acquirer has greater control over the selection, organization and pacing of the transmission. Now there are many implications of changes in framing which we cannot go into here. *Basically, changes in framing are changes in the modality of control.* Framing regulates the form of socialization into the category system, that is, into the positional structure, *and* into the *form* of the power relationships which constitute, maintain and reproduce the structure.

We can ask why there is any need to have concepts such as positional structure and transmission field when these concepts are defined in terms of classification and framing. The reason is this. The pupil does not experience directly a positional *structure* or a transmission *field*; the pupil experiences directly the classification and framing of local pedagogical relations. Our view is that in acquiring the Cs and Fs of these relationships, the pupil is *also* acquiring the macro representation of the code, the positional structure and the transmission field: the relations between the structure of power and the structure of control. We have previously indicated that there can be a range of variations in the values of classification and framing. Thus we can have at least[3]

(1) $+C +F$
(2) $+C -F$ forms of collection codes

(3) $-C -F$
(4) $-C +F$ forms of integrated codes.

It is crucial to determine what is the dominant educational code where variations exist.

It might seem, from both Figure 8.1 and the general discussion, that our analysis is based upon the notion that a school transmits only one code and therefore that there are no variations in its positional structure or transmission field. This may be the case. Certainly, this was the position for grammar schools, for elementary schools and for many public schools. In primary schools, which contained separate infant and junior departments, it was possible, and often in fact the case, that the shift from infant to junior also entailed a shift in the transmission code. In contemporary schools, particularly comprehensive schools, as we have indicated in chapter 5, we are likely to find a range of codes. Indeed, any one department which is part of a school with a dominant collection code may well find itself transmitting forms of collection and forms of integrated codes, depending upon the age, or curriculum selection procedures, of the school. However, in such cases, we would expect the transmission codes to be themselves strongly classified, that is, the more 'able' the student was considered, the more likely he/she would be to acquire a collection code ($+C +F$). Variation within and between codes entails both variation in content *and* variation in forms of control.

Summary

We are now going to say that the educational *code* is determined by the values of classification and framing. *A code is a regulative principle, tacitly acquired, which integrates relevant meanings, the form of their realization and their evoking contexts.* As a code changes, so do what count as relevant meanings, what count as appropriate realizations and what count as evoking contexts. As classification and framing change, so do relevant meanings, realizations and contexts. Inherent in the classification is the distribution of power; inherent in the framing is the principle of control.

We can ask what are the origins of the dominant power and control relations of the school? What is the origin, that is, of the dominant code? What is it maintaining and repeating? In capitalist societies— or, for that matter, in *any* society—it is repeating the dominant cultural category. In capitalist societies this is class. Class structure and relationships constitute and regulate both the distribution of power and the principles of control; that is, constitute and regulate the relationships between categories, the hierarchical form of their constitution *and* regulate the realization of the categories—that is, the principles of control. We can ask who acquires the dominant code and who acquires the dominated variation? Here we are concerned with the *distribution* of dominating and dominated codes in terms of the class origins of the receivers.

Classification and framing of the codes of production

What we shall attempt now is to use the language of codes (Cs and Fs) in order to examine the relationships between the form of production and the form of education.

We can use the concepts classification and framing to indicate the codes of education *and* the codes of production. We can then consider the nature of the relationship between the code regulating the form of education and the code regulating the form of production for any category (pupil) in the social division of labour of education and any category (worker) in the social division of labour of production. For example, what are the values of the classification and framing of education in the case of the 'less able' and the 'able', and what are the corresponding values regulating their future occupational positions? We can consider the social relationships constituted by the mode of production in terms of classification and framing. We can ask what are the relationships between the various categories of production: that is, the relationships between the various agents, unskilled, skilled, technologists, managers, administrators, etc. The relationships between these categories can be strongly or weakly classified. If the former, then the relationships are stable and sharply distinguished, the functions well insulated from each other, and the agents are not interchangeable. If the latter, then the relationships between agents are less sharply distinguished, there is reduced insulation between functions and agents are more inter-changeable between categories. In the same way, we can consider the framing of the mode of production. This refers to the regulation on the realization of the categories; that is, to the form of communica-tion constituted by the category system of the mode of production. If the primary unit of production is a repetitive, individually per-formed, strongly paced, explicitly sequenced *divisive act*, we can say that this is strong framing. If the primary unit of production is relatively co-operative, group based, where there is opportunity to vary the conditions and perhaps sequencing and pacing, where the outcome is less a fraction of the total object of production but bears a more direct relation to it, we can say that this represents weak framing.

We have considered initially the basic *unit* of production, that is the basic social relations of production at the level of the shop floor. We have distinguished between the *form* of the productive *act*—what is *made*, what a worker produces—and the form of the *relation* between agents of production (workers). We have distinguished between *what* is made and the *relationships* between those who are involved in making it. We have called what is made, what is produced —that is, the *social act of production—a realization* of an agent. We have examined the act in terms of the degree of fragmentation or divisiveness it entails. The degree of fragmentation or divisiveness refers to the relationship between the act and the final product. The more fragmented or divisive the act(s), the less like the final product is its realization. The more integrated the act, the more like the final product is its realization, that is, its consequence. The act is a *socially regulated realization* of a category (agent). The act of pro-duction is a communicative consequence of an agent. We can there-fore consider the regulation of the act in terms of framing. The more fragmented or *divisive* the act, the stronger the framing; the less fragmented or divisive, the weaker the framing.

The form of the social relationship between agents of the basic unit of production can be referred to the concept classification, because here we are considering the principle of the relationships between the categories (agents) of the social division of labour. The relationships between agents have two features, horizontal and vertical. The horizontal feature refers to the relationship between agents who share membership of a *common* category—e.g. unskilled, skilled, supervisory, managerial. The vertical feature refers to the relationship between agents who are members of *different* categories. The vertical feature may, *but not necessarily always*, create a hierarchical ordering of the relationships between the categories.

We can generate the following relationships between the primary agents of production in terms of the principle of their classification.

Very strong classification $(++C)$
The primary act is the result of an *isolated* agent.
The *unit* is an isolated agent.

Strong classification $(+C)$
The primary act is the result of *related* agents within a category; e.g. a group of workers who are members of a common category. The *unit* is a group.

Less strong classification (C)
The primary act is the result of *related agents between adjacent categories*.
The *unit* is a team of workers: unskilled, semi-skilled, various skilled.

Weak classification $(-C)$
The primary act is the result of *integrated agents across categories*. The *unit* entails an integration of workers of various skills, and levels of supervision/management in policy and practice of production.

Now, if we put together the nature of the primary act in terms of its framing (divisive/integrated) and the form of the relation between agents in terms of the principle of their classification (isolated/integrated), we can obtain at least five forms of regulation of the basic unit of production.

Codes of production

(1) Isolated agents; divisive act. $++C$ $++F$
(2) Related agents *within* a category; divisive act. $+C$ $+F$
(3) Related agents *between adjacent* categories;
     integrated act. C $-F$

184 CHANGES IN THE CODING OF EDUCATIONAL TRANSMISSIONS

(4) Integrated agents *across* categories; divisive act. $-C$ $+F$
(5) Integrated agents *across* categories; integrated
      act. $-C$ $-F$

We can now identify four forms of ideological control over the mode of production in class societies.

We can identify a historical process in the development of these production codes, from entrepreneurial to corporate capitalism, from code 1 to code 3. We would argue that codes 4 and 5 would constitute a qualitative change in the production code were they to be *fully* implemented and *generalized* throughout the system of production. A necessary condition for this would be a change in the dominant cultural category—that is a change in class structure. In capitalist societies, in the same way as we noted the relation between class (as the dominant cultural category) and the codes of education, we can note the relation between class and the codes of production.

We could link theories of control, which both legitimize and provide a scientific basis for the exploitation of production, to the codes.

(1) We might connect Taylorism with (1).
(2) We might connect the Human Relation School with (2).
(3) We might connect the Socio-Technical System theory with (3).
(4) We might connect industrial democracy as a worker-based theory in opposition to the others.

Further, we could broadly distinguish between two qualitatively different production codes, strongly and weakly classified. It is relevant to point out that there are as yet few even isolated examples of integrated production (weakly classified) in the West.

We can now return to our question of the relationships between the mode of education and the mode of production. To do this, we shall have to ask the question in terms of the form of regulation of the act of educational acquisition (C/Fs) and the form of regulation (C/Fs) of the act of production. Further, we must do this separately for different agents of production (levels of skill, technology, supervision, management, administration). As soon as we consider, in these terms, the relationships between the mode of education and the mode of education under conditions of advanced capitalism, the more complex they become to unravel in detail, although in general one can find at different levels a broad correspondence, but also apparent contradictions. For example, there has been a general movement, certainly in England, towards a relaxing of the Cs and Fs which regulate secondary-school transmissions to the 'less able' pupils, and a similar relaxing for all pupils at the primary stage. However, the regulation of the primary unit of production to which these secondary students are destined is $++C + +F$. The elite curriculum (academic) of the secondary school is regulated by $+Cs$ and $+Fs$, *irrespective* of the regulation of the unit of production. This contradiction between the regulation of education and production in the case of the 'less able' student is an indication of the relative autonomy of education, or its relative independence of production. In general, however, there is correspondence between the dominant educational code *collection* and the dominant code of production; that is, between the strong, hierarchically based classification of education and the strong, hierarchically based classification of the mode of production. A society of some considerable interest in this respect is Sweden. We can note here that there is a pronounced attempt to de-classify, employ weak framing, realized by an invisible pedagogy in education ($-C -F$), and an attempt towards integrated agents/divisive act ($-C +F$) in the mode of production. Further, there are signs that industrial training is moving towards an invisible pedagogy. We should remember that, irrespective of the correspondences or contradictions between the regulation of the mode of education and the mode of production, the class basis of the social relationships of the division of labour is still reproduced. Further, whatever the dominant educational code, the middle class are much more likely to possess the means of its appropriation and reproduction (see *note (a)*).

Aspects of the relationship between education and production

We shall now consider, in terms of the principle of its classification, the relationships between the category education and the category production.

Education is a class-allocatory device, socially creating, maintaining and reproducing non-specialized and specialized skills, and specialized dispositions which have an *approximate* relevance to the mode of production. Whereas the device may be highly efficient in regulating the class basis of the social relations of the mode of production, education may and does create contradictions and discrepancies with reference to:

(a) the relationships between the distribution of the categories it creates and the distribution of the required categories of the mode of production;

(b) the relationships *between the categories* it creates and the relationships *between the categories* required by the mode of production;

(c) the realization of its categories (skills and dispositions) and the expected realizations of the categories of the mode of production.

We shall say that (a), (b) and (c) constitute the *systemic* relationships between education and the mode of production. This refers to the role of education in its approximate reproduction of the work force. The state, historically, has gained increasing control over the *systemic* relationships whilst maintaining the educational system in its essential role as a class distributor of the social relationships of production.[4] The class-based distribution of power and modalities of control are made substantive in the form of transmission/acquisition *irrespective* of variations in the systematic relationships between the modes of education and production. In this way, the educational system maintains the dominating principle of the social structure.

It is clear that the *systemic* relationships between education and production create for education the form of its economic or material base. In this way, the mode of production is anterior to the mode of education. Further, the strong classification between producers and reproducers of knowledge (between researchers and teachers in schools) parallels the strong classification between the dominating and dominated categories of the mode of production. The strong classification between the producers and reproducers of knowledge also ensures that the *recontextualizing* of knowledge; that is, the creation of textbooks, etc. for schools, is carried out by *reproducers*, not producers. In this way, the concept of, and production of, science in schools may be different from the concept of, and production of, scientific activity shared by researchers. Further, as we have indicated before, there are parallels (approximate correspondences) between the controls on the context of production and controls on the context of acquisition in education. These parallels in structures and contexts indicate the approximate or relative correspondence between education and production, establish the causal direction and show the form of the material basis of education.

We have argued that the systemic relationships between education and production constitute both the class and the material basis of education. Inasmuch as this is the case, this relation indicates the dependency of education upon the mode of production. However, we shall also argue that education is relatively independent, or relatively autonomous of production.

Initially, when education as a specialized and separate agency was constituted in Europe (Durkheim, 1938), it was subordinate to the church. The conflict during the pre-industrial period centred upon the independence of education from the church. The autonomy of education from the church was followed by the increasing dependency of education on the mode of production, and thus on the state. If we examine this dependency more closely, we can note the following:

(1) The hierarchical features of the school, the gradual separation and distinctiveness of specialized forms of discourse, the valued attributes of acquirers, were already constituted *before* entrepreneurial capitalism. These features were not created by capitalism, but they took on a new significance in the disciplining of an appropriate proletariat amenable to factory discipline.

(2) We have previously argued that there is a contradiction, at least in England, between the regulation on the 'less able' student $(-C -F)$ in education, and the regulation of the unit of production $(++C ++F)$. This indicates an independence of education from production in the area of regulation. Further, the school, rather than equipping the worker with appropriate attitudes and discipline, may indirectly and unwittingly provide a range of countervailing strategies. A $+C +F$ educational code is likely to create countervailing strategies in the pupil; e.g. fixing pupil-based production norms, resistance to discipline, avoidance techniques, implicit and possibly explicit sabotage of the means of education, operating just on the margin of acceptable conduct.[5]

(3) We would further argue that only a small fraction of the output of education bears a *direct* relation to the mode of production in terms of the appropriateness of skill and disposition.

(4) It could be argued that today the dispositions appropriate to the mode of production are already socially constituted in the family.

We therefore do not accept entirely Bowles and Gintis's argument, as this relates to the correspondence between dispositions valued in the school and the dispositions required by agents of the work force in capitalist societies. We agree that the school may well *legitimize* values and attitudes relevant to the mode of production, but this does not mean that these are so internalized as to constitute *specific personalities*. Consider various forms of industrial action over the last hundred years. The school in this respect is highly inefficient in creating a docile, deferential and subservient work force. The school today has difficulty in disciplining its pupils.

The classification of production and education

We shall suggest that the crucial relation between education and production is the strength of the classification between these two categories. Where this classification is strong, then the principles, contexts and possibilities of education are not integrated with the contexts, processes and possibilities of production. Where the classification is weak, the principles, contexts and possibilities of production are integrated with the principles, contexts and possibilities of education. Under such conditions, education is a crucial integrator of the social relationships of work, learning and research. Where the classification is strong, work (production) and 'knowledge' (education) are insulated from each other. It is crucial to distinguish between the *systemic* relationships of education and production and the *principle of the classification* between education and production. Indeed, we are told that education is for 'life', for the 'mind', for 'leisure', for the development of the 'self'. This is the language realized by a strong classification, of the relation between education and production. *We shall define the relative autonomy of education in terms of the strength of the classification between the category education and the category production.*

We have made a distinction between:
(1) The *classification* of the categories education and production.
(2) The *systemic* relationships between education and production.
On this basis we can distinguish at least between:
(a) strong classification and simple systemic relationships (nineteenth-century entrepreneurial capitalism);
(b) strong classification and extended systemic relationships (twentieth-century capitalism);
(c) weak classification and extended systemic relationships (China, Romania, Cuba).

Further, we can have, and do have, strong classification with *extended* systemic relationships in social structures with different dominating cultural categories. Thus we can change from:
(1) simple to extended systemic relationships;

(2) private property as the dominant cultural category of the
     social structure to various forms of collective property *without
     the strength of the classification between the category education
     and production undergoing fundamental disturbances.*

This suggests that we can make a fundamental distinction between
societies where education no longer possesses relative autonomy
(weak classification of the relations between education and production) and societies where education *does* possess relative
autonomy (strong classification of the relation between education
and production). We can make a further crucial distinction between
societies where the production code is integrated ($-$C) and where the
production code is divisive ($+$C). In the former, we have a fundamental difference, a radical change in the dominant cultural category.
Further, we can consider the relationships between the production
codes and the education codes in terms of their correspondence.
On this basis we do have cases where there has been a radical change
in the mode of production ($-$C) and so in the dominant cultural
category, a major reduction in the autonomy of education, but *no*
correspondence in the code of production and the codes of education.
In this situation, we have an educational code $+$C $+$F as a preparation for at least a $-$C production code.[6] This raises the fundamental question of whether the integration of education with production (reducing the autonomy of education) is for the purpose of
increasing the efficiency of production and so raising the material
level of the society, or it is intended to change the *social* relations
of production. This is not the place to consider this possible contradiction, Our aim is to show that the analysis we have been developing
can be applied to societies with very different dominant cultural categories. We are also raising the question of whether there are any
features of the relative autonomy of education in Western capitalist
societies which apply to societies with very different dominating
cultural categories but where education occupies a *similar* structural
relation.

Relative autonomy of education

We shall now examine some implications of the relative autonomy of
education. In this situation the principles, contexts and possibilities
of production are not directly constituted in the principles, contexts
and possibilities of education. Education, that is, is not directly in

rapport with a material base, although it is affected by such a base. Here the principle or form of transmission of education is related only indirectly to a material base. That is, there is an attenuation of the relationships between the symbolic structures of education and its material base. (A parallel with the relationships between the base and the superstructure.)

The relative autonomy of education gives to its values an apparent autonomy; the appearance of objectivity, of neutrality, and at the same time, of altruistic purpose and dedication. And these become the attributes of its superior agents (Bourdieu and Passerson, 1970). It is not difficult to see the role of education in creating, disseminating and legitimating the professional ethic. The relative autonomy of education is the basic means whereby the consciousness of the agents of symbolic control is legitimatized ánd maintained and, in co-operation with the family, reproduced. We consider this attenuation (the indirect relation of education to a material base) the crucial fundamental ideological message of the educational system. The *expression of the message* reflects the social group who have appropriated the forms of educational transmission. Thus, historically, the message may be realized in the concept of the gentleman, the cultivated man, the autonomy of self or mind, the independence of thought from a material basis. In more contemporary terms, education for life, education for leisure, education for personal autonomy. Always education is about discipline, but that which is subject to the discipline, and the *form* of the discipline, varies historically. The condition has remained unchanged; strong classification between the category education and the category production.

In its original form, the school contained the contradiction between faith and reason. After nearly 1,000 years, this contradiction is institutionalized in the form of the contradiction between intrinsic and extrinsic features of education. The intrinsic features refer to education as structurally distinct and separate from production with distinct and separate values.[7] The extrinsic features refer to what we have called the *systemic* relationships with production. This socially constituted division between the sacred and profane is integral to the form and process of cultural reproduction instituted in education. That which constitutes the sacred takes on a different expression in different historical periods. *Plus ça change, plus c'est la même chose.*

Class and the dual educational message

The ruling class—that is, those who dominate production by deciding its means, contexts and possibilities—have necessarily a direct relation to production but an *indirect* relation to education, in particular, and cultural reproduction in general. *And this relationship determines the particular significance of the educational code for their experience.* This group is concerned with:

(1) the systemic relation between education and production;
(2) maintaining the class basis of the social relations of production.

They are *essentially* concerned with perpetuating the relationships between the principles of classification and the dominant cultural category. In general, these interests are realized in attempts to influence and control the state. Explicitly, this class regulate directly the codes of production but are related only indirectly to the codes of education.

Within the middle class (those who have appropriated access to, and control over, specialized forms of communication) we have distinguished those whose function is directly related to the mode of production and those who function in the various agencies of cultural reproduction. That is we have distinguished between those who are categories of the social division of labour of production and those who are categories of the social division of labour of symbolic control. Now it follows that the latter fraction has a *direct* relation to cultural reproduction but an *indirect* relation to production. This fraction enjoys a relative autonomy of production in the constituting of principles, contexts and possibilities of cultural reproduction *and* in the constituting and disseminating of its codes of transmission. This fraction accepts (at different historical periods, with different degrees of ambivalence) the basic principles of the classification and is essentially concerned with the relationships between the *principles* of control and the dominant cultural category. And this relationship determines the particular significance of the educational code for its experience.[8] We are arguing that there is a division between dominating power (production) and dominating control (cultural reproduction) and that *the former limits the latter.*

The structural relationships between symbolic control and production is parallel to the relationships between education and production. That is, education is dependent upon production but also possesses a specific independence or *relative* autonomy in the constituting of its codes. We are arguing, like others, that the location in the class structure of the agents of symbolic control is an ambiguous one and *is a structural parallel to the ambiguous relation between education and production*. The stronger the systemic relationships of education, the stronger the grip of the mode of production on the codes of education and the more direct the relation between the material base and the codings of education. Education no longer has a problem of relevance, but it is the relevance created by the mode of production (see *note (b)*). On the other hand, the forms historically taken by the relative autonomy of education become a distinguishing feature of the mental structures of the agents of symbolic control which is constituted, legitimized and reproduced by the transmission codes of education which are regulated by these self-same agents. This becomes something like a chicken-and-egg problem. A solution is to see that an arena is constituted by the strength of the classification between education and production which makes available the basis for variations in modalities of control whose origins lie outside education, but which are institutionalized, coded and generalized by the educational systems. Thus, if the systemic relations of education are strengthened, then this increases the penetration of power relationships into education. If relative autonomy is preserved or strengthened, then it reduces the direct penetration of power (production) but maintains the power *indirectly* through forms of middle-class control realized in the codes of education. The middle class are specialists in the theory, practice and dissemination of symbolic control. Their development and internal ideological differentiation have their origins in the development and internal differentiation of capitalism. The theories they develop are selectively incorporated in the codes of production and in this way they become features of the systemic relationships between education and production as elements of business studies and management training.

Finally, different contradictions arise out of differences in the relationship between the classificatory and systemic relationships of education in different historical periods and in social structures with different dominating categories.

We have noted the significance of the relation between education and production for the formation and reproduction of the consciousness of that fraction of the middle class who function as agents of cultural reproduction. We can raise the question of whether the integration of the principles, contexts and possibilities of education and production will change that consciousness and its social basis. Presumably weakening the classification between education and production should also blur the definition of worker; a crucial category in socialist societies. Inasmuch as teachers, researchers, etc. are now also producers, it would seem that the traditional opposition between the categories intellectual and worker should be resolved. Under conditions of strong classification of the relation between education and production, the categories, worker and intellectual, are sharply distinguishable and so is the social basis of their consciousness. The disappearance of the category, intellectual, is brought about by widening the area and penetration of explicit social control in which *education is a crucial ideological force*. (We should also consider the agencies of youth.) In China and Romania such movements are proceeding; more established in China than Romania. In both societies there is a conflict between raising the material base (increasing the gross national product) and changing the social relationships of production. In such societies there is, on the one hand, a pressure to transform an agrarian into an industrial base and, on the other, an ideological imperative to transform the social relationships of production. However, if the dominating pressure is efficiency (linked, of course, to economic self-determination), then it is difficult to see how education can become a crucial ideological force, because the above conditions are likely to lead to an increase in bureaucratic and technological control which it is unlikely that education will escape. If education cannot play the rôle required, then how is the consciousness required to create and maintain the transformation of the social relations of production to be generated?

Note (a)

Class and the acquisition of educational codes

Appropriation of the means of education entails successful socialization into the dual messages which underlie and are realized in its codes of transmission. From this perspective we can gain a further understanding of the origins and reproduction of restricted and elaborated sociolinguistic codes in the family. Briefly, according to the theory, restricted codes realize context-dependent principles and meanings. The principles and meanings are embedded in local contexts, in local social relationships, practices, activities. To this extent they are relatively strongly related to a *specific* material base. Elaborated codes realize context-independent meanings through the media of explicit principles. These explicit principles and meanings are less embedded in a local context, in local social relationships, practices, activities. To this extent the principles and meanings are less related, indeed related only indirectly, to a specific material base. Now inasmuch as these principles and meanings are indirectly related to a specific material base, such explicit principles and meanings become objects of special significance in their own right, and become a means of identity, relevance and achievement.

If we now look at the hypothesized relationships between familial socio-linguistic codes and social class, then the children of the middle class will receive a transmission where the realizations (the codings) have an indirect relation to a specific material base as a consequence of the families' structural relation to the mode of production and the parents' experience of the class-regulated educational codes. These children become sensitive to, incorporate as crucially relevant, principles which construct texts that are related only indirectly to a specific material base. Further, they become sensitive to the social relationships which induce, regulate and call for such realizations, codings or texts, either in the family or the school. We must again point out that the familial socio-linguistic code orients the child to the relevance of the systemic relationships between education and production *and* to the classificatory relationships between education and production; that is to both the dependent and the relatively autonomous relationships between education and production. The systemic relationships translate into the motivation of the child towards education, irrespective of its immediate relevance or the level of the child's performance. The relative autonomous relationship translates into the child's orientation towards the context-independent meanings of the educational codes and to the social relationships which constitute and regulate the transmission of its specific texts. Social class creates a fundamental correspondence between familial and educational codes.

In the case of the lower-working-class child we would argue that the realizations of the transmission are more directly related to a material base as a consequence of the families' structural relation to the mode of production and to the parents' experience of education. These children would be more likely to become sensitive to, incorporate as *initially* relevant, principles and meanings more directly related to a specific material base, that is to a restricted code. However, as we have argued repeatedly, the educational code, its form and content, its sequencing rules, pacing and content may and often do invalidate the experience and consciousness the children bring to the school. The school discounts the experience of the child, to be followed by the child discounting the experience of the school. It may well be for the lower-working-class child or pupil, relative to the middle-class child or pupil, that the dominant message of the educational code is that constituted by the *internal* classificatory features of the code *rather* than by the specific pedagogic feature, i.e. its framing. If this is the case, then the lower-working-class child is not able to appropriate the means to produce what counts as legitimate texts but the pupil is made aware of the power relationships which underpin the classificatory features *and* his/her place within them. Here we can identify a major source of resistance and challenge on the part of such pupils. These hypotheses may help us to understand some of the results of the SRU research:

(1) If we consider verbal IQ tests, middle-class children are oriented to offering context-independent meanings in that context, and score high; lower-working-class children, who are oriented to context-dependent meanings, score *low*.

(2) When children were asked in a formal experimental context to describe, explain or instruct, our research shows that when we control for verbal IQ, middle-class children, relative to lower-working-class children of seven years of age, are much more likely to produce speech realizing context-independent meanings.

(3) In a situation where children aged eight had to group photographs of food common to both classes, middle-class children were much more likely to group them according to a taxonomic principle, and lower-working-class children were more likely to group them according to their everyday relationships (eggs and bacon, fish fingers and chips). The experiment was designed in such a way so as to encourage the children to switch the principle of their groupings, and a number of lower-working-class children did switch to a taxomatic principle.

Now when we look at the instructions given to the children, we can note that they are often of a very general, open kind, e.g. 'What is going on in the picture?' 'Can you tell somebody how to play "X" who doesn't know how to play?' 'Can you put the pictures together the way you think they go together? You can use all of the pictures, or just some of them.' In the language we have used here, the instruction is regulated apparently by weak classification and weak framing. What appears to happen is something like this. The middle-class child does not accept the instruction in terms of a request for a $-C$ $-F$ regulated response ('Do it in any way you like' ($-C$) and 'Talk about it in any way you want' ($-F$)). On the contrary, the child interprets it as requiring a response regulated by $+C$ $+Fs$ ('Do it *one* way and talk about it in a *particular* way'). Thus when he/she is talking about the picture cards, the child uses not a narrative form but explicit speech to describe, often very accurately, what he/she takes to be the objective feature of the picture according to criteria of true/false. The child does not attempt to relate the details in the picture to his/her own life, practice or activities. When these children give the rules of a game, they, more often than the lower-working-class children, attempt to give the rules abstracted from any local context. In the same way, the middle-class children, relative to the lower-working-class children, grouped the food items according to the principles of a taxonomy rather than according to their associations in meals of various kinds. We believe that what we are witnessing here has little to do with the 'measured intelligence' of the children, but is the result of a communication code in which symbolic realizations are *indirectly* related to a material base, which directs the child in certain contexts to *select* a performance rule which creates a context-independent text. In other words, the middle-class child is aware that the adult does not require the response that the instruction at the surface level is apparently calling for. The lower-working-class child on the other hand interprets the instruction at its *surface value* ($-C$ $-F$) and so creates a context-dependent text. If such an explanation is correct, then it also shows how class relations penetrate familial transmission but not in any final or irrevocable form. Indeed, it shows the social basis of what are often considered to be 'abstract cognitions'. And inasmuch as it does this, it points both to potential *and* to its class regulation.

Finally, as I have stated elsewhere, the sequencing rules of educational transmissions, the pacing of the transmission (the rate of expected acquisition), its future relevance and its immediate irrelevance are, to say the least, based upon performance rules which the middle-class child embryonically possesses. Class regulates the elaborated codes of education and in the family. However, if we start from the view that all children possess common competence, are eager to find out about their world and control it, we might come to understand the social basis of differences in children's *performances*, how performances are socially constituted, how and why some are legitimized and others not, which might then create conditions for change, at least in education.

Note (b)

The issue here is which features of the codes are affected: the classificatory or the framing features or both. It is crucial to know why the systemic features are being strengthened; that is the nature of the economic and social conditions. Under deteriorating economic conditions we would expect:

(a) Classification: (1) a reduction in the number of discourse categories (subjects);
(2) a change in their hierarchical relationships and a shift from pure to applied categories;
(3) an increase in the strength of the classification between transmitters and between acquirers.

(b) Framing: (1) an increase in the strength of sequencing rules;
(2) an increase in the pacing of the transmission;
(3) an increase in the explicitness of criteria.

In other words, a general increase in the strength of classification and framing and a reduction in the number of variants. This will make more explicit and strengthen all hierarchical features, reduce the economic costs of the transmission, perhaps alter the distribution of the various outputs of the educational system *and* tighten the grip of the state upon educational agencies. We might hypothesize that movements to weaken classification and framing (relatively expensive codes) are more likely to develop under conditions of relatively full employment. To strengthen the systemic relations does not constitute an *integration* of education and production but strengthens the regulation of education by the state. Indeed the concept of an educational system as itself a producer is possible only where the profit motive has been abolished. Consider that the production of goods by prisoners is carefully regulated so as not to compete with industrial products. The integration of education with production as a crucial means of transforming the social relations of the division of labour requires a change in the dominant cultural category. At a fundamental level, the relative autonomy of education may well be a constituent feature of class societies.

Note (c)

On imposition, provocation and change

Now we have argued that class relationships determine the principle of the distribution of power and the modalities of control. How? The principle of the distribution of power is made substantive in the principle of the classification which in turn creates the social division of labour of education and production. The modality of control is made substantive in the principle of the framing, which determines the social relations within production, the rules of communication and so their realizations which then regulate consciousness. From this point of view, the reproduction of class relationships is effected through the codes of transmission. These codes may be written formally in terms of the *values of and relationships between classification and framing*. (See Figure 8.2, which sets out diagrammatically the basic relationships. The codes are constituted by the relations and values of classification and framing through which power and control are made substantive at the level of consciousness and which give the latter its distinctive features. The model holds both for production and education and their relation to each other.)

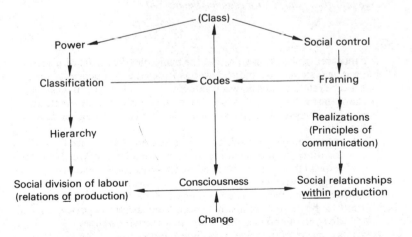

Figure 8.2   The dominating cultural category

Let us look briefly at the relationships between power and control (that is, classification and framing) in terms of change. We shall take our example from *education*, remembering that classification refers to the principle of the relationships between *categories* and framing to the public regulation on communication.

Classification regulates the relationships between (1) agencies, (2) agents, (3) discourse, (4) practices, (5) acts. Now if framing weakens and the classification remains unchanged, then at some point the classification will be challenged because the relationships between categories will be challenged. At that point, power will be exerted to retain the classification. Changes in framing will at some point challenge the principle of the classification and so the power relationships which it is transmitting. *We must distinguish whether a change in the classification and framing is imposed or provoked*, because the ideological significance will depend upon whether it is the result of imposition or provocation. Consider education. If the Schools Council wishes to weaken Cs and Fs, then the ideological significance may well be different from a desire to weaken Cs and Fs on the part of, say, rank-and-file teachers. In other words, the apparent weakening of Cs and Fs may simply indicate *a change in the modality of control*, rather than a major change in the distribution of power. Consider production. A firm may decide to weaken the Cs and Fs which regulate the process. Workers may also be concerned to weaken the Cs and Fs. The ideological interests, however, may be very different. The former case may be more a change in the modality of control; the latter may represent an attempt to change the distribution of power. Consider the move towards integrated educational codes at the secondary level. Such a move may be supported by both the political right and left, but for different reasons. One way to decide the significance of a weakening of Cs and Fs is to consider the relationships between the categories which have undergone a change and *those which have remained unaltered*.

Notes

1   We must remember, however, that the principle of classification creates a message system which indirectly constitutes the experiences of the pupil. The relationships between categories is itself a crucial message, perhaps the most crucial if these come to be considered inevitable and legitimate. Consider that in a strongly classified educational code we will find:

 (a)   insulation between subjects, the creation of specialized identities, their explicit hierarchical organization, which creates a social division of labour of *both* the transmission and acquisition of knowledge.

 (b)   a concept of *progression* in time (five years, six years, seven years old; boys, girls are distinct specialized social categories; a social division of knowledge and competence within time).

 (c)   a concept of sacred and profane knowledge.

Power is never more eloquent and penetrating than in the insulation it produces between categories. From this point of view, research which focuses upon communication within a classroom (that is, upon framing) misses entirely the complex messages transmitted *indirectly* by the principle of classification.

2 Framing regulates not only *what and how* the knowledge is to be communicated by the pupil but also the procedures and processes of evaluation (assessment).

3 See 'On the classification and framing of educational knowledge', chapter 5 of this book.

4 One of the solutions to the problem of creating an adequate work force under conditions of advanced capitalism is the acceptance of a meritocratic ideology of education.

5 It is possible that education is relatively more successful in the *constituting* of specific personalities only in the case of high-level agents of reproduction, whereas for manual workers it is rather more *regulative* of the expression of, than constituting, the personality.

6 Here we have a situation where the educational context is non-participatory as a preparation for a participatory work context.

7 It is clear that education is regulated and limited by the state, which is a dominating centre of conflicting interests. The form the regulation takes varies. For example in England there is *as yet* relatively little direct regulation of the content (except for religion) or regulation of the forms of transmission, whereas (for example in Sweden) certainly the content and to some extent the form of transmission is centrally directed. It is important to note that *relative autonomy* as used in this paper does *not* refer to the relations between education and the state. That is, it does not refer to the degree of delegation which constitutes in Althusserian terms a 'space'. It refers to a crucial relationship between education and production *and* the consequences of this relationship for the creation of, and variations in, educational codes, which are considered as constituting the ambiguous consciousness of agents of cultural reproduction. The ambiguity of the relationships between education and production repeats itself in the identity, values and interests of agents of cultural reproduction. The history of this fraction of the middle class reveals the archaeology of their consciousness. Thus we can find today the ideology of the old middle class : *radical individualism*, the *meritocratic* ideology of the socially mobile necessary for their access to the educational system, the ideology of *radical personalizing* celebrating the apparent release of the person from the structure which, we have argued, informs the shift towards weakening classification and framing.

8 From this point of view we would argue that, for the ruling class— those who dominate the principles, contexts and possibilities of production—their consciousness is less dominated by the mode of education but is constituted essentially by the *mode of production*. In the same way we consider that the consciousness of the working class, especially the lower working class, is less dominated by the mode of education but is essentially constituted by the mode of production.

However, and in contrast, the consciousness of the agents of symbolic control is directly constituted by the mode of education and *indirectly* constituted by the mode of production. Here again we can see crucial differences in the location of the structuring of consciousness of this fraction of the middle class which regulate its relationships to both the ruling class and the working class. This difference may create as a distinguishing feature of its consciousness a primary focus upon the principles of social control rather than a primary focus upon the principles of the distribution of power.

References

ALTHUSSER, L. (1971), 'Ideology and the ideological state apparatus', in *Lenin and Philosophy* (trans. B. Brewster), New Left Books.

BERNSTEIN, B. (1977), Introduction to *Code in Context*, Diana S. Adlam *et al.*, Routledge & Kegan Paul.

BOURDIEU, P. and PASSERON, J. C. (1970), *La Réproduction: éléments pour une théorie du système d'enseignement*, Paris: Éditions de Minuit.

BOWLES, S. and GINTIS, H. (1976), *Schooling in Capitalist America*, London: Routledge & Kegan Paul; New York: Basic Books.

DURKHEIM, É. (1938), *L'Évolution pedagogique en France*, Paris: Alcan.

VLASCEANU, L. (1976), 'Decision and Innovation in the Romanian Educational System: a theoretical exploration of teachers' orientation', Ph.D. thesis, University of London.

Acknowledgments

I would like to acknowledge the value of discussions with Lazar Vlasceanu, Daniel Kallos and Staf Callewaert on the problems of the integration of education with production. I am also most grateful to Madeleine MacDonald for a critical reading of the first draft of this chapter.

Index

Adelstein, David, 112
Adlam, Diana, 26
aesthetics, 119, 125, 139, 169–70
age grouping, 37–8, 55–9, 61, 65, 69, 75, 114, 118, 135, 140, 178
Althusser, Louis, 174, 199
Anderson, C. A., 164
anti-school peer group, 39, 45–6
approaches, sociological, 20, 157–8, 166–8, 171
architecture, 70, 72, 134, 139–40
art studies, 148, 170
assessment, *see* pedagogy, evaluation

Banks, O., 164
Berger, P., 167, 169
Bernstein Basil, 85; *et al.*, 40, 51
biological theories, 122, 125–6, 166
Blacks, 29, 163
Bourdieu, Pierre, 14–15, 17, 100, 125, 128, 146, 149, 174; and Passeron, J. C., 190
Bowles, S. and Gintis, H., 174, 187
Brandis, W., 32, 112
Brierley, Molly, 132
Britain: liberalism, 29; middle class, 18; public schools, 18; sociology in, 168; sociology of education in, 17, 85, 160–4, 169; student protest, 169; universities, 64, 166; *see also* England; Scotland
bureaucratization, 5, 55, 63–5, 158, 193

Burns, T. and Stalker, G. M., 19

Cage, John, 148, 169
Callewaert, S., 200
capitalism, 127, 131, 181, 184, 187, 188–9, 192, 199
Centre de Sociologie Européenne, 14–15, 146
Chelsea Centre for Science Education, 100
China, 188, 193
Chomsky, Noam, 123
church and education, 58, 74, 128–9, 187, 190
class, social: and code, 22–4, 26–31, 145–6, 175, 178, 184, 191–4, 196–7; definition, viii, 175; and division of labour, 185–6; and educational knowledge, 13, 164–5; and English studies, 170; and family-school relations, 43; and the instrumental order, 38–9; and organic solidarity, 18; and pedagogies, viii, 21, 124–5, 135–7, 139; and play, 122; and pupil role, 44, 49; reproduction of relations, 1, 16, 32, 131, 144, 149, 174; and social control, 11, 14, 170, 181
classification and framing (Cs and Fs), 6–7, 8–12, 86, 169; of aesthetic experience, 170; in education, viii, 21, 24, 30, 184–5, 199; between education and

Routledge Social Science Series

Routledge & Kegan Paul   London, Henley and Boston

39 Store Street, London WC1E 7DD
Broadway House, Newtown Road, Henley-on-Thames,
Oxon RG9 1EN
9 Park Street, Boston, Mass. 02108

Contents

Authors wishing to submit manuscripts for any series in
this catalogue should send them to the Social Science Editor,
Routledge & Kegan Paul Ltd, 39 Store Street,
London WC1E 7DD

● *Books so marked are available in paperback*
All books are in Metric Demy 8vo format (216 × 138mm approx.)

International Library of Sociology

General Editor John Rex

GENERAL SOCIOLOGY

Barnsley, J. H. The Social Reality of Ethics. *464 pp.*
Belshaw, Cyril. The Conditions of Social Performance. *An Exploratory Theory. 144 pp.*
Brown, Robert. Explanation in Social Science. *208 pp.*
● Rules and Laws in Sociology. *192 pp.*
Bruford, W. H. Chekhov and His Russia. *A Sociological Study. 244 pp.*
Cain, Maureen E. Society and the Policeman's Role. *326 pp.*
●**Fletcher, Colin.** Beneath the Surface. *An Account of Three Styles of Sociological Research. 221 pp.*
Gibson, Quentin. The Logic of Social Enquiry. *240 pp.*
Glucksmann, M. Structuralist Analysis in Contemporary Social Thought. *212 pp.*
Gurvitch, Georges. Sociology of Law. *Preface by Roscoe Pound. 264 pp.*
Hodge, H. A. Wilhelm Dilthey. *An Introduction. 184 pp.*
Homans, George C. Sentiments and Activities. *336 pp.*
Johnson, Harry M. Sociology: *a Systematic Introduction. Foreword by Robert K. Merton. 710 pp.*
●**Keat, Russell,** and **Urry, John.** Social Theory as Science. *278 pp.*
Mannheim, Karl. Essays on Sociology and Social Psychology. *Edited by Paul Keckskemeti. With Editorial Note by Adolph Lowe. 344 pp.*
Systematic Sociology: *An Introduction to the Study of Society. Edited by J. S. Erös and Professor W. A. C. Stewart. 220 pp.*
Martindale, Don. The Nature and Types of Sociological Theory. *292 pp.*
●**Maus, Heinz.** A Short History of Sociology. *234 pp.*
Mey, Harald. Field-Theory. *A Study of its Application in the Social Sciences. 352 pp.*
Myrdal, Gunnar. Value in Social Theory: *A Collection of Essays on Methodology. Edited by Paul Streeten. 332 pp.*
Ogburn, William F., and **Nimkoff, Meyer F.** A Handbook of Sociology. *Preface by Karl Mannheim. 656 pp. 46 figures. 35 tables.*
Parsons, Talcott, and **Smelser, Neil J.** Economy and Society: *A Study in the Integration of Economic and Social Theory. 362 pp.*
Podgórecki, Adam. Practical Social Sciences. *About 200 pp.*
●**Rex, John.** Key Problems of Sociological Theory. *220 pp.*
Sociology and the Demystification of the Modern World. *282 pp.*
●**Rex, John** (Ed.) Approaches to Sociology. *Contributions by Peter Abell, Frank Bechhofer, Basil Bernstein, Ronald Fletcher, David Frisby, Miriam Glucksmann, Peter Lassman, Herminio Martins, John Rex, Roland Robertson, John Westergaard and Jock Young. 302 pp.*
Rigby, A. Alternative Realities. *352 pp.*
Roche, M. Phenomenology, Language and the Social Sciences. *374 pp.*

Sahay, A. Sociological Analysis. *220 pp.*
Simirenko, Alex (Ed.) Soviet Sociology. *Historical Antecedents and Current Appraisals. Introduction by Alex Simirenko. 376 pp.*
Strasser, Hermann. The Normative Structure of Sociology. *Conservative and Emancipatory Themes in Social Thought. About 340 pp.*
Urry, John. Reference Groups and the Theory of Revolution. *244 pp.*
Weinberg, E. Development of Sociology in the Soviet Union. *173 pp.*

FOREIGN CLASSICS OF SOCIOLOGY

●**Durkheim, Emile.** Suicide. *A Study in Sociology. Edited and with an Introduction by George Simpson. 404 pp.*
●**Gerth, H. H.,** and **Mills, C. Wright.** From Max Weber: *Essays in Sociology. 502 pp.*
●**Tönnies, Ferdinand.** Community and Association. (*Gemeinschaft und Gesellschaft.*) *Translated and Supplemented by Charles P. Loomis. Foreword by Pitirim A. Sorokin. 334 pp.*

SOCIAL STRUCTURE

Andreski, Stanislav. Military Organization and Society. *Foreword by Professor A. R. Radcliffe-Brown. 226 pp. 1 folder.*
Carlton, Eric. Ideology and Social Order. *Preface by Professor Philip Abrahams. About 320 pp.*
Coontz, Sydney H. Population Theories and the Economic Interpretation. *202 pp.*
Coser, Lewis. The Functions of Social Conflict. *204 pp.*
Dickie-Clark, H. F. Marginal Situation: *A Sociological Study of a Coloured Group. 240 pp. 11 tables.*
Glaser, Barney, and **Strauss, Anselm L.** Status Passage. *A Formal Theory. 208 pp.*
Glass, D. V. (Ed.) Social Mobility in Britain. *Contributions by J. Berent, T. Bottomore, R. C. Chambers, J. Floud, D. V. Glass, J. R. Hall, H. T. Himmelweit, R. K. Kelsall, F. M. Martin, C. A. Moser, R. Mukherjee, and W. Ziegel. 420 pp.*
Johnstone, Frederick A. Class, Race and Gold. *A Study of Class Relations and Racial Discrimination in South Africa. 312 pp.*
Jones, Garth N. Planned Organizational Change: *An Exploratory Study Using an Empirical Approach. 268 pp.*
Kelsall, R. K. Higher Civil Servants in Britain: *From 1870 to the Present Day. 268 pp. 31 tables.*
König, René. The Community. *232 pp. Illustrated.*
●**Lawton, Denis.** Social Class, Language and Education. *192 pp.*
McLeish, John. The Theory of Social Change: *Four Views Considered. 128 pp.*
Marsh, David C. The Changing Social Structure of England and Wales, 1871-1961. *288 pp.*
Menzies, Ken. Talcott Parsons and the Social Image of Man. *About 208 pp.*

●**Mouzelis, Nicos.** Organization and Bureaucracy. *An Analysis of Modern Theories. 240 pp.*

Mulkay, M. J. Functionalism, Exchange and Theoretical Strategy. *272 pp.*

Ossowski, Stanislaw. Class Structure in the Social Consciousness. *210 pp.*

●**Podgórecki, Adam.** Law and Society. *302 pp.*

Renner, Karl. Institutions of Private Law and Their Social Functions. *Edited, with an Introduction and Notes, by O. Kahn-Freud. Translated by Agnes Schwarzschild. 316 pp.*

SOCIOLOGY AND POLITICS

Acton, T. A. Gypsy Politics and Social Change. *316 pp.*

Clegg, Stuart. Power, Rule and Domination. *A Critical and Empirical Understanding of Power in Sociological Theory and Organisational Life. About 300 pp.*

Hechter, Michael. Internal Colonialism. *The Celtic Fringe in British National Development, 1536–1966. 361 pp.*

Hertz, Frederick. Nationality in History and Politics: *A Psychology and Sociology of National Sentiment and Nationalism. 432 pp.*

Kornhauser, William. The Politics of Mass Society. *272 pp. 20 tables.*

●**Kroes, R.** Soldiers and Students. *A Study of Right- and Left-wing Students. 174 pp.*

Laidler, Harry W. History of Socialism. *Social-Economic Movements: An Historical and Comparative Survey of Socialism, Communism, Co-operation, Utopianism; and other Systems of Reform and Reconstruction. 992 pp.*

Lasswell, H. D. Analysis of Political Behaviour. *324 pp.*

Martin, David A. Pacifism: *an Historical and Sociological Study. 262 pp.*

Martin, Roderick. Sociology of Power. *About 272 pp.*

Myrdal, Gunnar. The Political Element in the Development of Economic Theory. *Translated from the German by Paul Streeten. 282 pp.*

Wilson, H. T. The American Ideology. *Science, Technology and Organization of Modes of Rationality. About 280 pp.*

Wootton, Graham. Workers, Unions and the State. *188 pp.*

CRIMINOLOGY

Ancel, Marc. Social Defence: *A Modern Approach to Criminal Problems. Foreword by Leon Radzinowicz. 240 pp.*

Cain, Maureen E. Society and the Policeman's Role. *326 pp.*

Cloward, Richard A., and Ohlin, Lloyd E. Delinquency and Opportunity: *A Theory of Delinquent Gangs. 248 pp.*

Downes, David M. The Delinquent Solution. *A Study in Subcultural Theory. 296 pp.*

Dunlop, A. B., and McCabe, S. Young Men in Detention Centres. *192 pp.*

Friedlander, Kate. The Psycho-Analytical Approach to Juvenile Delinquency: *Theory, Case Studies, Treatment. 320 pp.*

Glueck, Sheldon, and Eleanor. Family Environment and Delinquency. *With the statistical assistance of Rose W. Kneznek. 340 pp.*

5

Lopez-Rey, Manuel. Crime. *An Analytical Appraisal. 288 pp.*

Mannheim, Hermann. Comparative Criminology: *a Text Book. Two volumes. 442 pp. and 380 pp.*

Morris, Terence. The Criminal Area: *A Study in Social Ecology. Foreword by Hermann Mannheim. 232 pp. 25 tables. 4 maps.*

Rock, Paul. Making People Pay. *338 pp.*

●Taylor, Ian, Walton, Paul, and Young, Jock. The New Criminology. *For a Social Theory of Deviance. 325 pp.*

●Taylor, Ian, Walton, Paul, and Young, Jock (Eds). Critical Criminology. *268 pp.*

SOCIAL PSYCHOLOGY

Bagley, Christopher. The Social Psychology of the Epileptic Child. *320 pp.*

Barbu, Zevedei. Problems of Historical Psychology. *248 pp.*

Blackburn, Julian. Psychology and the Social Pattern. *184 pp.*

●Brittan, Arthur. Meanings and Situations. *224 pp.*

Carroll, J. Break-Out from the Crystal Palace. *200 pp.*

●Fleming, C. M. Adolescence: Its Social Psychology. *With an Introduction to recent findings from the fields of Anthropology, Physiology, Medicine, Psychometrics and Sociometry. 288 pp.*

● The Social Psychology of Education: *An Introduction and Guide to Its Study. 136 pp.*

●Homans, George C. The Human Group. *Foreword by Bernard DeVoto. Introduction by Robert K. Merton. 526 pp.*

● Social Behaviour: *its Elementary Forms. 416 pp.*

●Klein, Josephine. The Study of Groups. *226 pp. 31 figures. 5 tables.*

Linton, Ralph. The Cultural Background of Personality. *132 pp.*

●Mayo, Elton. The Social Problems of an Industrial Civilization. *With an appendix on the Political Problem. 180 pp.*

Ottaway, A. K. C. Learning Through Group Experience. *176 pp.*

Plummer, Ken. Sexual Stigma. *An Interactionist Account. 254 pp.*

●Rose, Arnold M. (Ed.) Human Behaviour and Social Processes: *an Interactionist Approach. Contributions by Arnold M. Rose, Ralph H. Turner, Anselm Strauss, Everett C. Hughes, E. Franklin Frazier, Howard S. Becker, et al. 696 pp.*

Smelser, Neil J. Theory of Collective Behaviour. *448 pp.*

Stephenson, Geoffrey M. The Development of Conscience. *128 pp.*

Young, Kimball. Handbook of Social Psychology. *658 pp. 16 figures. 10 tables.*

SOCIOLOGY OF THE FAMILY

Banks, J. A. Prosperity and Parenthood: *A Study of Family Planning among The Victorian Middle Classes. 262 pp.*

Bell, Colin R. Middle Class Families: *Social and Geographical Mobility. 224 pp.*

Burton, Lindy. Vulnerable Children. *272 pp.*
Gavron, Hannah. The Captive Wife: *Conflicts of Household Mothers.*
190 pp.
George, Victor, and **Wilding, Paul.** Motherless Families. *248 pp.*
Klein, Josephine. Samples from English Cultures.
   1. Three Preliminary Studies and Aspects of Adult Life in England.
   447 pp.
   2. Child-Rearing Practices and Index. *247 pp.*
Klein, Viola. The Feminine Character. *History of an Ideology. 244 pp.*
McWhinnie, Alexina M. Adopted Children. *How They Grow Up. 304 pp.*
● **Morgan, D. H. J.** Social Theory and the Family. *About 320 pp.*
● **Myrdal, Alva,** and **Klein, Viola.** Women's Two Roles: *Home and Work.*
238 pp. 27 tables.
Parsons, Talcott, and **Bales, Robert F.** Family: Socialization and Inter-
action Process. *In collaboration with James Olds, Morris Zelditch and
Philip E. Slater. 456 pp. 50 figures and tables.*

SOCIAL SERVICES

Bastide, Roger. The Sociology of Mental Disorder. *Translated from the
French by Jean McNeil. 260 pp.*
Carlebach, Julius. Caring For Children in Trouble. *266 pp.*
George, Victor. Foster Care. *Theory and Practice. 234 pp.*
   Social Security: *Beveridge and After. 258 pp.*
George, V., and **Wilding, P.** Motherless Families. *248 pp.*
● **Goetschius, George W.** Working with Community Groups. *256 pp.*
Goetschius, George W., and **Tash, Joan.** Working with Unattached Youth.
416 pp.
Hall, M. P., and **Howes, I. V.** The Church in Social Work. *A Study of
Moral Welfare Work undertaken by the Church of England. 320 pp.*
Heywood, Jean S. Children in Care: *the Development of the Service for the
Deprived Child. 264 pp.*
Hoenig, J., and **Hamilton, Marian W.** The De-Segregation of the Mentally
Ill. *284 pp.*
Jones, Kathleen. Mental Health and Social Policy, 1845-1959. *264 pp.*
King, Roy D., Raynes, Norma V., and **Tizard, Jack.** Patterns of Residential
Care. *356 pp.*
Leigh, John. Young People and Leisure. *256 pp.*
● **Mays, John.** (Ed.) Penelope Hall's Social Services of England and Wales.
About 324 pp.
Morris, Mary. Voluntary Work and the Welfare State. *300 pp.*
Nokes, P. L. The Professional Task in Welfare Practice. *152 pp.*
Timms, Noel. Psychiatric Social Work in Great Britain (1939-1962).
280 pp.
● Social Casework: *Principles and Practice. 256 pp.*
Young, A. F. Social Services in British Industry. *272 pp.*

SOCIOLOGY OF EDUCATION

Banks, Olive. Parity and Prestige in English Secondary Education: a Study in Educational Sociology. *272 pp.*

Bentwich, Joseph. Education in Israel. *224 pp. 8 pp. plates.*

●**Blyth, W. A. L.** English Primary Education. *A Sociological Description.*
  1. Schools. *232 pp.*
  2. Background. *168 pp.*

Collier, K. G. The Social Purposes of Education: *Personal and Social Values in Education. 268 pp.*

Dale, R. R., and **Griffith, S.** Down Stream: *Failure in the Grammar School. 108 pp.*

Evans, K. M. Sociometry and Education. *158 pp.*

●**Ford, Julienne.** Social Class and the Comprehensive School. *192 pp.*

Foster, P. J. Education and Social Change in Ghana. *336 pp. 3 maps.*

Fraser, W. R. Education and Society in Modern France. *150 pp.*

Grace, Gerald R. Role Conflict and the Teacher. *150 pp.*

Hans, Nicholas. New Trends in Education in the Eighteenth Century. *278 pp. 19 tables.*

● Comparative Education: *A Study of Educational Factors and Traditions. 360 pp.*

●**Hargreaves, David.** Interpersonal Relations and Education. *432 pp.*

● Social Relations in a Secondary School. *240 pp.*

Holmes, Brian. Problems in Education. *A Comparative Approach. 336 pp.*

King, Ronald. Values and Involvement in a Grammar School. *164 pp.*

  School Organization and Pupil Involvement. *A Study of Secondary Schools.*

●**Mannheim, Karl,** and **Stewart, W. A. C.** An Introduction to the Sociology of Education. *206 pp.*

Morris, Raymond N. The Sixth Form and College Entrance. *231 pp.*

●**Musgrove, F.** Youth and the Social Order. *176 pp.*

●**Ottaway, A. K. C.** Education and Society: An Introduction to the Sociology of Education. *With an Introduction by W. O. Lester Smith. 212 pp.*

Peers, Robert. Adult Education: *A Comparative Study. 398 pp.*

Pritchard, D. G. Education and the Handicapped: *1760 to 1960. 258 pp.*

Stratta, Erica. The Education of Borstal Boys. *A Study of their Educational Experiences prior to, and during, Borstal Training. 256 pp.*

Taylor, P. H., Reid, W. A., and **Holley, B. J.** The English Sixth Form. *A Case Study in Curriculum Research. 200 pp.*

SOCIOLOGY OF CULTURE

Eppel, E. M., and **M.** Adolescents and Morality: *A Study of some Moral Values and Dilemmas of Working Adolescents in the Context of a changing Climate of Opinion. Foreword by W. J. H. Sprott. 268 pp. 39 tables.*

●**Fromm, Erich.** The Fear of Freedom. *286 pp.*

● The Sane Society. *400 pp.*

Mannheim, Karl. Essays on the Sociology of Culture. *Edited by Ernst Mannheim in co-operation with Paul Kecskemeti. Editorial Note by Adolph Lowe. 280 pp.*

Weber, Alfred. Farewell to European History: *or The Conquest of Nihilism. Translated from the German by R. F. C. Hull. 224 pp.*

SOCIOLOGY OF RELIGION

Argyle, Michael and **Beit-Hallahmi, Benjamin.** The Social Psychology of Religion. *About 256 pp.*

Glasner, Peter E. The Sociology of Secularisation. *A Critique of a Concept. About 180 pp.*

Nelson, G. K. Spiritualism and Society. *313 pp.*

Stark, Werner. The Sociology of Religion. *A Study of Christendom.*
   Volume I. *Established Religion. 248 pp.*
   Volume II. *Sectarian Religion. 368 pp.*
   Volume III. *The Universal Church. 464 pp.*
   Volume IV. *Types of Religious Man. 352 pp.*
   Volume V. *Types of Religious Culture. 464 pp.*

Turner, B. S. Weber and Islam. *216 pp.*

Watt, W. Montgomery. Islam and the Integration of Society. *320 pp.*

SOCIOLOGY OF ART AND LITERATURE

Jarvie, Ian C. Towards a Sociology of the Cinema. *A Comparative Essay on the Structure and Functioning of a Major Entertainment Industry. 405 pp.*

Rust, Frances S. Dance in Society. *An Analysis of the Relationships between the Social Dance and Society in England from the Middle Ages to the Present Day. 256 pp. 8 pp. of plates.*

Schücking, L. L. The Sociology of Literary Taste. *112 pp.*

Wolff, Janet. Hermeneutic Philosophy and the Sociology of Art. *150 pp.*

SOCIOLOGY OF KNOWLEDGE

Diesing, P. Patterns of Discovery in the Social Sciences. *262 pp.*

●**Douglas, J. D.** (Ed.) Understanding Everyday Life. *370 pp.*

●**Hamilton, P.** Knowledge and Social Structure. *174 pp.*

Jarvie, I. C. Concepts and Society. *232 pp.*

Mannheim, Karl. Essays on the Sociology of Knowledge. *Edited by Paul Kecskemeti. Editorial Note by Adolph Lowe. 353 pp.*

Remmling, Gunter W. The Sociology of Karl Mannheim. *With a Bibliographical Guide to the Sociology of Knowledge, Ideological Analysis, and Social Planning. 255 pp.*

9

Remmling, Gunter W. (Ed.) Towards the Sociology of Knowledge. *Origin and Development of a Sociological Thought Style. 463 pp.*

Stark, Werner. The Sociology of Knowledge: *An Essay in Aid of a Deeper Understanding of the History of Ideas. 384 pp.*

URBAN SOCIOLOGY

Ashworth, William. The Genesis of Modern British Town Planning: *A Study in Economic and Social History of the Nineteenth and Twentieth Centuries. 288 pp.*

Cullingworth, J. B. Housing Needs and Planning Policy: *A Restatement of the Problems of Housing Need and 'Overspill' in England and Wales. 232 pp. 44 tables. 8 maps.*

Dickinson, Robert E. City and Region: *A Geographical Interpretation 608 pp. 125 figures.*

The West European City: *A Geographical Interpretation. 600 pp. 129 maps. 29 plates.*

● The City Region in Western Europe. *320 pp. Maps.*

Humphreys, Alexander J. New Dubliners: *Urbanization and the Irish Family. Foreword by George C. Homans. 304 pp.*

Jackson, Brian. Working Class Community: *Some General Notions raised by a Series of Studies in Northern England. 192 pp.*

Jennings, Hilda. Societies in the Making: *a Study of Development and Re-development within a County Borough. Foreword by D. A. Clark. 286 pp.*

●**Mann, P. H.** An Approach to Urban Sociology. *240 pp.*

Morris, R. N., and **Mogey, J.** The Sociology of Housing. *Studies at Berinsfield. 232 pp. 4 pp. plates.*

Rosser, C., and **Harris, C.** The Family and Social Change. *A Study of Family and Kinship in a South Wales Town. 352 pp. 8 maps.*

●**Stacey, Margaret, Batsone, Eric, Bell, Colin,** and **Thurcott, Anne.** Power, Persistence and Change. *A Second Study of Banbury. 196 pp.*

RURAL SOCIOLOGY

Haswell, M. R. The Economics of Development in Village India. *120 pp.*

Littlejohn, James. Westrigg: *the Sociology of a Cheviot Parish. 172 pp. 5 figures.*

Mayer, Adrian C. Peasants in the Pacific. *A Study of Fiji Indian Rural Society. 248 pp. 20 plates.*

Williams, W. M. The Sociology of an English Village: *Gosforth. 272 pp. 12 figures. 13 tables.*

SOCIOLOGY OF INDUSTRY AND DISTRIBUTION

Anderson, Nels. Work and Leisure. *280 pp.*

●**Blau, Peter M.**, and **Scott, W. Richard.** Formal Organizations: *a Comparative approach. Introduction and Additional Bibliography by J. H. Smith.* 326 *pp.*

Dunkerley, David. The Foreman. *Aspects of Task and Structure. 192 pp.*

Eldridge, J. E. T. Industrial Disputes. *Essays in the Sociology of Industrial Relations. 288 pp.*

Hetzler, Stanley. Applied Measures for Promoting Technological Growth. *352 pp.*

Technological Growth and Social Change. *Achieving Modernization. 269 pp.*

Hollowell, Peter G. The Lorry Driver. *272 pp.*

●**Oxaal, I., Barnett, T.**, and **Booth, D.** (Eds). Beyond the Sociology of Development. *Economy and Society in Latin America and Africa. 295 pp.*

Smelser, Neil J. Social Change in the Industrial Revolution: *An Application of Theory to the Lancashire Cotton Industry, 1770–1840. 468 pp. 12 figures. 14 tables.*

ANTHROPOLOGY

Ammar, Hamed. Growing up in an Egyptian Village: *Silwa, Province of Aswan. 336 pp.*

Brandel-Syrier, Mia. Reeftown Elite. *A Study of Social Mobility in a Modern African Community on the Reef. 376 pp.*

Dickie-Clark, H. F. The Marginal Situation. *A Sociological Study of a Coloured Group. 236 pp.*

Dube, S. C. Indian Village. *Foreword by Morris Edward Opler. 276 pp. 4 plates.*

India's Changing Villages: *Human Factors in Community Development. 260 pp. 8 plates. 1 map.*

Firth, Raymond. Malay Fishermen. *Their Peasant Economy. 420 pp. 17 pp. plates.*

Gulliver, P. H. Social Control in an African Society: a Study of the Arusha, Agricultural Masai of Northern Tanganyika. *320 pp. 8 plates. 10 figures.*

Family Herds. *288 pp.*

Ishwaran, K. Tradition and Economy in Village India: *An Interactionist Approach.*
Foreword by Conrad Arensburg. 176 pp.

Jarvie, Ian C. The Revolution in Anthropology. *268 pp.*

Little, Kenneth L. Mende of Sierra Leone. *308 pp. and folder.*

Negroes in Britain. *With a New Introduction and Contemporary Study by Leonard Bloom. 320 pp.*

Lowie, Robert H. Social Organization. *494 pp.*

Mayer, A. C. Peasants in the Pacific. *A Study of Fiji Indian Rural Society. 248 pp.*

Meer, Fatima. Race and Suicide in South Africa. *325 pp.*

Smith, Raymond T. The Negro Family in British Guiana: *Family Structure and Social Status in the Villages. With a Foreword by Meyer Fortes. 314 pp. 8 plates. 1 figure. 4 maps.*

Smooha, Sammy. Israel: Pluralism and Conflict. *About 320 pp.*

SOCIOLOGY AND PHILOSOPHY

Barnsley, John H. The Social Reality of Ethics. *A Comparative Analysis of Moral Codes. 448 pp.*

Diesing, Paul. Patterns of Discovery in the Social Sciences. *362 pp.*

●**Douglas, Jack D.** (Ed.) Understanding Everyday Life. *Toward the Reconstruction of Sociological Knowledge. Contributions by Alan F. Blum. Aaron W. Cicourel, Norman K. Denzin, Jack D. Douglas, John Heeren, Peter McHugh, Peter K. Manning, Melvin Power, Matthew Speier, Roy Turner, D. Lawrence Wieder, Thomas P. Wilson and Don H. Zimmerman. 370 pp.*

Gorman, Robert A. The Dual Vision. *Alfred Schutz and the Myth of Phenomenological Social Science. About 300 pp.*

Jarvie, Ian C. Concepts and Society. *216 pp.*

●**Pelz, Werner.** The Scope of Understanding in Sociology. *Towards a more radical reorientation in the social humanistic sciences. 283 pp.*

Roche, Maurice. Phenomenology, Language and the Social Sciences. *371 pp.*

Sahay, Arun. Sociological Analysis. *212 pp.*

Sklair, Leslie. The Sociology of Progress. *320 pp.*

Slater, P. Origin and Significance of the Frankfurt School. *A Marxist Perspective. About 192 pp.*

Smart, Barry. Sociology, Phenomenology and Marxian Analysis. *A Critical Discussion of the Theory and Practice of a Science of Society. 220 pp.*

International Library of Anthropology

General Editor Adam Kuper

Ahmed, A. S. Millenium and Charisma Among Pathans. *A Critical Essay in Social Anthropology. 192 pp.*

Brown, Paula. The Chimbu. *A Study of Change in the New Guinea Highlands. 151 pp.*

Gudeman, Stephen. Relationships, Residence and the Individual. *A Rural Panamanian Community. 288 pp. 11 Plates, 5 Figures, 2 Maps, 10 Tables.*

Hamnett, Ian. Chieftainship and Legitimacy. *An Anthropological Study of Executive Law in Lesotho. 163 pp.*

Hanson, F. Allan. Meaning in Culture. *127 pp.*

Lloyd, P. C. Power and Independence. *Urban Africans' Perception of Social Inequality. 264 pp.*

Pettigrew, Joyce. Robber Noblemen. *A Study of the Political System of the Sikh Jats. 284 pp.*

Street, Brian V. The Savage in Literature. *Representations of 'Primitive' Society in English Fiction, 1858–1920. 207 pp.*

Van Den Berghe, Pierre L. Power and Privilege at an African University. *278 pp.*

International Library of Social Policy

General Editor Kathleen Jones

Bayley, M. Mental Handicap and Community Care. *426 pp.*

Bottoms, A. E., and **McClean, J. D.** Defendants in the Criminal Process. *284 pp.*

Butler, J. R. Family Doctors and Public Policy. *208 pp.*

Davies, Martin. Prisoners of Society. *Attitudes and Aftercare. 204 pp.*

Gittus, Elizabeth. Flats, Families and the Under-Fives. *285 pp.*

Holman, Robert. Trading in Children. *A Study of Private Fostering. 355 pp.*

Jones, Howard, and **Cornes, Paul.** Open Prisons. *About 248 pp.*

Jones, Kathleen. History of the Mental Health Service. *428 pp.*

Jones, Kathleen, with **Brown, John, Cunningham, W. J., Roberts, Julian,** and **Williams, Peter.** Opening the Door. *A Study of New Policies for the Mentally Handicapped. 278 pp.*

Karn, Valerie. Retiring to the Seaside. *About 280 pp. 2 maps. Numerous tables.*

Thomas, J. E. The English Prison Officer since 1850: *A Study in Conflict. 258 pp.*

Walton, R. G. Women in Social Work. *303 pp.*

Woodward, J. To Do the Sick No Harm. *A Study of the British Voluntary Hospital System to 1875. 221 pp.*

International Library of Welfare and Philosophy

General Editors Noel Timms and David Watson

● **Plant, Raymond.** Community and Ideology. *104 pp.*

● **McDermott, F. E.** (Ed.) Self-Determination in Social Work. *A Collection of Essays on Self-determination and Related Concepts by Philosophers and Social Work Theorists. Contributors: F. P. Biestek, S. Bernstein, A. Keith-Lucas, D. Sayer, H. H. Perelman, C. Whittington, R. F. Stalley, F. E. McDermott, I. Berlin, H. J. McCloskey, H. L. A. Hart, J. Wilson, A. I. Melden, S. I. Benn. 254 pp.*

Ragg, Nicholas M. People Not Cases. *A Philosophical Approach to Social Work. About 250 pp.*

● **Timms, Noel,** and **Watson, David** (Eds). Talking About Welfare. *Readings in Philosophy and Social Policy. Contributors: T. H. Marshall, R. B. Brandt, G. H. von Wright, K. Nielsen, M. Cranston, R. M. Titmuss, R. S. Downie, E. Telfer, D. Donnison, J. Benson, P. Leonard, A. Keith-Lucas, D. Walsh, I. T. Ramsey. 320 pp.*

Primary Socialization, Language and Education

General Editor Basil Bernstein

Adlam, Diana S., *with the assistance of Geoffrey Turner and Lesley Lineker.* Code in Context. *About 272 pp.*

Bernstein, Basil. Class, Codes and Control. *3 volumes.*
  1. *Theoretical Studies Towards a Sociology of Language. 254 pp.*
  2. *Applied Studies Towards a Sociology of Language. 377 pp.*
● 3. *Towards a Theory of Educatiomal Transmission. 167 pp.*

Brandis, W., and **Bernstein, B.** Selection and Control. *176 pp.*

Brandis, Walter, and **Henderson, Dorothy.** Social Class, Language and Communication. *288 pp.*

Cook-Gumperz, Jenny. Social Control and Socialization. *A Study of Class Differences in the Language of Maternal Control. 290 pp.*

●**Gahagan, D. M.,** and **G. A.** Talk Reform. *Exploration in Language for Infant School Children. 160 pp.*

Hawkins, P. R. Social Class, the Nominal Group and Verbal Strategies. *About 220 pp.*

Robinson, W. P., and **Rackstraw, Susan D. A.** A Question of Answers. *2 volumes. 192 pp. and 180 pp.*

Turner, Geoffrey J., and **Mohan, Bernard A.** A Linguistic Description and Computer Programme for Children's Speech. *208 pp.*

Reports of the Institute of Community Studies

●**Cartwright, Ann.** Parents and Family Planning Services. *306 pp.*
  Patients and their Doctors. *A Study of General Practice. 304 pp.*

Dench, Geoff. Maltese in London. *A Case-study in the Erosion of Ethnic Consciousness. 302 pp.*

●**Jackson, Brian.** Streaming: *an Education System in Miniature. 168 pp.*

Jackson, Brian, and **Marsden, Dennis.** Education and the Working Class: *Some General Themes raised by a Study of 88 Working-class Children in a Northern Industrial City. 268 pp. 2 folders.*

Marris, Peter. The Experience of Higher Education. *232 pp. 27 tables.*
  Loss and Change. *192 pp.*

Marris, Peter, and **Rein, Martin.** Dilemmas of Social Reform. *Poverty and Community Action in the United States. 256 pp.*

Marris, Peter, and **Somerset, Anthony.** African Businessmen. *A Study of Entrepreneurship and Development in Kenya. 256 pp.*

Mills, Richard. Young Outsiders: *a Study in Alternative Communities. 216 pp.*

Runciman, W. G. Relative Deprivation and Social Justice. *A Study of Attitudes to Social Inequality in Twentieth-Century England. 352 pp.*

Willmott, Peter. Adolescent Boys in East London. *230 pp.*

Willmott, Peter, and **Young, Michael.** Family and Class in a London Suburb. *202 pp. 47 tables.*

Young, Michael. Innovation and Research in Education. *192 pp.*

●**Young, Michael,** and **McGeeney, Patrick.** Learning Begins at Home. *A Study of a Junior School and its Parents. 128 pp.*

Young, Michael, and **Willmott, Peter.** Family and Kinship in East London. *Foreword by Richard M. Titmuss. 252 pp. 39 tables.*
The Symmetrical Family. *410 pp.*

Reports of the Institute for Social Studies in Medical Care

Cartwright, Ann, Hockey, Lisbeth, and **Anderson, John L.** Life Before Death. *310 pp.*

Dunnell, Karen, and **Cartwright, Ann.** Medicine Takers, Prescribers and Hoarders. *190 pp.*

Medicine, Illness and Society

General Editor W. M. Williams

Robinson, David. The Process of Becoming Ill. *142 pp.*

Stacey, Margaret, *et al.* Hospitals, Children and Their Families. *The Report of a Pilot Study. 202 pp.*

Stimson, G. V., and **Webb, B.** Going to See the Doctor. *The Consultation Process in General Practice. 155 pp.*

Monographs in Social Theory

General Editor Arthur Brittan

●**Barnes, B.** Scientific Knowledge and Sociological Theory. *192 pp.*

Bauman, Zygmunt. Culture as Praxis. *204 pp.*

●**Dixon, Keith.** Sociological Theory. *Pretence and Possibility. 142 pp.*

Meltzer, B. N., Petras, J. W., and **Reynolds, L. T.** Symbolic Interactionism. *Genesis, Varieties and Criticisms. 144 pp.*

●**Smith, Anthony D.** The Concept of Social Change. *A Critique of the Functionalist Theory of Social Change. 208 pp.*

Routledge Social Science Journals

The British Journal of Sociology. *Editor – Angus Stewart; Associate Editor – Leslie Sklair. Vol. 1, No. 1 – March 1950 and Quarterly. Roy. 8vo. All back issues available. An international journal publishing original papers in the field of sociology and related areas.*
Community Work. *Edited by David Jones and Marjorie Mayo. 1973. Published annually.*
Economy and Society. *Vol. 1, No. 1. February 1972 and Quarterly. Metric Roy. 8vo. A journal for all social scientists covering sociology, philosophy, anthropology, economics and history. All back numbers available.*
Religion. Journal of Religion and Religions. *Chairman of Editorial Board, Ninian Smart. Vol. 1, No. 1, Spring 1971. A journal with an inter-disciplinary approach to the study of the phenomena of religion. All back numbers available.*
Year Book of Social Policy in Britain, The. *Edited by Kathleen Jones. 1971. Published annually.*

Social and Psychological Aspects of Medical Practice

Editor   Trevor Silverstone

Lader, Malcolm. Psychophysiology of Mental Illness. *280 pp.*
● **Silverstone, Trevor,** and **Turner, Paul.** Drug Treatment in Psychiatry. *232 pp.*

Printed in Great Britain by
Lowe & Brydone Printers Limited, Thetford, Norfolk